P9-DXE-917

The COMPLETE Outdoor Wedding Planner

From Rustic Settings to Elegant Garden Parties, Everything You Need to Know to Make Your Day Special

Sharon Naylor

PRIMA PUBLISHING

Copyright © 2001 by Sharon Naylor

All rights reserved. No part of this book may be reproduced or transmitted in any form or by any means, electronic or mechanical, including photocopying, recording, or by any information storage or retrieval system, without written permission from Random House, Inc., except for the inclusion of brief quotations in a review.

Published by Prima Publishing, Roseville, California. Member of the Crown Publishing Group, a division of Random House, Inc.

PRIMA PUBLISHING and colophon are trademarks of Random House, Inc., registered with the United States Patent and Trademark Office.

Library of Congress Cataloging-in-Publication Data
Naylor, Sharon.
   The complete outdoor wedding planner : from rustic settings to elegant garden parties, everything you need to know to make your day special / Sharon Naylor.
     p. cm.
   Includes index.
   ISBN 0-7615-3598-5
   1. Weddings—Planning. I. Title.
HQ745.N386   2001
395.2'2   2001051152

01 02 03 04 DD 10 9 8 7 6 5 4 3 2 1
Printed in the United States of America

First Edition

Visit us online at www.primapublishing.com

*For Madison
and Kevin*

Contents

Acknowledgments

In my previous books, I have thanked my family and friends for their loyalty, support, and love as I have ridden the waves of joy, elation, and frustration that is a writer's life. In this book, they are all thanked once again.

As I could not create this without them, I must thank from the bottom of my heart the wonderful editorial team at Prima. Denise Sternad, thank you for your efforts on my behalf, for pushing my contracts through legal, and for allowing me to bring my own concepts into your lineup. Michelle McCormack, I have never had such a wonderful editing relationship as I have had with you, and I thank you for allowing me so much freedom with my manuscripts. Jennifer Dougherty Hart, thank you for your tireless and thorough publicity efforts. Every author should be so lucky.

For their contributions to this book, I thank the many wedding professionals and brides and grooms who lent their personal experiences, advice, materials, and resources for my use. Special thanks go to Linda Zec Prajka of An Invitation to Buy Nationwide; Michelle Roth and Henry Roth; Rich Penrose of Dean Michaels Studios; Gail

Watson of Gail Watson Custom Cakes; Monica Zaslower of Event Works; Sarah Stitham of Charmed Places; Alain Pinon of Salon AKS; Marcia Peters of Finetica Child; Stacey David of Castle Hill in Newport, Rhode Island; Steve Blahitka of Back East Productions; Lisa Price; and Stevanne Auerbach.

Special thanks go to the many brides and grooms who shared their outdoor-wedding stories with me, particularly Patricia and Anthony Padovano, Nadia and Darryl Marin, and Jeffrey and Shana Landi.

For his kindness, patience, and talent, I thank Mike Napolitan for creating a Web site that is even more beautiful and more complete than I could have imagined.

For their supportive writers' community and quick willingness to help a fellow author, I thank the many members and leadership of the American Society of Journalists and Authors.

And to my always supportive and loving extended family, including Terry, George, and Renee McGuire; Jeanine and Jeffrey Condon; Linda Messina; Pattie Miles; Sue and Vic Gonnelli; Millie Somers; Anne and Nick Fagone; Annette and Ralph Corrao; Lydia and Andy Stec; Chris and George Balynsky; and all of my cousins.

Much love and gratitude go to my dearest friends Susan Cefolo-McDermott; Jill Althouse-Wood; Pamela Bishop; Jennifer Stinson; Susan DeLong; and to my always inspiring and hard-working students Mike, Kristen, Nick, Patty, and Helena.

And thanks to my Madison and to my Kevin, who always make me smile.

Your Wedding-Planning Timetable

ONE YEAR BEFORE THE WEDDING

- [ ] Announce your engagement
- [ ] Attend engagement parties
- [ ] Discuss as a couple what your shared wishes are for the wedding of your dreams
- [ ] Begin looking through magazines and books for wedding-day ideas
- [ ] Choose the wedding date (and backup dates for booking purposes)
- [ ] Research weather conditions at your location for the wedding date
- [ ] Inform your family and friends of the wedding date
- [ ] Assess your wedding budget
- [ ] Decide who will pay for what
- [ ] Decide what part of your budget will get the most money (i.e., gown, reception, flowers, etc.)
- [ ] Begin online and phone research for dates, prices, and options
- [ ] Request brochures for destination weddings

- ❏ Create an organization system for all wedding plans (using file folders, computer programs, etc.)
- ❏ Decide on a level of formality
- ❏ Make up your own personal guest list
- ❏ Request guests lists from parents, fiancé's parents, and siblings
- ❏ Create final guest list
- ❏ Select and book your ceremony location
- ❏ Select and book your ceremony officiant
- ❏ Find out about your ceremony site's regulations
- ❏ Select and book your reception site
- ❏ Find out about your reception site's regulations
- ❏ Find out township or park department's permits and law requirements for your sites
- ❏ Research and book rental-item agency
- ❏ Create rental-item needs list
- ❏ Visit with rental-agency planner to look at supplies, choose linen colors, china patterns, etc.
- ❏ Choose the members of your bridal party and inform them of their roles
- ❏ Choose and order your wedding gown and veil
- ❏ Collect bridesmaids' size cards and ordering information
- ❏ Choose and order your bridesmaids' gowns
- ❏ Hire a wedding coordinator (if you so choose)
- ❏ Choose a florist and meet with the floral consultant
- ❏ Choose and book a caterer
- ❏ Choose and book a cake baker
- ❏ Choose and book a photographer
- ❏ Choose and book a videographer
- ❏ Choose and book your reception entertainment, DJ, or band
- ❏ Choose and book a limousine or classic-car company
- ❏ Start looking at invitation samples, and select your desired design
- ❏ Place engagement photo and announcement in local newspapers

❏ Notify your boss about your upcoming wedding and arrange for time off for the wedding week or weeks

NINE MONTHS BEFORE THE WEDDING

❏ Find out your local marriage-license requirements
❏ Meet with officiant about ceremony elements and prewedding classes
❏ Meet with caterer to discuss menu, outdoor-wedding setup, requirements, etc.
❏ Plan beverage requirements and bar setup
❏ Select packages with photographer and videographer
❏ Select packages with entertainment
❏ Meet with florist to design bouquets and floral décor
❏ Choose and book your honeymoon
❏ Apply for passports and travel visas, if necessary
❏ Notify out-of-town guests of the wedding date so that they may make travel plans
❏ Order your invitations
❏ Order your wedding programs
❏ Order your stationery
❏ Order wedding rings
❏ Have wedding rings engraved (if you so choose)
❏ Reserve all rental equipment (tents, chairs, tables, linens, etc.)
❏ Choose and reserve a block of rooms for your guests at a nearby hotel
❏ Book your honeymoon suite for the wedding night

SIX MONTHS BEFORE THE WEDDING

❏ Order preprinted napkins, matchbooks, etc.
❏ Create maps to ceremony and reception locations for enclosure in the invitations
❏ Begin to plan the rehearsal dinner

❑ Begin writing vows

❑ Select ceremony music

❑ Select ceremony readings

❑ Audition ceremony music performers

❑ Book musical performers for ceremony

❑ Register for wedding gifts

❑ Send for name-change information, if necessary

❑ Book hotel rooms for guests

❑ Book wedding-night accommodations for bride and groom

❑ Arrange for transportation for guests

❑ Plan "wedding weekend" activities, such as brunches, sporting events, barbecues, children's events, etc.

❑ Begin prewedding beauty treatments: skin care, relaxation, massage, tanning, etc.

❑ If holding an at-home wedding, hire a landscaper to level your lawn, remove weeds, trim shrubs, add extra plants or flower beds, mulch, etc.

THREE MONTHS BEFORE THE WEDDING

❑ Obtain marriage license, according to your state's requirements

❑ Go for blood tests, according to your state's time requirements

❑ Attend premarital classes, if required by your faith

❑ Address invitations to guests

❑ Assemble invitations packages

❑ Buy "Love" stamps at the post office

❑ Mail invitations to guests

❑ Order or make wedding programs

❑ Order wedding favors

❑ Arrange for team of helpers to make wedding favors with you

❑ Choose and rent groom's wedding wardrobe

❑ Begin wedding gown fittings

❑ Choose shoes and accessories for wedding day

❑ Start bridesmaid's fittings

❑ Help bride's and groom's parents choose their wedding-day attire

❑ Choose children's wedding-day attire

❑ Consult with wedding coordinator for updates and confirmations

❑ Consult with caterer or banquet-hall manager for update

❑ Complete your vows

❑ Ask honored relatives and friends to perform readings at the ceremony

❑ Finalize selections of ceremony readings and music

❑ Submit song "wish list" to DJ or band you've hired

❑ Submit picture "wish list" to photographer

❑ Submit video "wish list" to videographer

❑ Arrange for a baby-sitter to watch guests' kids on the wedding day (have several baby-sitters if there will be a lot of children)

❑ Finalize and book plans for rehearsal dinner

TWO MONTHS BEFORE THE WEDDING

❑ Go for fittings of wedding gown

❑ Choose and purchase your "going away" outfit and honeymoon clothes

❑ Meet with ceremony musician about song list

❑ Have attendants' shoes dyed in one dye lot

❑ Formally ask friends to participate in wedding, such as attending the guest book, transporting wedding gifts from reception to home, etc.

❑ Send for all name-change documents, such as passport, credit cards, driver's license, etc., if necessary

❑ Pose for formal prewedding portrait

❑ Enlarge and frame portrait of the two of you for ceremony entrance

❑ Purchase gifts for each other, parents, bridal party, honored guests

❑ Wrap and label gifts

ONE MONTH BEFORE THE WEDDING

❑ Get marriage license

❑ Meet with officiant to get the final information on ceremony elements, rules of the location, etc.

❑ Invite officiant to rehearsal dinner

❑ Plan the rehearsal

❑ Invite bridal party and involved guests to the rehearsal and rehearsal dinner

❑ Scout outdoor-wedding site to make sure all elements are in working order

❑ Arrange for house- and pet-sitters

❑ Inquire about town parking permits, gathering permits, etc.

❑ Confirm honeymoon plans

❑ Confirm wedding-night hotel reservations

❑ Get all incoming guests' arrival times at airports and train stations

❑ Arrange for transportation of guests to their hotel

❑ Arrange for transportation needs of guests throughout the wedding weekend

❑ Make beauty appointment for wedding day

❑ Visit your hairstylist to "practice" with hairstyles for the big day

❑ Get prewedding haircut

❑ Have fitting for wedding gown

❑ Pick up wedding bands

❑ Attend showers

❑ Write thank-yous for shower gifts (by hand, no shortcuts!)

❑ Call guests who have not RSVP'd to get the final headcount

❑ Make up seating chart for reception

❑ Write up seating place cards and table numbers

❑ Pick up honeymoon travel tickets and information books

❑ Make up welcome gift baskets for guests

❑ Arrange for wedding-day transportation for the bridal party if they will not be in limos

- ❑ Purchase unity candle
- ❑ Purchase garters (get two—one for keeping, one for tossing)
- ❑ Purchase toasting flutes
- ❑ Purchase cake knife
- ❑ Purchase guest book
- ❑ Purchase post-wedding toss-its (bird seed, flower petals, bubbles, bells, etc.) and decorate small containers (if you so choose)
- ❑ Purchase throwaway wedding cameras

One Week Before the Wedding

- ❑ Confirm all wedding plans with all wedding vendors, having them tell you what date, time, and place they have on record:
  - ❑ Caterer (give final headcount now!)
  - ❑ Florist (give delivery instructions now!)
  - ❑ Cake baker
  - ❑ Photographer
  - ❑ Videographer
  - ❑ Ceremony musicians
  - ❑ Reception entertainers
  - ❑ Officiant
  - ❑ Ceremony-site manager
  - ❑ Reception-site manager
  - ❑ Wedding coordinator
  - ❑ Limousine company (give directions now!)
  - ❑ Rental-company agent
- ❑ Pay final deposits for all services
- ❑ Place tips and fees in marked envelopes for such participants as the officiant, ceremony musicians, coordinator, valets, etc.
- ❑ If supplying your own beverages, conduct a shopping trip (with plenty of assistants) to the local liquor and beverage-supply house for a major spree
- ❑ Drop off guest welcome baskets at hotel
- ❑ Pick up wedding gown

- ❏ Groom picks up tux
- ❏ Groom and ushers pick up tux accessories, socks, shoes, etc.
- ❏ Pack for honeymoon
- ❏ Break in your wedding-day shoes
- ❏ Remind groom to get new shoes for the wedding day
- ❏ Remind groom to get a haircut for the wedding day
- ❏ Notify the local police department of your upcoming absence, so that they can patrol your neighborhood
- ❏ Get travelers' checks (if you so choose)
- ❏ Plan wedding-day brunch and inform bridal party about it
- ❏ Plan your special toasts
- ❏ Get ahead on wedding thank-yous by sending notes out to those who have sent gifts
- ❏ Submit address-change notification to the post office (if you will be moving after the honeymoon)
- ❏ Attend bachelor's/bachelorette's party (be sure to tell attendants and friends in advance that this week would be good for you, as you do not want to be out the night before your wedding)

The Day Before the Wedding

- ❏ If holding an at-home wedding, have the lawn freshly mowed
- ❏ Remove outdoor furniture, kids' toys, lawn tools from the yard
- ❏ Supervise delivery of rental items
- ❏ Supervise setup of tent and dance floor
- ❏ Supervise setup of portable toilets
- ❏ Visually inspect all delivered linens, china, crystal, flatware, etc.
- ❏ Request immediate replacement if items are not in top condition
- ❏ Decorate site as appropriate (e.g., hanging strings of white lights inside of tents, etc.)
- ❏ Have someone inspect the grounds for flaws in the walking areas (i.e., in case your dog has used the backyard recently . . .)

❑ Turn off lawn-sprinkler system, remove lawn-sprinkler heads

❑ Try out your wedding-day shoes on the lawn and walkways to see if your heels sink into the ground (it may be time for flats)

❑ Invite photographer, videographer, caterer, and entertainment to the site for a last-minute inspection of their work space for tomorrow

❑ Make sure everything you need is packed

❑ Lay out all wedding-day wardrobe and accessories

❑ Discuss with all residents in your home the shower-time schedule for the next day (very important!)

❑ Hand out printed directions to all family members and bridal-party members

❑ Confirm times for all attendants to show up on the wedding day, as well as where to go

❑ Arrange for a reliable relative to transport wedding gifts to his or her home for safekeeping

❑ Arrange for a reliable relative to be in charge of handing out payment envelopes

❑ Hit ATM to get cash on hand for emergencies, tips, valet, etc.

❑ Assemble emergency bag with extra stockings, lipstick, pressed powder, emery boards, and medical items such as aspirin or insulin

❑ Put a cell phone in the emergency bag

❑ Gas up the cars

❑ Go to the beauty salon to get waxed and tweezed

❑ Stock up on supplies for wedding-morning breakfast

❑ Place last call to caterer or coordinator to answer last-minute questions

❑ Attend rehearsal

❑ Attend rehearsal dinner

❑ If holding an at-home wedding, check the lighting system at night

❑ Get a good night's sleep!

ON THE WEDDING DAY

- ❏ Decorate wedding site (i.e., arrange chairs, set tables, assemble gift table, etc.)
- ❏ Set up heaters or air conditioners
- ❏ Receive delivery of ice
- ❏ Set out favors
- ❏ Set out place cards
- ❏ Set out post-wedding toss-its
- ❏ Set out guest book and pen
- ❏ Attend bridal brunch
- ❏ Have hair and nails done at beauty salon, and have a massage there as well
- ❏ Have photos taken at home
- ❏ Make sure someone responsible has arranged for your suitcases to go to your hotel room or in the car that will be taking you to the airport
- ❏ Make sure someone has the wedding rings
- ❏ Make sure someone has the car keys
- ❏ Relax and know that everything will be fine!

THE DAY AFTER THE WEDDING

This is for parents, friends, etc., of the bride and groom (who are now off on vacation—finally!)

- ❏ Have someone supervise the rental company's cleanup of the site
- ❏ Get a signed receipt for the return of all rented items
- ❏ Have tuxes returned to rental store
- ❏ Hold day-after breakfast for guests and bridal party
- ❏ Graciously accept all the compliments on the wedding
- ❏ Transport guests to airports, train stations, etc., for their rides home

Introduction

WHAT COULD be more beautiful than an outdoor wedding? Under a clear blue sky with perhaps a few wispy clouds of white, the bride and groom exchange vows surrounded by the natural beauty of their environment. A gentle breeze plays with the curled tendrils of the bride's hair, and the warmth of the sun is matched only by the warmth of the moment.

Who can forget that lovely television commercial where the happy, beaming couple strolls through a flower-specked field, the barefoot bride playfully kicks a soccer ball around with the stunning, *GQ*-worthy groomsmen, elegant ladies in wide-brimmed hats take a gentle glide on a garden swing, and a dozen too-cute-for-words flower girls wave shyly at the camera? It's an image favored by all of advertising right now, as the marketing geniuses on Madison Avenue know that the images of the outdoor wedding are captivating and lasting. Though you may not be up for a game of soccer on your wedding day, you'll certainly favor the elegance and natural beauty of an outdoor wedding.

If that commercial doesn't ring a bell, perhaps you remember the photos of Cindy Crawford in her bare feet and a barely-there white slipdress at her beach wedding to restaurateur Rande Gerber. With the nod from Cindy, beach weddings grew in popularity, now leading the way as the most popular outdoor-wedding choice among marrying couples.

Whatever your style, be it a beach bash or a classic tented wedding in your own backyard, you're sure to have a wedding your guests will talk about for years to come. There's something about an outdoor wedding that pleases the crowd and the couple alike. Perhaps it's that it's something different, not the same from-the-church-to-the-reception-hall event that everyone's been to so many times before. Different locations, different elements, but still boxed in among four walls. Perhaps it's the natural beauty of the location, making the most of the surrounding scenery such as flowering trees, bubbling brooks, wishing wells, tulip borders, and great views of the sunset. Certainly, it's a mix of these reasons plus a whole lot more.

The brides I spoke to said they wanted an outdoor wedding from the very start. Their reasons are as follows:

• "I've always wanted an outdoor wedding. There's something about being married out in nature that's always appealed to me, like you should be out there where things are growing and changing at every minute."

• "I didn't want my wedding to be held in a church or reception hall where we would be just a number. A friend was once rushed out of the church so that a funeral could be held the next hour. How depressing that she stepped out of her receiving line to see a hearse roll up to the curb. I also wouldn't want my reception to be one of five taking place at the same site on a Saturday afternoon. I want the day to be all mine."

• "I just wanted to have an original wedding, not like the ultra-traditional one my sister had and definitely not like the one I had for my first wedding. I wanted a new style, a new look, a good reflection of what I love now."

- "I knew there were going to be five weddings in my family that summer, and I wanted mine to stand out as the best."

- "I wanted my pictures to be amazing, not the same stuffy at-the-altar shots my parents have in their wedding albums. I wanted natural shots, lots of greenery in the background, and great lighting."

- "Celebrities have outdoor weddings all the time. This is my once-in-a-lifetime day, and I wanted it to be that special."

Perhaps you see yourself in one or more of the reasons listed above, or perhaps you have your own reasons. One bride I interviewed said that she and her new husband were always outdoorsy people, and they wanted to get married and celebrate their vows outside. Another bride said that being outdoors made her feel like her grand-parents and her mother could look down from heaven to watch the entire event.

We've all seen outdoor weddings glorified and featured in our favorite movies, television shows, and yes, in the most memorable commercials. The media knows what hits us where we live and what's attractive to us, and as the trend continues to grow hotter we'll all see many more outdoor-wedding scenes on the screen and on magazine covers. The best thing is, this is a trend that will never die. Indeed, it's growing stronger right this moment. Wedding experts such as myself are thrilled at the growing popularity of outdoor nuptials, as this type of wedding allows for more creativity, more originality, and more personality in the wedding celebration. Although some houses of worship and established reception sites come equipped with lists of rules—some even forbidding floral décor and pictures!—the outdoor wedding opens up a whole world of possibilities and few limits. Your options expand, and your dream ideas are more than just a possibility. And you're going to look great in those pictures!

As beautiful and as worthwhile as it is, coordinating an outdoor wedding starts off with a whirlwind of questions right from the start. I've collected some of the most common questions posed to me on my Web site, along with the very responses you may need now to get all of the arrangements underway.

Q. *Is planning an outdoor wedding more involved than planning a traditional, indoor wedding?*

A. Planning *any* wedding is always an involved process, but the scales are tipped to the side of extra work for this style of wedding. Aside from all of the many details of planning a ceremony and reception, you'll also add a few hundred more issues to your to-do list. For instance, because an outdoor wedding is prey to the threats of inclement weather, you'll have to plan for a backup location in case the skies open and the rain pours down. That said, planning your reception as you'd like it, and then handling all the details of preparing and moving the shindig to a second location, really amounts to planning *one and a half* weddings! Though it's a monumental task, say, to arrange the caterer's menu, preparation, and serving of the food, you'll also have to cover the instructions for moving the food, moving the serving tables, and moving the servers to a whole new location. And that location needs to be checked for power availability, ovens big enough for the caterer's trays, and so on. You get the picture.

Yes, planning an outdoor wedding means having to have a second backup plan in case of the worst, and that takes a lot of tough "what if" thinking that traditional, indoor brides do not have to heed (except for who's going to hold the umbrella as she dashes into the church). Indeed, the weather is a formidable foe to the outdoor-wedding couple, but with this book and the input of experienced wedding coordinators and recently outdoor-married couples who will share their advice with you here, you'll have a solid plan and assurance to put all your fears to rest.

Aside from the weather factor and the shuffling of locations, there are also the added elements of renting a tent, tables and chairs, linens, a dance floor, and a hundred other items you'll need for your big day. Add in the issues of locating or providing adequate parking and restroom facilities, bringing in enough power to light the tent and allow everyone to hear the band, securing parking permits for your guests, and much, much more—all of which is pretty much taken care of for you at a standard, basic (and boring, to some) indoor reception hall—and you're looking at a very long to-do list.

More work? Certainly. You may be the busiest you've ever been, but the results will be worth it. Plus, you'll have this book as a tool to guide you through the challenging steps of arranging your wedding elements well and preventing those menacing outdoor issues from ruining a single moment of your day.

Q. *What are the menacing challenges of the outdoors?*

A. Well, besides the obvious challenge that rain provides, you're also going to deal with other weather factors such as wind and humidity. On a windy day, the bride's veil can dance around above her head like a ghost, and especially at beach weddings the wind can carry the musicians' melodies and the couple's vows right out to sea. Many an outdoor wedding have been threatened, if not postponed, by an unwelcome guest—a hurricane or tropical storm, for instance. Flooding may close roads, and threatening lightning makes the outdoors unsafe.

An even greater outdoor wedding foe is, simply put, too much of a good thing. Glaring sun that reaches top temperatures can cause sweating, fainting, and heat that's unbearable to some guests. Metal chairs that have been out since 9 A.M. may actually burn some guests' legs, and the cake may melt right off the table.

Outdoor weddings also introduce the hazards of insects, particularly if you live in a region that's prone to mosquitoes. You don't want spray bottles of Off to be your wedding favors, so how do you handle the annoying little buggers?

And don't forget about mud from the rainstorm that cleared three days ago and left your backyard a soggy mess.

It sounds like a whirlwind of potential disasters—or it may just be something to deal with when the time comes. In this book, you'll learn how to overcome the hazards of Mother Nature with some smart timing and some smart action. As I stated earlier, outdoor weddings require a lot of work and a lot of attention to many "what ifs." The biggest mistake comes in not addressing all of these worries. It's the unprepared bride and groom who wind up having to postpone their wedding, or who wind up sun-baked and bitten up just in time for their honeymoon. With this book, you're ahead of the game, and even old Mother Nature and her blaring sun, pouring rains, and hair-frizzing humidity can't defeat you.

The faint of heart may shy away from the whole process at this point, deeming it too much trouble to worry about the weather and insects and 375-degree silverware baking on the tables. But if you're the kind of bride who is not daunted by a challenge—especially one that's been easily handled by millions of brides and grooms before you *and* to which you already hold the key to many of the biggest outdoor-wedding solutions—and if you will hold true to your desired dream of the perfect outdoor wedding, then welcome to the process. Sit down, get ready, and let's begin to plan your gorgeous day.

Q. *You said that outdoor weddings open up whole new potential for great planning ideas. I've just read about the hazards of planning a wedding in the open air. Now what are the benefits? What's the advantage?*

A. In addition to the originality of an outdoor wedding, no matter what the location and style, an outdoor wedding allows you and your wedding professionals a wider range of freedom. Your florist can do more than just place centerpieces on your tables and place a bouquet in your hand. Now, there are flower-strewn trellises, elaborate floral arrangements on marble pedestals, strings of tiny white lights up in the trees to summon the romantic environment of Tavern on the Green. Even without a pricey floral designer, you have the advantage of natural landscaping and great views that inspire and enhance your day and night. In the case of a wedding held at a botanical garden, you can't pay anyone to create such lovely gardens, floral-lined pathways, and landscaping genius. If you'll be in your backyard, your mom's prize rosebushes will add to the décor and not cost you a cent.

As you'll see in the photography section, the great outdoors provides priceless shots you'll never capture if you plan an indoor event. For instance, an inspired photographer will scout the setting for such amazing shots as the two of you walking along a romantic cobblestone path past a wishing well, or sitting together on a detailed stone wall, throwing bread crumbs to the family of ducks who just swam up to your reception, or—if you're lucky—admiring the rainbow that just formed after a light misting over the ocean. Outdoor weddings seem to support the notion that if you get into a friendly challenge with Mother Nature and win, she will reward you greatly.

Wide open spaces are also a big benefit to the outdoor wedding. Say you're planning a large wedding for all of your relatives, friends, neighbors, and colleagues. Family is very important to you, and you want to allow the guests to bring their kids. An outdoor wedding provides the perfect environment for such a wieldy guest list. Whereas small children would be out of place (and perhaps out of control) at a formal indoor wedding, all cooped up with nothing but the ice at the buffet table to amuse themselves, at the more informal style of an outdoor wedding there's room for wandering, for tag among the trees, for a separate section to be designed as the kids' supervised entertainment area. So many couples, especially those with kids themselves, do not want to leave the children out of the festivities, and this wedding setup is ideal for the all-inclusive arrangement. Plus, you might join in on the game of tag with the kids. Imagine the pictures of that scene. Priceless.

This brings up an important advantage to outdoor weddings. There are more opportunities for spontaneous fun. At a beach wedding, you might decide as a couple to take a short, intimate walk together along the shoreline just after your ceremony concludes. These valuable few moments alone together, especially in a romantic and idyllic setting as a pristine beach with gently breaking waves, are a luxury that few couples get to enjoy. Most get a three-minute limo ride alone to the reception, where they're mobbed by guests for the rest of the evening. Or, like that commercial I mentioned earlier, an impromptu game of soccer might break out and you can make all the jokes you want about the groom "scoring" just an hour after the ceremony.

Planning an outdoor wedding *does* have a major upside. If you're planning an at-home wedding or an outdoor wedding at a unique location, you will not have to get on a four-year waiting list such as at a traditional reception site. Your backyard is not likely to be booked for anything major a year from now, and that lovely estate home in the next town will be far more available than the best-known banquet hall. This alone is a great relief to some brides, as they simply don't have time to make hundreds of phone calls and check dozens of Web sites to find a Saturday that's available before 2006. Other perks: Having the ceremony and reception in that one outdoor location means you won't have to book and pay for transportation between the two places. You won't have to arrange for your guests to get from point A to point B either, and you won't have to worry about printing out more than one set of directions. It's one-stop celebrating and worth the hassles elsewhere to balance out the huge value of this component.

But perhaps the greatest advantage of all is that you can choose the setting of your dreams and fill it with the images of your dreams. You can create a wedding as beautiful as that of any celebrity's, and you can close it off by slow-dancing under the stars. The real stars.

No doubt you'll discover countless advantages as we move together through the pages of this book, plus some more of your own that you'll discover along the way. Obviously, an outdoor wedding holds many advantages. Why else would celebrities choose this type of wedding from their limitless options?

Q. *And this book will help us put it all together?*

A. From day one, you'll have all of the information and resources at your disposal, as well as expert advice from many top wedding professionals from all over the country. The pros consulted here have handled countless weddings, organized celebrity charity and personal events, had their work featured in magazines and on television, and even planned outdoor soirees for former presidents and first ladies.

Real-life couples will share their triumphs and wish-we-knew-better stories from every area of their own wedding-planning process, so that you can learn from their experiences. You'll find ways to cut costs on such outdoor-wedding issues as rentals, site permits, destination weddings, and outdoor-appropriate wedding gowns, tuxes, and décor. You'll learn which menu items are right for the different styles of outdoor weddings and the different weather factors, and you'll learn how to weatherproof your hair and makeup for a flawless look on your big day.

At the end of the book, you'll find worksheets, checklists, and extensive lists of resources for your research use and bargain finds.

And now, let's start creating your perfect outdoor wedding.

Other Books by Sharon Naylor

How to Plan an Elegant Wedding in 6 Months or Less

The Mother-of-the-Bride Book

1,001 Ways to Have a Dazzling Second Wedding

1001 Ways to Save Money and Still Have a Dazzling Wedding

The Bridal Party Handbook

For more wedding-planning and cost-cutting information, plus a free subscription to Sharon Naylor's *Wedding Tips* newsletter, visit www.sharonnaylor.net.

What Kind of Wedding Do You Want?

THIS IS the fun part. Here, you get to consider all the different ideal images of your perfect wedding in order to assess what your planning process will entail. This book covers the five general categories of outdoor weddings:

1. The True Outdoor Wedding, Open-Air Style
2. The Outdoor Wedding "On Location" with Tent
3. The At-Home Outdoor Wedding
4. The Beach Wedding
5. The Boat Wedding

You've undoubtedly seen glossy, beautiful images of all of these types of weddings, and now it's time to choose which one is right for you.

The True Outdoor Wedding, Open-Air Style

Imagine this . . .

A beautiful stretch of green landscape, surrounded by flowering trees, is transformed into the perfect wedding location. The collection

I

of tables set with crisp white tablecloths, flawless china, and crystal that sparkles in the sun provides a stunning contrast against the bright green lawn and foliage. Your flowers add a touch of elegance to the scene, and your guests mill about with champagne in their hands. Perhaps a trio of violinists strolls through the crowd, while tuxedoed butlers offer (with a gracious bow) selections of Brie-en-croute, bacon-wrapped scallops, and shrimp on silver platters. The sun shines down, and a gentle breeze wisps past.

Nearby, the children—all adorably dressed and laughing—are playing tag or peering over the edge of a stone wall to see the babbling brook and its promise of minnows and tadpoles.

The wedding of your dreams, open-air style, is held out in the glory of nature. No tents, just the canopy of the trees.

The Outdoor Wedding "On Location" with Tent

Now, imagine that same scene with a majestic white tent opening up to invite the guests to step inside. Perhaps this tent is located on the grounds of a beautiful arboretum or botanical garden. Smooth stone walkways lead to the festivities and also provide guests with paths for strolling past lavishly floral borders, fountains, ponds, and fields of lilies.

The tent provides shelter from the glare of the sun and the work of the wind, but it also provides a "room of one's own" that is transformed into your own vision of the perfect ballroom. Shimmering fabric swags transform the ceiling of the tent into a soft upper field, with not a hint of circuses or county fairs. The draped walls of the tent afford privacy, and the entire affair is as grand as can be. You have created your own five-star surroundings, whether in the middle of a paradise of flowers or with a view of the sea.

The At-Home Outdoor Wedding

Take the above-mentioned wedding and put it in your own backyard. The spacious lawn where you once played kickball as a kid, or where you've grown your own daisies for years, becomes transformed into an exquisite setting for your big day. Perhaps you'll hold your ceremony on the front lawn, walking down the gardenia-lined front walkway to a trellis where your minister awaits. A tent covers your backyard, again transforming the area into your own personalized ballroom.

What's even more meaningful is that this is "home." This is where you've shared many years of memories with your family—whether it's their home or yours—and now you are embedding your home with everlasting memories of this beautiful event.

Many brides love the symbolism of marrying at home, not to mention the convenience of not having to worry about finding an available date. Another advantage is that the entire affair can be easily moved indoors in case of truly inclement weather. So another thing to consider is the ease of adaptation. Plus, you'll love watching your home and all of its surroundings get a complete makeover. Your guests will be in awe.

The Beach Wedding

Your guests are gathered on a white-sand beach, watching your approach with wide smiles and tears in their eyes. As the music accompanies your procession, the ocean provides a rolling backdrop of its own brand of music. Seabirds call out, and the sun shines down. You're barefoot, your groom is casually dressed (he always did look great in a pair of chinos), and your maids are in comfortable sundresses—sans shoes—as well.

You couldn't ask for a more relaxed or more natural atmosphere, as your ceremony comes to a close and your wedding party moves to a tented or outdoor reception. The view of the seascape is magnificent. The sun may be setting over the water, turning the sky into a wash of vivid purples and pinks, and the stars begin to shine brightly over the clean ocean sky.

Wedding experts from all areas of the industry tell me that the beach wedding is running away with the prize for most popular style of outdoor wedding. Couples love the relaxed setting and not having to be all buttoned-up and proper. Brides love having the freedom to choose a flattering dress that doesn't make them look like a chandelier, and guests love a great night out at the beach.

After the wedding is over, you'll all be able to go back to your seaside hotels and enjoy the nightlife, the outdoor swimming pools and Jacuzzis, or perhaps a midnight sail aboard a yacht. It doesn't get much better than that.

The Boat Wedding

Your ceremony is performed on the top deck of a cruiser yacht as your guests watch you take your vows with a scrolling view of the cityscape passing all around you. The champagne corks pop, and the party begins. Some of the larger boats offer enclosed ballrooms downstairs for weather-protected celebration (an option if raindrops require you to move your ceremony into the interior of the boat), and the schooners and cabin cruisers invite you to stroll the decks and perhaps hoist the sails for a wind-spirited ride through the most gorgeous waterways available.

Whether it's an open-air sail through New York Harbor, a whisk around Martha's Vineyard or the Hamptons, or an all-day/all-night sail off the shores of Monterey, the boat wedding is a unique and memorable experience. The caterer might whip up a seafarer's delight in menu options: king crab legs, lobster claws, stuffed clams, Caesar salads. And you'll toast each other with a fine vintage as you sail off into the sunset surrounded by your loved ones.

Of course, these are just general snapshots of the five basic types of outdoor weddings, just to get your wheels turning. At this point, you're probably wondering which type would offer the best odds of beating the weather—a big concern of every couple planning an outdoor wedding, whose greatest fear just may be, What if it rains? Any tent wedding offers you ample protection against the wind and rain, and blinding sun for that matter. A beach wedding can be planned using a nearby beachside restaurant with an outdoor terrace as an adjunct reception location. The yacht you choose should have a sheltered indoors level, or else you risk the complete nightmare of being stuck on a boat in the rain for a long time until you reach the dock again, sitting in a puddle, freezing and miserable.

Fear of the weather is a big factor for any bride considering an outdoor wedding, but it does not have to be. The solutions are there. All of these types of weddings have workable solutions—you just need to plan for a bit of extra work, as well as be mindful of plan B as you plan your big day.

One of the best solutions for couples who are truly nervous about the weather, or who know they live in a finicky weather area, is to split the wedding in half. Have the ceremony outside and the reception inside. Or, have the ceremony inside, perhaps in a church or synagogue, and then hold the reception outdoors at home or in a garden.

If you truly want an outdoor wedding, it would be a shame to let a projected "what if?" fear take that possibility away from you. No one can guarantee the weather, but you can guarantee yourself the wedding of your dreams if you plan ahead, plan for alternatives, and make smart choices each step along the way.

The ideas are probably already flowing through your mind right now. So, let's start by brainstorming your ideal images and wished-for elements of your day. On the following page, you'll find a worksheet

Make It a Joint Effort

To allow the groom his say in the planning of the wedding, make a photocopy of the worksheet below and ask for his input. Some grooms are eager to be involved in the planning process, and some just want to show up on the wedding day. But whatever the case may be, the groom should at least have the *option* of a say in the matter. One groom I spoke to said, "All of my friends are going to be there, and I don't want a poofy frou-frou wedding. I want some elements that my buddies are going to enjoy, like prime rib on the menu instead of foie gras. I don't even know what foie gras is." We've come a long way from the days when *all* grooms just put on their tuxes and showed up. It's not just the bride's day anymore. The guys want to make some plans too, as well they should in the creation of the perfect day for both the bride and the groom.

where you can start writing down your ideas for each aspect of the wedding. Whatever comes to mind—whether it's that Vera Wang gown you saw in the pages of a bridal magazine, that Gail Watson wedding cake your cousin had at her wedding, or the wedding bands from the Tiffany catalog—write it all down. I can't tell you how important it is—*especially* for the planning of an outdoor, customized wedding—to know what you want and to be able to describe it.

What kind of outdoor setting do you want for your wedding—a botanical garden? A beach? The backyard transformed by tents and great landscaping?

What kind of outdoor setting do you want for your wedding *(continued)*

How big is the wedding (i.e., how many people are going to be on your list)?

_____ Immediate family

_____ Extended family

_____ Friends

_____ Colleagues

_____ Clients

_____ Neighbors

_____ Parents' lists

_____ Siblings' lists

Do you want a large wedding, where everyone has to be invited, including their kids, or do you want a small, intimate gathering of your closest friends and relatives?

Who will you choose for your bridal party?

Describe the perfect gown for the wedding you're envisioning.

How will you wear your hair?

What kind of jewelry will you wear with the gown?

Will you wear a veil?

What will the bridesmaids be wearing—full-length gowns? Cocktail dresses? Sundresses?

What will the men be wearing—tuxedoes? Dinner jackets? Khaki pants and navy jackets? Khaki pants and white, button-down shirts?

What will your wedding colors be?

Describe the elements of your ceremony. Will you want a full, traditional, religious ceremony or a more custom-planned style?

What kinds of food do you want at your reception?

Will you want a sit-down dinner? A cocktail hour with passed hors d'oeuvres? A buffet? Dessert only?

What kind of cake do you want—three tiers? Six tiers? Chocolate ganache? A different cake flavor on every level?

What will the entertainment be like—DJ? Band? Orchestra? Strolling musicians?

Name some songs you'd like to dance to with your partner.

Will you want a limo to whisk you away? A horse and carriage? Your convertible with the top down and a "Just Married" sign on the back?

What other ideas do you have?

Again, this worksheet is just a tool to get you to keep track of your vision for your wedding. Each of these questions is very important, as the elements of any wedding all come together to form the wedding's style, as well as determine the suitability of your wedding location. Location is an all-important thing for an outdoor wedding, so your wishes may determine the style of wedding you'll ultimately have.

As you move through the months of planning, you'll undoubtedly adapt these wishes, perhaps add more detail to them, or decide you want something different altogether. Be flexible! Be spontaneous! Follow the ideas in your imagination, and you'll have a ball watching your dream wedding come together with each decision you make.

Size Does Matter

One of the most important questions you've just been asked is: How big do you want your wedding to be? The size of your guest list determines many of the plans for your wedding. Not only does a larger guest list mean a bigger bridal budget, but it also sets the stage for the location of your wedding. For instance, if you're only planning on having twenty close relatives attend your wedding, then the smaller yacht may be the setting for you. If your guest list tops 250, then that outdoor wedding at the arboretum may be a better fit than the backyard bash at home.

For most couples, the budget alone determines the guest list, and then the reception hall is chosen to accommodate that number. In this situation, many couples planning traditional indoor weddings find that their guest lists are restricted due to space limitations. They may not be able to invite all of the guests they'd like because their banquet room only seats 120. For you, planning your outdoor wedding, you're less limited by the constraints of your guest list as far as space is concerned. Out in a garden or on the beach, space is unlimited. You've removed one obstacle toward having the full attendance you desire.

> ### Wedding Day Reflections
>
> I kept going back over my original ideas sheet, adding in new ideas that I'd gotten from my planner, from my friends, from televised wedding specials. In the end, I was amazed at how little I imagined for myself in the beginning, how few details I could actually name. It made me see my own progress as my ideas sheet turned into a true blueprint of what I wanted from my day.
>
> —Allison

So, now that you've considered whether you want a small, intimate wedding or an enormous one, you have a better idea of what kinds of locations you'll be looking at. You'll thus have a better idea of where to start your search.

A Question of Children

A great many brides I've spoken to said that their desire to include children in their weddings led them to choose an outdoor location. For brides and grooms who are fortunate enough to be part of large, loving families, they wouldn't dream of having a wedding where children are not included.

Whether or not to include children at a wedding poses a big question for etiquette experts. When you consider that caterers charge by the plate, inviting fifty children at $75 a plate—when they'll probably just pick at the cheese platter—means that you're going to spend a fortune for all of those kids to be there. Some brides and grooms agonize over the decision of which kids get to come. Some may naturally include all their nieces and nephews, but what about the first-cousins' kids? How do you tell your cousin no when you'd like your best friend to bring her two sons? How do you avoid hurting feelings? And how do you indicate on the invitation that kids aren't invited?

These are the sticky relational situations that can make a bride's head spin. When the size of the wedding is an issue—whether due

Wedding Day Reflections

When Allison put this sheet in front of me and asked me to write down my ideas for the wedding, I kind of humored her and just wrote down: I want to show up on time. But as I watched her having so much fun with the planning, and as we talked about all the different ideas she was having, I just found myself piping in with suggestions about how to light the tent, what kind of meal we'd have, and all kinds of other things. Maybe it was because we had planning checklists and idea sheets, and we weren't just sitting down for tea at her mom's and gushing about the silverware, that it was much more fun for me to be involved. We still look back on those idea sheets and see how our wishes changed from the beginning of the process to the end . . . especially once we realized the beach wedding thing was possible. Then it was an explosion of ideas from there.

—Jeff

to space, budget, or just general matters of sanity—solid decisions are going to have to be made about children attending the wedding and reception. Some couples draw the line at their own children and those kids who are part of the bridal party. Period. They arrange for day care during the hours of the ceremony and reception, and they indicate that kids aren't invited to the wedding by following the long-held etiquette rule: Write only the parents' names on the invitation. Case closed.

Inviting children to the wedding is a big proposition. Not only do you need to arrange for extra space while you're eating—they can run wild in the gardens after the meal—you'll also have to take some extra steps:

• Arrange for several kid-friendly options on the menu.

• Provide adequate day care with trained and licensed baby-sitters.

• Ensure the children's safety, especially at outdoor parks where bridges and slopes can cause falls.

• Arrange for entertainment for the kids during the reception. Have children brought around to the side of the tent, or to a separate area of the park, for special activities just for kids. Some ideas: puppet shows, a visit from costumed characters, even the screening of a popular children's movie on videotape.

Children are happy just to be running in a pack together, and they're mesmerized by the idea of chasing fireflies and butterflies, or collecting shells on the beach. Put in the time and effort now to arrange for some kind of organized entertainment and supervision for

---

Wedding Day Reflections

My family lives all over the country, and we haven't seen some of our cousins for years. I haven't even seen my college roommate's new baby yet. So we're having a big outdoor wedding where the guests can bring their children, and the kids can play together. A wedding, to us, is a family affair. And it's not family without the kids.

—Sarah

But What About the Children?

My friend just called to say she'd be coming to the wedding with her husband, and they wanted to bring their eight-year-old son. The kid's a holy terror and is certain to cause disruptions. What do I do?

You'll have to explain to your friend that you're in a tough situation here. Although you'd love to include all the kids in the wedding day, you've had to draw the line and say "adults only." Promise her that you've arranged for high-quality day care during the wedding, and you'd be happy to arrange for a sitter for her son. Just be lighthearted about it, mention that you've had to turn down several relatives' similar requests, and that you're sure a few hours out together alone would be fun for her and her husband. Be firm, and don't cave in. You'd be surprised how news of a flip-flop spreads like wildfire, and all of your friends and relatives will be calling for an exemption from your rule. This is one of the toughest parts of planning an important family event. You have to keep your own best interests in mind, and you have to establish boundaries.

the kids. A big crowd, tired kids, and "old people's music" can add up to major tantrums and disruptions to your wedding.

Another option to consider is the wedding weekend. All of those kids can be safely left out of the wedding-day (and night) festivities if you've planned the new, popular "wedding weekend." This trend has couples planning three days' worth of activities for guests who come into town for the big bash. The activities may include free passes to a ball game, a museum, or a zoo; casual dinners or barbecues; or a friendly game of badminton or softball at the local park. Filling up a weekend with activities makes the trip to your wedding location even more enjoyable and allows for family togetherness on a much more relaxed and informal basis. Plus, everyone gets to show off their kids, and everyone gets to have a good time. Your wedding day, then, becomes a more official event, where the parents happily get a break from the kids, and you don't have to worry about screaming babies during your vows or tantrums during the best man's toast.

WHO MAKES THE CUT?

Now that you've decided whether the kids are in or out, it's time to figure out just who makes the cut for your wedding guest list. For this step, you'll be dealing with three lists: yours, your parents', and the groom's parents'. If this isn't your first wedding, you may be lucky enough to just be dealing with your own list. Whatever the case, it's important to do a complete job with your guest list so that you have a starting point for your budget, your location scouting, your catering ideas, and various other aspects of your wedding as they pop up later.

When creating the guest list, it's important that you be organized. When you're listing 200 names, compiling three different lists, and dealing with kids, for example, you might end up with duplicate listings. So comb through the list first and verify that you have single listings for everyone.

Next, create "tiers" for your wedding list. Tiers are established to classify each guest according to where they fit in your life. No, this isn't where you give your relatives A's or B's for how kind they've been to you and whether or not they sent you a birthday card this year. It establishes where they stand. The usual tier arrangement looks something like this:

Wedding Day Reflections

We rented some outdoor activity sets, like the air-filled Moonwalk for the bigger kids to play on. For the little ones, we rented one of those tubs filled with the brightly colored plastic balls. We didn't want anyone getting hurt, so we put the trampoline away. More for our drunk ushers' safety than the kids'.

—Melanie

Wedding Weekend Activities

Here are some activity ideas for the typical wedding weekend:

Sporting-event tickets

Museum trips

Boating and fishing

Family sports competitions, such as
    softball or miniature golf

Taking in a kids' theater production

Broadway-type play tickets

Free movie passes

Golf outings

Horseback riding

Shopping outings at the nearby
    outlets or posh mall

Brunch buffets

Barbecues

Pizza night

Theme-restaurant nights

Home-movie night

1. Immediate family—grandparents, parents, stepparents, brothers, sisters, children
2. Bridal party and their guests
3. Closest friends and their guests
4. First cousins
5. First-cousins' kids
6. Clients
7. Colleagues
8. Distant relatives with whom I speak regularly
9. Friends who have not quite completely faded from my life
10. Neighbors

These tiers are just in place in case the location you love has a capacity limit. This categorizing will make it easier to eliminate categories of people from your list from the bottom up. It's just a way to organize the "cut" list so that you don't waste too much time flipping coins while pointing to people's names.

Help! The Parents' Guest List Is Twenty Pages Long!

Simply asking your parents for their list can be the introduction to a major headache. Parents always want everyone they've ever known on their list, and their final headcount alone can total more than your original entire guest list. So here are some tips for establishing rules for the parents' lists:

• Tell them you've already got the relatives you're inviting on your list. Give them a limit above the duplicate names from your list. Say, "We're doing the guest list now, and we have just a little bit of room to spare. So just let me know the ten extra people (friends or clients) you'd like to invite."

• Remind them that the guest list is a fluid thing. Even though you have ample space at your disposal with an outdoor wedding, the budget is still a big issue for you. Let them know that you may have to trim down the guest list in the future, so if they could put a star next to the names they really want at the wedding, you'll try to keep them on the list.

• Inform them of your rules for selection. Parents are notorious for applying the "trade-off" approach, as in, "Well, you were invited to Marge and Tony's wedding thirteen years ago, so they have to come to yours." If you don't know Marge and Tony's last name, they don't make the list. Explain that you want to have all of your closest friends and family at your wedding, and though you'd love to accommodate them, you just don't have room for people you don't really know.

• Be prepared for battle. Some parents don't know how to separate their wants from your needs, especially if they are paying for the wedding, and they have a funny way of manipulating their adult kids with the old line "Well, we're paying for it, so what we say goes." Unfortunately, no matter what your age and independence level, it's all too common for parents to wield their power with that one and squeeze those extra guests onto the list. When you must say no to protect your own interests (and friendships), just stand firm, explain that you're doing all you can, and don't take any grief. If Mom comes out with the usual, "Well, how would that look?" then you can respond with, "It'll look like the wedding I want."

Don't forget about your guests' guests. You'll certainly want to allow your bridal party and older guests to invite their partners to the wedding. As a general rule, guests under 18 do not bring a date, but you can bend that rule for siblings or cousins that you know are in long-term relationships. Here's a bright idea from one couple: "If you have children and are planning a large, outdoor family-oriented party, then why not allow your kids to invite one or two of their school friends for familiar company?"

Guest List Worksheet

(Copy this page for your own list, parents' lists, combined lists, and final list.)

Name of guest	Who this person is	Tier placement

A Formal Question

Another determining factor in what kind of outdoor wedding you'll plan is the level of formality of the event itself. If you want an ultra-formal wedding, with all of the accoutrements such as guests in long gowns and tuxes; exorbitant fare such as lobster tails, caviar, and champagne; and a string orchestra, then your outdoor event will take on a certain shape (and accompanying budget!). If your style is more to the other extreme, and you prefer a more relaxed, informal wedding or even a tea or brunch, then your plans will reflect that level as well.

It really depends upon your personal tastes and your vision for the perfect wedding.

Generally, outdoor weddings take place during the day, or during the transition from day to night. According to the standard rules of formality based on the time of day (see chapter 4), outdoor weddings are perfect for less formal receptions.

An outdoor wedding usually means the attire will be more informal. Generally, although you do have the freedom to create the wedding you want, where you want it, the location determines what the formality level will be. Some locations just call out for a more formal dress code and décor. For example, an elegant mansion with fountains and marble stairs will certainly demand highly formal elements for your day. A beach wedding, on the other hand, is no place for long ball gowns and full tuxedoes with vests and tails. An arboretum wedding may be too ornate for an informal wedding. Your location will directly affect the formality of your wedding, so once you pinpoint the level you'd like to achieve, then you'll better know what kinds of locations to scout. The level of formality may be determined in part by your location, but it's more a matter of what your ideal wedding details entail. All of the details must match the wedding's level of formality, and as we proceed through the book you'll be able to choose each element according to how it fits into the formality level of your day as well as your own wishes.

Simplify It

A computer program can greatly simplify the task of your wedding list, as you can classify each name according to where people "rank" on your list. The computer will then rank according to your classifications and deliver an organized list at the touch of a button. Some wedding-planning software programs do offer this kind of tracking system, but you can do it yourself with Microsoft Access on your own home or work computer.

The Neighbors Can Hear You!

We're having an outdoor wedding in my backyard. I'm close with my neighbors and have gone out to dinner with them on occasion, but I don't have enough room on my guest list to invite them to the wedding. I don't want them to hate me for not inviting them. What do I do?

If you truly cannot invite your neighbors to the wedding, then it would be good form for you to let them know ahead of time that you are planning a backyard reception and are thus limited in space. Why say anything at all? Well, these neighbors are going to be the ones dealing with all the cars parked on the street, the kids straying into their yard, the noise and the lights until 11 P.M. It's best to let them know of your plans so that they can expect the crowd. Let them know what time the party is scheduled to end, so that they don't fear an all-nighter and call the police to shut down your fun. As for the damage done to the relationship, make up for it by asking the neighbors to dinner at your place when you return from your honeymoon, no gifts allowed. I'm sure the peace will be restored.

Help! This Is Too Much!

Considering all that you'll be doing—planning an outdoor wedding (which includes making your backup plans for an alternate location in case of weather problems), in addition to all of the many other details involved—you might favor the idea of hiring a wedding coordinator. Some brides and grooms appreciate the knowledge and wisdom an experienced planner brings to the process, and they find it worth the expense to leave the details to a pro. Some couples are just way too busy with their career and family obligations to devote the necessary time to planning every little aspect of such an involved task. Some may be finishing up school and planning to marry after graduation, and studying for the bar or for finals does not allow much time for interviewing bands. So hiring a planner may be the way to go.

A professional wedding planner can take the reins for the long planning road ahead, and the brides I've spoken to said that their planners made the whole experience both much more successful and much more enjoyable.

The raves about good planners keep coming in, and that's because most couples *are* extremely busy running the rest of their lives. Wedding coordinators take on the dirty work, the research, the phone calls, the checking, the reminding, all so that we don't have to do it. Their time *is* money, however, you might find that your particular life situation is such that the investment is worth your peace of mind.

> ## *Wedding Day Reflections*
>
> A *word to the wise: Don't let other people see your guest list. You're sure to hear 'Why am I tier B when Aunt Zelda is tier A?' Ranking your guests is great for managing your guest list, but it's hell for family diplomacy. So leave it at home.*
>
> —Renee

CRITERIA FOR HIRING A WEDDING COORDINATOR

The wedding coordinator, as is the case with any wedding professional, is subject to his or her customers' great scrutiny. After all, you'll be spending a lot of money on your wedding, and your emotional investment is even greater. Consider hiring a coordinator to be akin to hiring a nanny or an investment specialist. You'd ask plenty of questions, ask for references, demand experience, and the ultimate in service. For a wedding coordinator, the values are much the same.

Just Ask!

According to the Association of Bridal Consultants, the average couple spends 15% of their wedding budget on their bridal consultant, and brides older than 30 are much more likely to hire a professional wedding planner than to get help from their relatives and friends.

WHERE DOES ONE FIND A WEDDING COORDINATOR?

Start your wedding coordinator search by asking recently married friends, relatives, and coworkers for the names of their event coordinators. Very often, wedding coordinators also do corporate events, so don't count out your unmarried friends for their advice on this one. Ask if anyone has worked with a great planner, and add those names to your investigations list.

Once you have your list of candidates, it's time to do some research. Phone inquiries can reveal what should be your main concern: whether or not that particular planner belongs to an event-planning association. The Association of Bridal Consultants (ABC) (860-355-0464, www.weddingchannel.com) and the Association of Certified Professional Wedding Consultants (408-528-9000, www.acpwc.com) are just two of the most prestigious event-planning associations out there, and membership in these groups means that your potential planner has been well screened, well trained, and has years of experience and credentials. These associations can also recommend planners in your area, provide the details of those planners' services, and give you all contact information. Any

Simplify It

A less formal wedding held during the day will cost less than an ultraformal wedding held at night. Everything from the menu to the décor to the entertainment relies upon the level of formality, and that directly affects the budget.

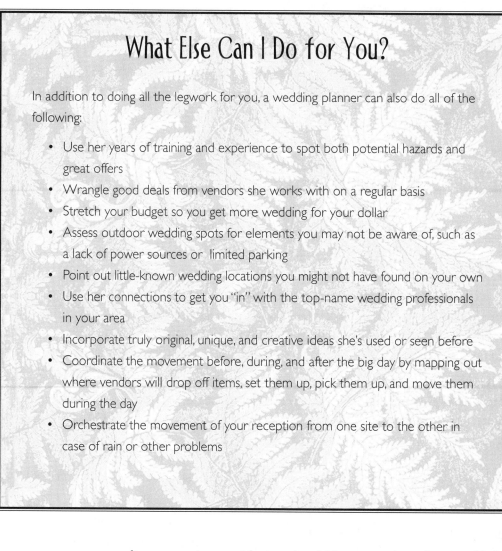

What Else Can I Do for You?

In addition to doing all the legwork for you, a wedding planner can also do all of the following:

- Use her years of training and experience to spot both potential hazards and great offers
- Wrangle good deals from vendors she works with on a regular basis
- Stretch your budget so you get more wedding for your dollar
- Assess outdoor wedding spots for elements you may not be aware of, such as a lack of power sources or limited parking
- Point out little-known wedding locations you might not have found on your own
- Use her connections to get you "in" with the top-name wedding professionals in your area
- Incorporate truly original, unique, and creative ideas she's used or seen before
- Coordinate the movement before, during, and after the big day by mapping out where vendors will drop off items, set them up, pick them up, and move them during the day
- Orchestrate the movement of your reception from one site to the other in case of rain or other problems

coordinator you're considering should be a member of an established organization in the field, so that you know your professional comes well prepared to do a good job on your wedding.

WHAT ARE THE QUALITIES OF A GOOD WEDDING COORDINATOR?

Although you can begin your research process over the phone, such as winnowing down the field by asking if the coordinator is

- Track down an errant delivery on the day of the wedding so you don't have to make last-minute frantic calls
- Diplomatically get you discounts or slashed fees for any vendors' wedding-day mistakes
- Read and request changes to vendor contracts in order to protect your best interests (Note: Be sure to be involved in this process also, as you have to protect your own best interests as well!)
- Advise you on matters of etiquette
- Handle specific wedding item orders
- Make sure everything goes smoothly on the big day so that you don't have to worry

That's just the short list of the advantages of hiring a good wedding coordinator. And notice I said a *good* wedding coordinator. The wedding industry is a large one— a $32 billion-dollar industry, by the way—and there exists both good apples and bad apples. A good coordinator can do all of the above and more, and a bad coordinator can create more problems than you might have otherwise had. The key lies in making the investment of time to find and interview top-rated coordinators. There is no better way to ruin your wedding than to try to speed through this process and hire the first planner you find. This is the person who will be in large part responsible for the success of your wedding—for the creation of your wedding dream come true. So take the selection process very seriously.

available on your wedding date, a face-to-face meeting at the planner's office is crucial for making the big decision.

It is here at the personal meeting that you'll get your first look at who the planner is, what she has to offer, what she's accomplished in the past, and—most importantly—how the two of you get along. Forging a good relationship is an important part of the planner-bride relationship. You'll want to make sure the planner is a friendly person, that she has a solid, professional manner, is a good listener, takes notes, explains her services and terms well, and just generally has her act together. You'll be working together for a long time and depending upon a lot of give-and-take. Any partnership requires good communication, similar working styles, and a great deal of respect. You also have to *like* the person you're working with. So a lengthy chat at the first consultation (which is usually free) is more than just a gathering of information; it's sort of like a blind date. You never know if you're going to hit it off. But when you do, you'll know it.

Another important element of this first visit to the planner's office is assessing what you see around you. Although not everyone can afford a lavishly decorated office straight out of the pages of *Martha Stewart Living*—and if they do have one, you might want to look at the price list for services—a good planner works in an organized office that's clean and functional. If you walk in to find stacks of folders piled waist-high, tons of message slips stuck to the desk, and days' worth of unopened mail, then you know that this particular planner isn't efficient enough to handle your wedding well.

A good planner also displays examples of her work, whether in framed pictures on the walls or in photo albums with extensive images from all of the different events she has done. Some planners display framed thank-you notes from celebrities, politicians, and well-known families, but you shouldn't be swayed simply on that basis. Look at the work, look at the images, look at the details. See if they're pleasing to you. Most importantly, look at the pictures of the outdoor weddings and events

Wedding Day Reflections

At first, I was afraid to hire a planner. I thought the whole wedding would be taken over and I wouldn't have anything to say about it. I thought I'd be subjected to all kinds of out-there, artsy touches, but I was so surprised to find that my planner was not Franck from Father of the Bride. She was a regular person with great ideas, who listened to my ideas, and did everything she could to incorporate them. It was WAY better than letting my mother get involved.

—Angela

the planner has done. Ask her to tell you about her experience with outdoor weddings. You'll want to make sure she has a lot of events like yours under her belt, that she's experienced in the nuances of planning at an outdoor location, and that she's had much success with such arrangements in the past.

Ask to see letters of recommendation. Most planners also have these in a display book or in a file. Read through to see what the brides and grooms have had to say. Of course, no planner is going to include a bash letter that complains about unreturned phone calls, sloppy delivery, or incomplete service, so take these with a grain of salt. Are all of the brides thanking the planner for "listening to what I had to say" or "going above and beyond"? For "being reliable" and making the day "perfect"? Read the letters carefully and use them as just one part of your assessment.

If you're happy so far, ask to see the planner's package details. Most planners now offer a veritable menu of their services, including the following:

- *All-inclusive packages.* The planner will do just about everything—research vendors, help with the budget, book, arrange, order, confirm, and run the wedding day from start to finish.

- *Limited packages.* The planner will help you do your own research, do the booking and ordering, and run the wedding day.

Wedding Day Reflections

I visited a few planners before I came to Jenny, and it was amazing how we just hit it off from the start. She has a friendly, joking manner about her that just makes her fun to be around. But she's also all business. I liked how she spoke to her assistants, how she allowed her voice mail to take phone calls from other people while I was sitting there, and how she really listened to what I had to say. Her credentials, package information, and contract were included in an organized packet she gave to me, and she answered all my questions fully. We worked well together from the start.

—Celia

- *One-day packages.* The planner will act as ringleader on the wedding day to be sure the deliveries are made to the right places and that the vendors show up, to arrange the design of the location, and to direct guests to the right place.

Of course, many different packages exist, but these are the three most common. See if the packages match your needs, and talk openly about just how much assistance you expect. Planners know that today's brides and grooms are busy, and they're well trained to formulate a plan that works with your needs.

THE MONEY QUESTION

So, what does a good planner cost? Although some wedding coordinators charge a flat fee on retainer for the wedding-planning process, the norm is for the planner to charge 10% to 15% of the total bill for the wedding. To the cynical, it would seem that the planner would make more money if she got *you* to spend more money and, based on the principles of economics, that's true. But you can control that little issue by establishing a budget and sticking to it. Never give a planner carte blanche with your wedding budget, no matter how much you're tempted to splurge.

Always be in control of the expenses, and always speak up if you think she's planning too much for your floral budget, for example. Remember, no matter how professional she is or how impressive her credentials are, she works for you.

Wedding Day Reflections

We were planning a destination wedding, so we had to work with a planner from that area. It meant that we didn't get to have a face-to-face meeting with our coordinator, and that all of our communication was either over the phone or through e-mail. We just asked the resort for the best planner they had, checked her credentials with the Association of Bridal Consultants, asked for a packet of her work, and assessed her on her performance. She was great to work with, always returned calls within a few hours, sent what we needed, and generally did a great job. We met her on the wedding day and couldn't believe what a wonderful job she'd done. Everything was just as we'd asked.

—Tracy

THE CONTRACT

A good wedding coordinator will always provide a solid partnership contract that outlines the terms of her services, her fees, and a detailed list of extras. Make sure the contract is complete, that her full information is listed on the contract, that the wedding date and location are listed on the contract, and that you both sign it. Steer clear of coordinators who do not offer contracts, as that is an indication of past legal issues or an unwillingness to take responsibility for services promised. A true professional always offers a contract and always lets you take it home to review before signing.

So now you have an idea of your wedding's style, size, and formality, and you've hired some help to pull it off. Now we get to the big stuff. The money.

What's It Going to Cost?

THAT'S THE big question. It seems that every couple planning an outdoor wedding wonders at the outset if this is a way to save money. Does an outdoor wedding cost less than a traditional, indoor one? The answer is both yes and no.

Of course an informal outdoor wedding can cost less than a standard, traditional indoor wedding, but the expenses for planning any outdoor wedding depend upon the choices you make. Though you may save a lot by not having to pay for extra hours of transportation (having a limousine take you and your bridal party from a church to a faraway reception site, for example), all of those rental costs for tables and chairs and linens can add up to make up for and surpass the difference. An extravagant outdoor wedding can cost well above the current national average of $20,000 for a standard indoor wedding. If the couple chooses a lavish menu, a sea of floral décor, a $7,000 wedding gown, and a crate of Cristal champagne, then of course the outdoor wedding is going to cost more than the standard event.

Natural Averages for Wedding Elements

According to a recent survey run by *Bridal Guide* magazine, the average couple will spend . . .

- . . . more than a year planning their wedding, which gives them plenty of time to search out savings.
- . . . a great deal of time looking to the Internet (49.1%), magazines (84.7%), and wedding books (40.8%) for ways to get more wedding for their budget.

According to the most recent survey by the Association of Bridal Consultants:

- Ninety-four percent of all weddings are formal
- Ninety-eight percent of all couples will have a reception
- Fifty-three percent of all weddings are funded by both sets of parents and the couple, while twenty-seven percent of weddings are funded by the couple themselves, and nineteen percent are funded by the father of the bride

According to a survey of over 1,000 brides on my wedding Web site, couples will spend large chunks of their wedding budget on their reception. Following, I've also included in parentheses the national average amounts reported by the Association of Bridal Consultants (ABC):

Stop Right There! How Can We Afford All This?

So even though it's not a given that outdoor weddings will save you a buck, you can save plenty by making smart cost-cutting choices throughout your planning process. Included throughout this book are boxed savings hints from my book *1001 Ways to Save Money . . . and Still Have a Dazzling Wedding*. With these insider tips, you'll learn how to find discounts, make smart shopping choices,

- More than $800 for the wedding gown
- More than $200 for the veil
- More than $175 for shoes and accessories
- More than $150 for bridesmaids' gowns, shoes, and accessories
- More than $80 for men's wedding wardrobe and accessories
- More than $5,000 for catering at the reception (ABC figures: The average cost of a reception is $4,217)
- More than $1,000 for flowers and décor (ABC figures: National average is $200–$500, only 2.5% will pay more than $2,000 for their flowers)
- More than $1,000 for entertainment (ABC figures: 61.5% pay less than $1,000 for their music selection)
- More than $500 for limousines or classic cars
- More than $1,700 for photography
- More than $1,000 for videography
- More than $250 for the wedding cake
- More than $600 for the invitations, programs, and other printed materials (ABC figures: $275 for invitations alone)
- More than $2,000 on wedding rings
- More than $3,000 for the honeymoon (ABC figures: $2,250)
- More than $18,000 for the entire wedding budget

stretch your budget, and even wrangle some wedding services and products for free. So watch for those savings hints and make your plans accordingly.

Clearly a wedding of any style, shape, or location is going to cost you. There's no getting around that, unless you want a very, very simple wedding (which may be more your style). Before you panic about the prices quoted in the box above, remember that those are national averages, derived from factoring-in numbers way above and way below those figures. Regardless of your regional location and the going rates in each area of the industry, solid bargains are to be found.

WHERE DO WE START?

Though these figures can be quite intimidating, it's important not to let your financial fears get the best of you. Your first step is to sit down and figure out how much money you'll have to work with. Include the amounts you and your fiancé are able to contribute, plus the amounts your parents may be able to contribute. You may be in the advantageous position of having generous parents with an open-ended gold card at your disposal. Or, you're working with a limited budget that has been carefully culled from all givers. Whatever your tax bracket, the issue of "Where is this money coming from?" remains.

We'll start with the usual situation. The couple's parents will adhere to the standards of old, even in these modern times, and pay for portions of the wedding. This brings up issues of etiquette—you're all wondering who pays for what. Below, I've listed the traditional list of bride's family's expenses and groom's family's expenses:

Here is the traditional list of who pays for what:

THE BRIDE'S FAMILY PAYS FOR

- Wedding announcements
- Engagement party
- Bridal consultant
- Invitations
- Wedding gown and veil
- Bride's accessories and shoes
- Reception site
- Catering
- Flowers
- Photographer
- Videographer

- Reception entertainment
- Limousines
- Tips

THE GROOM'S FAMILY PAYS FOR

- Officiant
- Marriage license
- Bride's bouquet
- Boutonnieres
- Rehearsal dinner
- Honeymoon

This is the traditional list that has been passed down through the books of etiquette for years. Many families do stick to these rules, but the trend now is for more of a pick-and-choose approach to each expense. Remember those figures in the national averages box, where I reported that 53% of weddings are funded by both sets of parents and over a quarter of weddings are funded by the couple themselves? With individual families perhaps holding different financial statures, and with good intentions worth more than gold, a list of prescribed expenses may cause pressure, obligation, and strain. If, say, the groom's family is extremely wealthy, whereas the bride's family is of more modest means, you can't avoid hurt feelings if the groom's family pays for the entire wedding. For many couples, this becomes a diplomacy nightmare, creating ego-centered battles and long-term resentments. Funny how money can drive wedges between people, and that's the last thing you want as you're creating a new life together as an extended family.

My best advice to you, especially when dealing with differing financial levels, is to create a budget pool. If the parents wish to contribute to the expenses of the wedding, they get to throw their money into your collection for this purpose. This removes several big problems that universally crop up when family and money blend. No

Keep It To Yourselves!

For an even smoother process of eliminating the measuring stick of monetary contributions, keep the amounts given by each set of parents to yourselves. Make it a solid rule that the totals are not to be shared with anyone, even if one set of parents hands over a check that makes your jaw hit the floor.

longer will you have the entitlement speeches that come with the handing over of the check, the "Well, we're paying for the band, so we get to approve/confirm/object." The bride and groom are free to take the funds and budget them accordingly, so that they can plan the wedding of their dreams. Somehow this arrangement does manage to smooth over the rough spots where family members' egos and personal reflections are concerned, and it virtually erases all of the implicit competition between the two sides.

No, nothing is ever simple, not even when you are blessed with the advantage of having parents and stepparents, grandparents and godparents help out with the budget for the wedding. Neither is it a cakewalk (so to speak) to take on a wedding budget by yourselves, even absent the family squabbling. Some couples save for years, some use all their graduation-gift money, some take on extra part-time jobs to pay for their wedding and honeymoon. I must warn you not to take such risks as maxing out your credit cards, taking on extra credit cards, taking out another mortgage, or selling your valuable antiques collection. As important as a wedding is, it's not as important as your financial stability. Plus, if you figure-in interest rates, your beautiful $20,000 wedding could end up costing you $150,000 in the long run. Do yourself a favor and don't base your wedding on debt. Use what you have, and use it wisely.

Prioritizing Expenses

Before we get to setting a realistic budget, it's important to think about your priorities for your wedding. Certain elements of the day are going to be more important to you, depending upon your personal style and your vision of the day you want. If it's a five-star reception you desire, then you'll want a larger portion of your budget devoted toward the caterer, cake, and liquor. You'd scale down the flower order to a simpler level in order to push more money into the food column. Or, perhaps you've always wanted a Vera Wang gown, and as you're not going to have limos at your outdoor wedding, you can shove that allocation into the gown budget. (For that Vera Wang gown, you might have to scale down the cake as well.) Whatever your must-have is for the wedding, you'll certainly want more of your wedding budget designated for that purchase. You can trade off in other areas to get a good balance with your budget. Use the list provided below to figure out where your

Your Wedding Elements Priority List

____ Engagement announcement	____ Caterer's menu
____ Engagement party	____ Liquor
____ Ceremony site	____ Cake
____ Reception site	____ Flowers
____ Rental items	____ Reception entertainment
____ Wedding gown	____ Photography
____ Accessories and shoes	____ Videography
____ Groom's clothing	____ Limousines/Transportation
____ Wedding coordinator	____ Favors
____ Invitations	____ Gifts
____ Programs	____ Honeymoon

priorities lie. You'll rank the elements with either stars or numbers—depending on your own personal ranking system—so that you'll know where you'll be concentrating your funds. (A word of note: On average, most brides and grooms spend 50% of their wedding budgets on the reception, as that's what's going to wow their guests.)

Now that you know where you're going to devote significant portions of your wedding budget (i.e., which section gets the big bucks), it's time to create your working wedding budget. Bear in mind that the purpose of a wedding budget is to keep you on track. The best working budgets are somewhat flexible, allowing you some room to budge and never so stringent that you're bound to any hard number. Budgeting is a tough job, especially when there is so much emotion, meaning, and importance attached to each category of your wedding plans. So use this tool as a starter, and allow yourself the grace to play with the numbers as you go along.

Simplify It

For a great interactive budget tool that totals your categories, keeps track of your expenses, and offers you great efficiency, check out the free wedding budgeting spreadsheet at www.TheKnot.com.

WEDDING BUDGET

Items/service	Who's paying	Budgeted	Actual
Engagement announcement			
Engagement party			
Ceremony site			
Ceremony décor			
Officiant's fee			
Marriage license			
Blood tests			
Prewedding counseling/classes			
Reception site			

(continues)

Items/service	Who's paying	Budgeted	Actual
Rentals for reception site			
Preparation of reception site (landscaping, cleaning, etc)			
Additional permits for parking, etc.			
Wedding gown			
Wedding gown fittings			
Accessories and shoes			
Bride's manicure, pedicure, and hair			
Groom's clothing			
Groom's accessories			
Wedding coordinator			
Invitations			
Postage			
Programs			
Thank-you notes			
Caterer's menu			
Liquor			
Cake			
Flowers			
Reception décor			
Reception entertainment			
Photography			
Videography			
Wedding cameras			
Limousines or classic cars			
Other guest transportation			
Favors			
Gifts			
Toss-its			
Honeymoon			
Tips			

Smart Shopping for Brides and Grooms

Throughout this book, you'll find plenty of specific ways to cut costs on everything from your flowers to the cake to the band. But perhaps the best way to save money, to make the most of your budget, and—most importantly—to keep you from wasting money, is adhering to the rules of smart wedding shopping. As was mentioned earlier, the wedding industry is big business. You'll be shopping in many different areas of this conglomerate industry, dealing with many different vendors, striking deals left and right. We're talking about a lot of money here, and you'll want to make sure that you're not making uninformed decisions, making shopping mistakes, and perhaps getting taken for a ride (and not just in the back of a shiny new limousine).

SMART SHOPPING RULE #1: RESEARCH, RESEARCH, AND THEN RESEARCH AGAIN

For every purchase, every guarantee of service, and every consideration for the wedding day, research your options fully. That may mean Internet searches, checks with vendors' professional associations, getting referrals from friends and former clients, and running a search on the company through the Better Business Bureau. This is the best way to protect your investments and make smart hiring and buying choices. Never book the first vendor you interview. Always create a list of several options and research all thoroughly.

SMART SHOPPING RULE #2: ALLOW PLENTY OF TIME FOR PLANNING

Although a great wedding can be planned in six months or less, you'll need to allow yourself plenty of time for all the research and

Wedding Day Reflections

I *don't even want to talk about it. I'm an educated, intelligent person, but I got ripped off by a fly-by-night wedding boutique. I went for the too-good-to-be-true prices, didn't check the place out, and the place closed up and disappeared before I got my dress. We're still fighting with them in court.*

—Danielle

Don't Forget the Extras

As if the damage weren't already enough, you'll have to remember to factor in extra expenses for the following:

- Tips
  Site manager (such as arboretum manager): 15% to 20% of entire bill for the reception
  Valets: $1 per car
  Waiters: $20 to $30 each, depending upon quality of service
  Bartenders: 15% of liquor bill
  Limousine drivers: 15% of transportation bill
  Delivery workers: $10 each if just dropping items off, $20 each if dropping off and setting up to a great extent
  Tent assemblers and rental agency assemblers: $20 each
  Entertainers: $25 to $30 each
  Beauticians: 15% to 20% of beauty salon bill
  Cleanup crew: $20 each

- Permits. You'll need a permit to use a private beach for the ceremony and reception, for parking, for gathering, for use of park for ceremony and reception, for fireworks (in states where fireworks are legal—you could be looking at jail time and big fines if you use fireworks where prohibited by law).

- Delivery fees. For any purchase that requires delivery, such as flowers and rental items, always ask if delivery is free. Some vendors do deliver for free (which is nice, considering you just paid a mint for their services), and some do charge for the drop-off. Ask specifically for their delivery charge amount, look on their store brochures to see if the amount matches their published fees, and figure that into your expenses. Also, see if they charge separately for pick up.

- Surprise expenses. Such as having to pay inebriated guests' cabs at the end of the night, having to buy more ice for the reception, etc. It's a good idea for a responsible family member to keep some extra cash on hand for unexpected costs.

general planning discussed in rule #1. A rushed job may result in poor decision making, extra expenses, and the inability to locate the best deal available. The more time you devote to your planning process, the better off you'll be.

SMART SHOPPING RULE #3: READ YOUR CONTRACTS

Every high-quality wedding professional offers a written, complete contract. If you run into a vendor who does not provide a contract or who does not allow you to keep a copy for your own records, run away. A contract is a valid legal agreement guaranteeing the delivery of exactly what you're paying for. In the instance of a discrepancy or a vendor's failure to deliver, the contract is your only recourse in court. A good contract also keeps you organized and in control of your plans. Be sure you read the entire contract, even the small print, before signing. Ask for clarification if you do not understand something as written. Ask if you can take the unsigned contract home to review. If you see questionable clauses or promises you're not comfortable with, ask the vendor to cross off items and initial the changes. A good vendor will do that within professional reason.

Be sure the contract is complete, including your name and contact information, the wedding date and street location—every little detail of your agreement right down to the number and types of flowers used in the bouquets, the start and finish times of the vendor's service to you, overtime fee, gratuities, refund and cancellation clauses, payment schedules, and both your and the vendor's signatures. A complete contract is your promissory note that you'll be getting what you pay for.

Wedding Day Reflections

We wasted about $200 by tipping our limo driver, our coordinator, and our servers at the end of the night. What we didn't know was that a 19% gratuity had already been included in our bill, which my dad paid that night. It was all right there in our contracts, but we didn't pay attention.

—Jennifer

SMART SHOPPING RULE #4: USE YOUR PLASTIC

Though it's never a good idea to run up and max out your cards, you should use your credit cards to make your wedding purchases. For the consumer's protection, a credit card charge is traceable, enforceable, and subject to protection by the credit card company. Cash exchanges offer no such proof and can be argued over in court to a much greater degree. So, use your plastic for proof of purchase, and pay off your balances as you go.

SMART SHOPPING RULE #5: STICK TO THE BUDGET

Even though it's not unusual to go a bit over the top of your original wedding budget, particularly if you haven't researched the true average expenses of wedding services in your area, you should never throw the budget to the wind. There is a real temptation to splurge, to get only the best, to go above and beyond to plan the most beautiful day of your life. But some control is in order here. Be familiar with your budget, keep it in mind, and stay within the general neighborhood of the numbers you've set.

Wedding Day Reflections

We actually lost $350 because we couldn't prove that we'd already paid the final payment on our photography bill. We paid cash, thinking we were smart in using some of our wedding money and avoiding interest expenses. But that cash transaction was "lost" by the caterer and we were pressured under threat of a small claims lawsuit to pay even more money to that thief!

—Marly

SMART SHOPPING RULE #6: DON'T SHOP WHEN YOU'RE TIRED

If you're dragging at the end of the day, that's not a good time to go out and interview bands. You may be so tired that you won't give your full attention to the process, and your fatigue and impatience may lead you to make a quick decision just to get out of there. Too many couples, admittedly rushed and harried in their everyday lives, report that they made careless money decisions when they weren't at their best. They just wanted to cross something off their to-do list, and the gravity of their decision didn't hit them until they were more alert. So if you're wiped out when you're scheduled to interview a planner, change the appointment and go when you're more on top of your game. Tired buys are impulse buys, and those always lead to trouble.

SMART SHOPPING RULE #7: BE ORGANIZED

It doesn't matter whether you use a bunch of file folders, a computer program, or a handheld organizer. What does matter is that you remain organized throughout the entire wedding-planning process. You'll need to refer back to contracts and receipts, so you'd better know where they are. Couples who lose receipts very often lose their investments. Keep your bridal party on track through regular correspondence, and make full use of the checklists provided in this book. I can't emphasize enough how important it is to be efficient in the planning of your wedding, as disorganization is the number-one cause of added expense and stress. You want to enjoy this process, not beat yourself up because you lost your copy of the pickup form for your gown.

SMART SHOPPING RULE #8: NEGOTIATE

Some people are deathly afraid of negotiating. It's just not their strong point, and they'd rather spend more than risk a confrontation of any kind. But the wedding-planning industry is wide open to the spoils of negotiations. When you're buying a large amount of products from one vendor, especially, you have ample grounds to ask the vendor for a discount or for one item for free. Take the example of the groom who had eight men in his lineup for the bridal party. Upon the men's visit to the tuxedo-rental agency, the groom negotiated his tuxedo rental to be free, as he was bringing in so much business that day. A bride who notices a stain on the bottom edge of a gown in a boutique could surely negotiate a 10-percent discount off the dress, especially if that stain can be removed, camouflaged by the train, or cut away with the portion below her expected hem.

It can never hurt to ask for a break, as you'd be surprised how willing wedding vendors are to keep you happy. After all, the wedding business runs on word-of-mouth. Business owners know full well that brides are always asked by their newly engaged friends for the names and numbers of great vendors. They want to be on your short list. They want to get all of your friends' business, plus your sisters' and your sisters' friends'. One happy bride can equal a goldmine of future work, so many vendors will grant reasonable requests for the sake of your referral. Keep that in mind. You do have leverage, as long as you're polite and diplomatic, and your request is not too outrageous.

Smart Shopping Rule #9: Don't Cut Too Deeply

Of course you'll want to control your wedding budget, but it would be a shame if you tried so hard to save money that you wound up with a disappointing day. You don't want your cuts to show, and you don't want to spend years regretting the choices you made to save a buck.

Smart Shopping Rule #10: Assess Others' Offers to Help

Every bride gets plenty of offers from her family members and friends who'd love to help out with the wedding. Perhaps your cousin Ted is a film major and offers to videotape your wedding for a very small fee. Sounds like a great deal, but is it? Ted may be a film major, but have you seen his work? So many couples agree to family-help offers to try to save money, only to end up with a horrible final product. In your situation, you may be considering allowing your grandmother and your aunts to prepare some of the food for the wedding. Sounds great. But have they cooked for 150 people before? Consider all of the implications of the agreement, consider the kindhearted loved one's true talent, and consider the meaning of having them provide a

Online Shopping: Tips for Your Wedding

There's a wealth of information on the Web that can make planning your wedding a lot easier by saving you time and helping you find exactly what you want. But whenever you shop online, follow these tips to make your experience a good one:

- Pay for your order with a credit card. If you are unhappy with your order and don't get satisfactory resolution from the online store, your credit card company will go to bat for you.

- Shop with a store that uses a secure server. There are three ways to find this out:
  1. When you place your order, you'll see "http" in the browser's Web address bar change to "https."
  2. You'll see an icon of a locked padlock in the lower right-hand side of your browser window.
  3. The store will tell you that it uses a secure server.

- Order your wedding supplies as soon as possible. If you are a last-minute shopper, click on the store's "shipping" link to find out what delivery options are offered. (Remember, "overnight" shipping may not mean that you'll receive your order the next day. Sometimes it means that the online store will ship you the item overnight when it leaves their warehouse, which can take a few days.)

portion of your day as their gift to you. The decision is entirely up to you, but this smart shopping rule reminds you to think the offer through completely before saying yes. Talk with the volunteer to let him know the scope of what's needed, and ask for samples of the work beforehand. It's always risky to hire a friend rather than a professional. Professionals may be more expensive, but they're trained and experienced, and unlike your friend they're willing and prepared

- Save on delivery fees by ordering several items from one store at the same time.

- If you find a store or wedding service you like, sign up for its newsletter. This will alert you to special money-saving offers, such as sales and free shipping.

- Shop with established stores. It's likely that they made mistakes last year and learned how to bring you better service this year. If you want to see what other shoppers think about particular online stores, go to BizRate (www.bizrate.com) or Gomez (www.gomez.com) and compare.

- Look for live inventory-control buttons. These are little buttons next to the item that tell you whether the item is "in stock" or "out of stock."

- Check the store's return policy before you shop there. I'd also look for a telephone number so that if you have a question about your order, you can call and actually talk to a live person.

- Save all of your shopping receipts (the store will e-mail these to you). Either set up a folder in your e-mail program or print them out and put them in a safe place.

- Read the store's privacy policy. If you can't find one, don't shop there.

—LISA PRICE, ONLINE SHOPPING CONSULTANT AND
SPOKESPERSON; COAUTHOR OF THE BEST OF ONLINE SHOPPING

to work hard during your wedding day. Cousin Ted might shoot great stuff, but there's no telling if he'll have a steady hand after three hours at the reception. And Grandma may not want to spend hours in the kitchen. Think it out.

You might be laughing at some of the obvious blunders highlighted in the previous examples, but remember, only hindsight is 20/20. When you're dealing with so many different planning elements in a short time, it's easy to make some mistakes. Unfortunately, just one mistake can cost hundreds if not thousands of dollars when you're planning a wedding, and the repercussions last forever. So protect yourself now from making the most common wedding-shopping blunders and you'll protect your day, your self-esteem, and your credit rating.

3

The Legalities

A s IMPORTANT as the cake, the gown, the reception, and the honeymoon are to you, they pale in importance next to the fact that your marriage has to be legal. Each state has its own rules and standards for marriage licenses and required testing, and your hometown or wedding location has its own set of rules on permits and applications. At the very foundation of all of your planning lies the simple truth that you have to adhere to laws and regulations, or all of this fine and creative work you're doing is for naught.

This chapter will lead you through getting your legal validations at every step of the process. You already know you need a marriage license, but you might not be aware of your town's requirements for obtaining the necessary permits allowing large gatherings at your home. It would be a shame to spend months sculpting a lovely reception, and then learn at the last minute that your lack of a permit means you have to find another location.

Read on and take notes. It's time to take care of the fundamentals so that you can proceed with the fun stuff.

The Marriage License

Your marriage license is of the utmost importance, and each state has its own requirements for application and laws connected to the issuing of these important legal documents. Every state has its own list of requirements, waiting periods, fees, and mandatory tests, and although there are census Web sites that list state-by-state charts of what's needed when, you shouldn't rely on these printouts alone. Laws change every day, and "I didn't know" won't help matters when your marriage bureau refuses to grant you your license.

Instead, call your town hall or the marriage licensing bureau of the town or city where you will be married. Ask for its license-issuing rules, deadlines, required tests, and—most importantly—a brochure or printed copy of these regulations. Get the name of the person you've spoken to, plus the date and time of your conversation. You will receive information on the application process, including time of validity and a list of required tests.

The dates you are told are crucial. It may be that a marriage license is only valid for thirty days from the time of application. In that case, you'll have to mark on your extremely organized wedding calendar a timely date that will allow you both to apply and fulfill the requirements of the license process and still have the license remain valid on your wedding date.

When it is the right time to apply, you will have to appear in person—both of you—at the licensing counter in your town hall, and you will have to fill out your forms there. Call for an appointment ahead of time, as some bureaus operate during specific

---

Wedding Day Reflections

We *did it way too early. We didn't do our research, and we thought the marriage license was good for sixty days. It turns out that we had a thirty-day deadline and had to rush to get a new license in time. Luckily, we did, but it cost us a new filing fee, new blood-test fees, and a late fee. All wasted money and a great deal of stress.*

—Ashley

hours during the week, and ask which necessary documentation you will have to bring along. The registrar will want to see any or all of the following for both of you:

- Birth certificate
- Driver's license or photo ID
- Passport
- Divorce papers
- Death certificate (if one or both of you is widowed)

Once your paperwork has been copied and you've been given the forms, it's time to get the lowdown on the blood tests and required classes. Some states require HIV and hepatitis testing. Others require a full physical. And all have a time limitation for the validity of your test results. Schedule your testing wisely, making sure that all of your due-by dates coincide and that you'll be fully licensed to marry.

LICENSING AND BLOOD TESTS WHEN YOU'RE PLANNING FROM A DISTANCE

We don't all marry in the town in which we grew up, or even in the town in which we live. These days, couples are taking their weddings on the road, planning them to take place in distant cities or states, even in foreign countries. Planning from a distance requires a great amount of legwork to ensure that all of the legalities are covered. At the outset, call the location's town hall to ask about wedding-licensing procedures. You may be forwarded to a tourism department if you're planning to marry at a vacation spot or in a major city. If your wedding will be in an international destination, you will have to speak with the registrar at the embassy or consulate in that location.

During your initial conversation, always ask for a printed copy of the current wedding-license requirements for your location. Many locations receive this kind of request very often, depending upon their popularity as wedding sites, and they may be able to e-mail or fax you a copy of their complete list of rules. You'll find information on license applications, required testing, waiting periods, validity periods, the need for witnesses, and the like. Yet even though this printout may seem complete, there are still some questions you will need to ask. These are the tricky legal issues that have tripped up couples before you, and you must be aware of the official red tape that can snare all of your big plans.

1. Ask about the waiting period. Some locations require you to wait 24 to 72 hours after applying for a license before you can marry. This rule dates back to the days when society wanted to make sure people weren't rushing into marriage or marrying for the wrong reasons. This rule endures, and is an undeniable part of the legal process in some areas. Find out about this waiting period so that you do not force a postponement of your wedding due to timing constrictions.

2. Ask about the need for witnesses. Some locations will require you to bring along one or two witnesses who are known to you. It may not be good enough to pull someone off the beach and have that person stand up for you. With outdoor weddings in foreign locations especially, you'll need to be sure you have your bases covered. Get the facts in writing about who you need to bring with you.

3. Ask about the blood tests. Most states say that the tests have to be performed in the same state in which the ceremony will be performed. Some states do accept results from certain other states, but this can get confusing. In all cases, specifically ask if you'll need to have your blood tests performed in that particular state, or if that state will accept blood-test results from where you currently reside. When planning a destination wedding overseas, you'll want to be especially careful about ensuring the validity of your blood tests. Ask about the waiting period following the blood tests and any filing instructions of blood-test results (e.g., are they accepted through faxed forms, or does a physician have to call them in?), and always get a complete list of all of the blood tests needed. Many couples report

that they just thought they needed an HIV test, but different states require a whole list of different tests.

4. Be complete, be organized, and keep your schedule straight. Allow plenty of time for testing, physicals, and counseling, and keep track of your licensing process.

Bring the license with you on the wedding day for the officiant to sign.

Religious Requirements

You may not consider religious requirements to be legal matters, but to most houses of worship and officiants, their rules are law. If you are planning a ceremony of faith—which is not always the case with an outdoor wedding— then you will have to consult with your chosen priest, minister, rabbi, or other religious leader about his or her faith's rules and regulations. We'll talk more about choosing an officiant later and arranging for one to step out of the church and perform your ceremony in the outdoors or at your home, but for now we're talking about the rules of the cloth.

The officiant is certainly going to require at least one face-to-face meeting at which you will discuss the requirements for marriage ceremonies. You'll undoubtedly be asked to fill out some paperwork, which might include a lengthy questionnaire and essay questions. Some churches even require printed letters of referral from family members,

Simplify It

Call the officiant and ask for his or her printed brochure covering the religious requirements for marriage ceremonies. Most houses of worship offer checklists of the classes and counseling needed, fees, contracts, and document requirements. This brochure can usually answer most of your questions and give you a guideline for what needs to be handled in order to procure the valid services of your officiant.

stating that the couple is "fit" to be married. (I don't make these rules, I just report them!)

You'll be asked for a copy of your birth certificates, any divorce or annulment papers, and a death certificate if one or both of you is widowed. You might also be asked for proof of your membership in the church, as some houses of worship will only marry parishioners.

Unfortunately, the world of religious representation is not always perfect. The church may have strict rules for its marriage sites, and you may be met with some resistance by officiants who have strong personal preferences about who they marry and how they arrange the sites. Their rules are set up for a reason, even if you don't understand them or agree with them. That's just the way it is.

Most religious leaders will also require your attendance at a series of prewedding counseling or classes, during which you and your fiancé will discuss your plans for your future and your beliefs of the present. Find out the scheduling for these required classes, and make room in your calendar for them. In some faiths, no wedding will take place if you haven't been adequately counseled. In the case of the faraway wedding or the destination wedding, ask the officiant-on-site about counseling rules. Can you be counseled in the town in which you live, with a note of completion from the minister who led your classes? Will the officiant accept an out-of-state "diploma?" These major issues must be addressed if you are to fulfill all of the necessary requirements to make your marriage legal on all levels.

If you are planning an interfaith ceremony, you may have to double your workload, meeting with the two representatives of both

> ## *Wedding Day Reflections*
>
> We had such a hard time with the rules of our church. Even though we weren't asking for a mass, but rather a representative of our faith to perform the ceremony, the priest gave us a hard time because we weren't official members of his church. It really turned us off, and we hired the mayor to do our wedding instead.
>
> —Lisa and James

your faiths. Fulfill your obligations in order to meet your religious needs for your ceremony, and stay organized on each front.

Additional Licenses

Aside from the two most obvious licenses you need—the state marriage license and the earned permission to be married by a religious official—there are a large number of additional legal steps to take when planning an outdoor wedding.

Your outdoor wedding site may require a reservation permit. If you are holding your wedding in a state park, arboretum, botanical garden, or beach, you'll certainly need to acquire a valid permit for your use of that location. The permit application, which is obtained through the town hall or the site's main offices, will provide information on fees and site restrictions, such as use of the land until a designated time in the evening. You'll want to keep a keen focus on all of these crucial details, as it is formalities such as these that end up creating the bounds of your day.

When seeking permits, give some thought to all of the different elements of your day, the timing, the location. Meet with the permits registrar to discuss the many facets of your plans. Depending upon your township's or the location's rules, you may find that the following require permits from you:

- Public gathering
- Use of private beach
- Use of public beach
- Use of state-park land
- Use of private gardens
- Use of estate home
- Gathering on private property (for 100 or more people, for instance)

- Parking
- Food and drink on public grounds
- Liquor consumption in a controlled, designated-drinking area
- Installation of portable toilets for outdoor sites
- Fire use, such as torches, a bonfire on the beach, etc.
- Fireworks permit (only in states where fireworks are permitted)
- Exemption from local noise violation and curfew rules until a designated time

A Matter of Insurance

Wedding insurance is available to all brides and grooms, but as a couple planning an outdoor wedding, you especially might want to check out this option as a protection of your investments. Outdoor weddings do pose some greater financial and logistical risks, so the idea of insurance may be just the thing to erase your worries of huge losses due to weather-related or locational problems.

If, for instance, a tropical storm rolls through your area on the wedding day, you'll undoubtedly need to make use of your alternate plans or postpone the wedding altogether. Either option does entail some extra expenses, which would be well covered under the umbrella of a good insurance policy. So do your research on wedding-insurance policies. Ones that omit "acts of God" (in order words, weather) are useless to you. Inspect all terms as you would with any other insurance policy and consider such a plan's value to you.

Insurance is a big issue in the planning of outdoor weddings. If you will be holding your wedding at any location other than your or your family's home, you should always check to see if the site is in-

Simplify It

*O*ne source for wedding insurance is the Fireman's Fund Insurance Company (800-ENGAGED). Call for convenient details and a consultation.

Be a Good Neighbor

Some areas with neighborhood associations have strict rules in place in order to ensure a high quality of living for the residents. In some areas, for instance, residents need to seek the association's permission to put up rose trellises in their front yard. Though these associations do help keep standards in property areas high, they can present a problem when you are planning an at-home wedding within the "jurisdiction" of the board. If you're planning to hold your celebration at home, you will need to obtain a copy of the neighborhood association's set of printed rules. You may need to inform the association of your plans ahead of time, so that an exemption may be granted. And get ready for a diplomatic meeting of the minds, as you will undoubtedly have to endure a barrage of questions and a list of restrictions. Such is the price of living under the rule of the neighborhood association.

sured. When dealing with an arboretum or other established location, ask about its liability policies and coverage in the event of on-site injuries to guests or vendors. If you will be holding your wedding outdoors at home, call your homeowner's insurance agent to ask about your current policy's coverage for personal injury to people on your property. As you will have a large group of people, perhaps children, and a number of vendors running about your place, in addition to people cooking in your kitchen, the potential for personal injury is there. Ask what level your coverage reaches and decide if you need to purchase an extra rider for the wedding day. Your agent can advise you on the entire process.

While you have your insurance agent on the phone, also ask about travel insurance for your destination wedding or honeymoon. The question of insurance definitely needs to be addressed if you will be bringing your children or other family members along on a trip to your wedding location.

Choosing the Date

OR ANY bride and groom, choosing the date of the wedding is obviously one of the most important first steps toward planning the entire event. It's also the most complicated, as couples have to coordinate available ceremony and reception locations, allow enough time to plan the wedding as a whole, and choose an appropriate season that fits into their personal schedules and preferences. For you, as you plan your outdoor wedding, you have a huge added concern: You have to think about the weather. Whereas indoor brides and grooms do give the chance of rain or blinding sun a thought—insofar as to how it will affect their picture taking—so many more of the details of your day depend upon the whims of nature. Your location, the comfort of your guests (and yourselves!), even the entire wedding menu and the dress you'll wear are dictated by your choice of wedding date. Indeed, weather can even cause an outdoor wedding to be postponed when the skies open and everything from rain to hail to lightning crashes your big day.

Before you close this book and relinquish your dream of an outdoor wedding, frightened by the potential nightmares caused by a

57

force you can't control, let's just take this one step at a time. You might not be able to control the weather, but you can improve your odds tremendously by considering your options, making smart decisions, and handling the weather factor with a sense of preparedness. It all starts with choosing a suitable wedding date. Now, let's get started.

Choosing the Right Month

Obviously, you know which months are most seasonable in your area. If you live in the Northeast, you can just cross those harsh winter months off your list and narrow your choices. If you live in the balmy portions of Southern California, where the weather is most often mild, then your available months are more plentiful. Of course, no one can predict an unseasonable hot spell or a surprising cold snap, but if you know your area, you know which months would be the most desirable for you. Choose a season when the temperature is most comfortable—when it's not the wettest time of the year, nor the most scorching of days.

Knowing which months are most seasonable is fine for when you're marrying in your own hometown or in an area where you've lived for years and where you know the seasonal patterns. But what happens when you're marrying elsewhere? In our mobile society, many brides and grooms are choosing to marry in new locations. It may be the city where they've just relocated for a job less than six months ago. It may be a midpoint between their families' home-

Wedding Day Reflections

We were considering May for our New York City weather, as it's usually about 65 to 68 degrees at this time. But this past year's hot streak of 81 to 85 degrees, as unusual as it was, caused us to think about a better time of year. We chose late September, as it's usually still warm out but just leading into fall. Plus, the colors of the trees were just starting to turn, and we thought that would make for a better backdrop.

—Gabrielle

towns. It may be a destination or beach wedding at a location they've always loved and dreamt about, but are not deeply familiar with. In that case, you'll have to do some research. Take this step seriously, and never make your decision based on the fact that "I know the weather in Austin, Texas, is always nice." Call your intended location's tourism bureau (see the resources section at the back of this book) and ask if you can get a listing of the area's average temperature and rainfall amounts. Most tourism boards do include this type of chart in their informational packets, usually in a boxed graph or a descriptive text section. Many cities' travel and tourism Web sites also contain this kind of chart, although you're more likely to find the *current* weather listed there than an annual listing. If you are a member of AAA, you can get a free tour book for that area, in which you will also find descriptions or charts of seasonal temperatures and details of the area's most popular tourism seasons.

> ## Simplify It
>
> Rather than making long-distance calls or standing in line at a crowded AAA center, check www.worldclimate.com for annual temperatures and rainfall amounts. Just remember that Mother Nature isn't bound by charts and graphs of average temperatures and rainfall amounts. Use the information at this Web site to get a general idea of your destination's average weather patterns.

Once you've collected your information and asked questions of that location's tourism experts about rainy seasons, hurricane seasons, and the like, then you're ready to choose the month that works for your outdoor wedding.

Another factor related to your wedding date—and you've heard this before—is where it fits into the most popular months for weddings. "High wedding season," or those dates when weddings are much more plentiful due to weather and day-to-day scheduling, can be more expensive than at other times of the year. Call it the "supply and demand" factor. Wedding professionals and site managers know that June weddings, for instance, are a favorite of brides and grooms, so prices may be inflated a bit in order for the bridal industry to make more money. The wedding industry isn't a $32 *billion*-dollar industry for nothing. Wedding pros know how important weddings are to couples, and they know that in some cases, brides and grooms will pay the higher fees to get the wedding they want at the time they want.

Currently, the most popular wedding months are June, August, September, and October. May is creeping in there as a top choice now, but you'll find the greatest concentration of weddings during those four months. You may be nodding your head right about now, knowing that those months also coincide with the nicest weather months in your area—rest assured that there are probably a few million other brides out there right now thinking the same thing.

So take the timing factor into consideration when planning your outdoor wedding, knowing that while you do have extra issues to consider, it's still within your capability to choose a month that works best with your plans.

Some Special Dates

Just as there are high wedding-season months, several dates during the year are also highly popular for weddings. Valentine's Day, for instance, becomes more than the most romantic day of the year for many couples when they tie the knot on February 14th. Again, the wedding industry is one step ahead of you, knowing that this is a top choice of many brides, and thus the prices of flowers and location fees are likely to soar. Another favorite date is New Year's Eve. Some couples prefer the solstices, viewing their choice of date as a new beginning in tune with the new cycles of nature.

You might consider the anniversary of the date you met as your ideal wedding date, or the anniversary of the date you got engaged. These kinds of days are, in most cases, inflated only in meaning, not in price, and they lend a great sense of sentimentality to your entire event. One couple married on what would have been the bride's grandparents' wedding anniversary, making the announcement to

Now That's a Bad Day

Some dates to avoid:

• Friday the 13th. Because superstition is historically a big part of weddings, you might want to avoid this date, even if you're not the type to fear that kind of legend.

• Tax time (April 15th). Everyone may be stressed about getting their tax returns completed and returned in time, so this may also be a date you want to stay away from. Plus, your guests may have just shelled out thousands to the IRS and may be unwilling or unable to spend money to attend your wedding or get you the kind of gift they'd love to be able to afford.

• Holiday weekends. It may seem to make sense that having your wedding during a holiday weekend such as Memorial Day or Labor Day would mean that more people would come, but you'd be subjecting your guests to peak travel and hotel rates at these times. Keep your guests' preferences in mind.

• Spring break. Your lovely beach wedding may be roped off, but you'll still see and hear the rowdy college revelers speeding down the beach in their open-topped Jeeps, tapping kegs just a few hundred yards from your elegant seaside affair. Even if you have received assurances of complete privacy during your event, your guests will still have to deal with the traffic, the crowds, and the frat-party–like hotels.

• Dates of major events in the city where your wedding will be held. If your chosen city will be home to an NBA championship game, a NASCAR race, a firefighter's convention, or even the shooting of a movie, the entire location's atmosphere could completely change. With the increase in activity and visitors, the city becomes a crowded tourist trap with ultrainflated prices at hotels, restaurants, even gas stations in the area. Ask the tourism board of the location you're interested in whether or not there are any major events planned for that area during the *entire* weekend. Even if the big event is on Friday night, those tourists are going to stick around and continue the celebration. Take all possibilities into consideration.

their guests that they chose this date with the hopes that they would enjoy the same kind of close, loving relationship as the grandparents' model. There wasn't a dry eye in the house.

Choosing a Day of the Week

Though Saturday is the usual day for weddings, more and more couples are including the other weekend days in their selection process. And you might be surprised at the reasons.

Friday night weddings are rising in popularity, because it's both a more readily available time and because Friday night weddings are often less expensive. This type of wedding is usually a formal event, as it is held in the evening hours after your guests have had time to travel in from work.

Sunday weddings are also becoming very popular with the outdoor wedding set right now, as they very often do not have to take into consideration the availability of churches or synagogues. Outdoor wedding ceremonies take place perhaps at a special altar or decorated area of your site, in the outdoors, and are not constrained by a house of worship's mass schedules and church availability. Sunday weddings are also more available and less expensive, but they are usually held earlier in the day as luncheons, brunches, or cocktail parties. This gives your guests time to travel home and ready themselves for their workweek ahead. Here, the outdoor wedding gives you an advantage (finally!), and this is the first of many.

The concept of site availability on certain days of the week becomes more of an issue when you think about the types of locations you might choose. An arboretum or botanical garden is usually open to the public on Saturdays and Sundays, but it may have a policy wherein it closes to the public at 5 P.M. on Fridays. Wedding parties are then invited in when privacy can be afforded, and the wedding event then takes place at 6 or 7 P.M. When you're dealing with wedding locations suited to outdoor weddings—such as parks, arboretums, wineries, estate homes, and beachside sites—you're also dealing with *their* day-of-the-week availability schedule. And their availability may not just be limited to the ideal Sunday late afternoon. You may be faced with restrictions, or opportunities, you hadn't taken into consideration.

So don't limit yourself to the standard Saturday afternoon.

Thinking About Everyone's Schedules

Although I would never advise you to make your wedding plans according to what everyone else wants, it would be wise to take your loved ones' schedules into consideration if you want them to actually share your wedding day with you. Perhaps you're planning a destination outdoor wedding. Your kids would need to be off of school for traveling and event days, so you'll need to look at their vacation calendars. Other potential limits to keep in mind:

• Pregnant women's due dates. They may not be able to travel, or take any level of outdoor heat at all, if they will be in their later months of pregnancy.

• College-aged-kids' vacation schedules.

• College-aged-kids' exam schedules.

• Professional people's exam schedules. Will your sister be in the depths of studying for her medical or bar exam? Will *you?*

Wedding Day Reflections

Since our wedding was going to be small and informal, and since most of our guests are from around here, we actually chose a Thursday evening for our outdoor wedding. We knew that the restaurants in our area did a brisk Thursday night business with all of the college kids, so we decided to have it in our backyard. It actually saved us money on liquor, since most of our guests had to work the next day and didn't want to drink too much!

—Sarah and Rick

• Relatives' or friends' medical conditions. If a loved one is undergoing a medical treatment such as dialysis or chemotherapy, then consider basing your wedding date around what would be best for his or her comfort.

• Negative family anniversaries. Think hard about the date you choose, because you can't expect your sister to be festive if you're marrying on the anniversary of her divorce. (I know this sounds silly, but some people do slip into a type of mourning on some days of the year.) Know your family's "hot button" dates and steer clear.

• Your child's birthday. If your child already isn't too thrilled with the idea of you marrying again, overshadowing his or her birthday with your all-encompassing wedding plans is certain to cause additional headaches.

• The busy season at work. Yours *or* your loved ones'.

• Religious holidays. Even if you don't strictly adhere to the rules of your faith, perhaps your relatives or friends do. Some religious holidays require followers to avoid eating at certain times of the day, or to avoid eating certain kinds of food, such as meat on Fridays during Lent. Be aware of religious restrictions in place during your potential wedding dates. You don't want your guests to have to pick at the cheese platter all night because they can't eat the rest of the food on your menu.

> ## *Wedding Day Reflections*
>
> Everyone in my family is an accountant, and we're all just about insane during the months leading up to tax time. I knew that would be a terrible time to try to pull off, and enjoy, a wedding, so I skipped right to the later summer months.
>
> —Gail

What Time Is It?

Because your wedding will take place outdoors, the usual question of time of day matters more than for the average indoor wedding, when time of day just determines the formality of the event. In your case, time of day also affects your location, the weather (what else is new?), the menu, the lighting, and various other elements of your plans.

We'll tackle the most universal aspect first: the formality. The time of day of your wedding determines the level of formality and the style of your reception. Weddings taking place earlier in the day may be less formal, and therefore less expensive. Later-occurring weddings are traditionally more formal and more expensive. The chart below matches up the commonly accepted times of day for weddings with their coordinating types of receptions:

How Time of Day Affects Your Plans

Type of reception	Time of day (start time)
Brunch	11 A.M.–1 P.M.
Luncheon	12 P.M.–2 P.M.
Tea	3 P.M.–4 P.M.
Cocktail party	4 P.M.–7 P.M.
Dinner	5 P.M.–8 P.M.
Champagne and dessert	8 P.M.–10 P.M.
Late night	9 P.M.–12 A.M.

Because you're dealing with the outdoors, these times of day and related types of receptions will depend upon whether or not you want your event to take place during daylight hours, or whether you'd prefer a nighttime outdoor fest with dramatic lighting, candles, torches, and perhaps a bonfire on the beach. This aspect of your plans will work hand-in-hand with the availability of your site—remember that botanical garden that didn't admit wedding parties until 6 P.M.?

"We want a sunset" is a popular refrain heard from couples choosing an outdoor wedding. Planning your wedding to coincide with the dramatic effects and beautiful sky colors of a sunset over the mountains or the ocean is always a wonderful idea. It's what makes an outdoor wedding all the more special and—some brides say—completely worth all the extra effort required to plan an outdoor event in the first place.

If you wish to marry during the evening or nighttime hours, when there is no sun to heat the chairs or make your guests sweat, remember that the lack of natural lighting will bring up some new issues for you. Your photos will have to be well lit, and that might result in blinding spotlights as the videographer follows you through your event. Your décor also takes on a new planning level—and a new expense level—when you need to hang chandeliers or string lighting within and outside your tent to allow your guests, caterer, band, and other professionals to see. Lighting takes on a whole new dimension in this case, as will be discussed later in chapter 11 (just something important to keep in mind at this point). The timing of your wedding will affect all of your plans, and it may affect your budget to a great degree as well.

> ### Simplify It
>
> For an instant check of what the precise sunset time will be on the date of your wedding (so that you can plan your ceremony or a champagne toast to coincide with that beautiful lighting), go to www.usno.navy.mil. This is the official site of the U.S. Naval Observatory, and it offers a tool that allows you to plug in any date and receive the precise sunrise and sunset times for that day. For the outdoor-wedding bride and groom, this tool is a must!

Time Is Money

You've heard countless times (including here!) how an earlier occurring, less formal wedding will always be less expensive than a later, more formal wedding. In most cases, that is true, but it is not a solid rule. Especially with outdoor weddings. It is entirely possible to plan any kind of wedding at any formality level at any time of day—and still spend a fortune. Throughout this book, you'll receive tips on making the most of your wedding budget, no matter what style of wedding you're planning. I'm reminding you of this now because I don't want you to make your date and time choices based on the idea that you will automatically save money if you plan a Sunday brunch in your backyard. Depending upon your choices, it's entirely possible to spend even more than the national average! So make your date and time choice according to the style of wedding you want, and we'll deal with the money thing as we go along.

One More Thing About the Weather

Outdoor weddings may be among the most beautiful, but they can also be among the most stressful. With the very real factor of the weather involved, you may find yourself glued to the television, watching the five-day forecast and worrying yourself into knots about the potential for rain. I've spoken to many wedding coordinators about this, and they all say that countless brides have complete break-downs over the constantly changing weather forecasts on the news. One bride logged onto her computer over 100 times one day to check the predictions at a weather Web site. Yes, this is going to be a chal-lenge for you, but you'll have to just wait and see what happens. The best thing you can do is to adopt a "whatever happens with the weather, we have a backup plan and everything will be fine" ap-proach. You don't want to turn into a basket case over something completely unpredictable! The wedding experts assured me that with a solid backup plan in place and great helpers at the ready, even rained-out outdoor weddings ultimately turn into lovely events. Couples even turned philosophical, saying they made a great team in a crisis and nothing could stop them from marrying. After a short shower, and after the blood pressures have dropped, you might even get a glimpse of a rainbow arching high over your tent, or off into the distance over the ocean. It's a reminder that even that which seems to be your worst fear can actually be overcome and then deliver amazing gifts. It's a great lesson to learn right before marrying.

5

Choosing the Location

IT'S NOT simply the battle cry of the real estate agent. "Location, lo-cation, location" applies to the outdoor-wedding couple to a much greater degree than to any standard-wedding couple. You'll have to make sure that the location you choose—whether it's the gardens and terrace of an arboretum, a pavilion at the beach, or your own backyard—is suitable for your wedding in more ways than one. Whereas most couples simply have to make sure their ceremony and reception spots can accommodate their specific number of guests, you're looking at more complicated issues such as permits, parking, restrooms, ground level, drainage, and natural décor. It sounds like you're getting ready to build a house, but what you're really doing is laying the foundation for your dream outdoor wedding.

Any wedding location has to meet certain criteria in order to be a good choice for the day. An outdoor wedding just requires a bit more thought toward the mechanics of the setup and toward the mobility of your guests. Aside from those beautiful flowering trees or the clear koi pond that suits your wedding image perfectly, you'll have to engage in the rather unromantic, practical kind of thinking that wedding coordinators refer to as "the meat of the plans." You'll undoubtedly agree that the question "Where are we going to put the toilets?" hasn't really figured into your wedding fantasies, but you will find that the steps involved in finding the perfect outdoor wedding location are worth the work.

One-Stop Shopping

The beauty of outdoor weddings is that most require the choice and setup of only one location. You may decide to have your ceremony and reception on the same grounds, either at the same spot or at a different area of the site. Some brides and grooms set up a "ceremony area," complete with rows of white chairs facing a decorated "altar" or arch. When the ceremony is complete and you've kissed your new husband for the first time, the procession begins to the reception area round the bend or down a cobblestone path to a decked-out portion of the grounds. Or you might decide to take your vows in the center of the dance floor, with your wedding party standing beside you and your guests at their tables. With an outdoor wedding, the choice is up to you.

The Inside-Outside Question

At this point, your fear of weather problems may be very real for you. You might be questioning what your backup plan would be if a thunderstorm rolled through on your big day, and how would you reserve two reception areas—one outdoor and one indoor—just in case? Some couples with nerves (and stomachs) of steel do go for the all-outdoor wedding, with their tables set up under the clear blue sky and no tent in sight. Many set up the tent and the grounds around it, knowing that they've planned well enough for everything to be moved completely inside the tent for cover. Some plan the open-air backyard wedding, but also clear out the living room of their home in case the guests need to rush indoors and continue the party inside.

It's a bit impractical and expensive to reserve your outdoor space *and* at the same time reserve an indoor spot such as a banquet hall to be used in case of an emergency. Few couples can afford to plan and pay for what amounts to two weddings just to be on the safe side. Instead, you can save yourself the extra planning, extra expense, and extra head-aches by choosing a location that naturally offers an indoor-outdoor option. By this, I mean that the location you choose gives you access to its gardens, its terraces, its walk-ways, *and* its ballroom with one reservation. The ballroom might have large glass doors that open up to the terrace or lawn, bring-ing the outdoors in if the weather allows. Your guests can then mill about the premises, sometimes indoors, sometimes out. There are a great many suitable outdoor reception locations that do offer this type of arrangement, and they should be first on your list. They are set up to handle the incidence of rain, and their staff is already well trained to handle that last-minute deci-sion to bring all of the buffet stations and tables indoors to their best organization.

Even beach weddings lend themselves well to this type of indoor-outdoor arrangement, as you might choose a lovely restaurant right on the shoreline that opens its doors to the sounds of the surf. In good weather, you would take your vows on the beach, barefoot, with your friends and family, and then move up to the restaurant's beach-side terrace and indoor rooms for the reception.

Simplify It

Having your ceremony and reception at the same spot elimi-nates extra limousine and travel expenses. You save on flowers and décor as you only have to beautify one space, and you don't have to print out multiple maps for your guests. It also allows you to get right to the champagne toast!

If it's peace of mind you desire, then this indoor-outdoor setup works well, as you know your plan B is right there waiting for you. Why make things more difficult when you have a more viable option according to the location you choose?

Gotta Have It: The Location Criteria List

All brides and grooms have to assess their potential wedding sites for the most important criteria. Is it big enough to accommodate your 200 guests? Is there air-conditioning? You will certainly follow the usual guidelines for site consideration, but—as usual—your list is a little bit longer. And for you brides considering boat and beach weddings, I've added a few important points at the end of this list. So for any outdoor wedding location, ask the following questions, take notes, and base your big decision on your findings.

Simplify It

Before you start hunting for outdoor wedding locations, be sure your wedding must-haves are at the forefront of your mind. Some locations do have restrictions governing use of their space, such as no flash photography, no live butterflies released, no bird seed or rose petals thrown, and—gasp!—no alcohol. So keep your wish list in mind and be sure to ask early on for your site contenders' lists of site restrictions. If you've just got to have those butterflies, then some of those gardens or parks may have to be crossed off your list.

• *Is it big enough?* Your site may have to be big enough both to seat your 100 guests for the ceremony in rows and *then* accommodate them when they move to a different area for the reception. Is there enough space? A good tent rental company will help you measure your backyard, for instance, with regard to fitting 125 people back there, so consider the size of your space according to your needs.

• *Is it flat enough?* Wedding coordinators and tent specialists strongly recommend you choose a very flat surface for your entire wedding area. Some couples do have flat areas in their backyards, but that hill you used to sled down when you were a kid will present a challenge to your guests. If you will be laying a parquet dance floor down for your reception, be sure the land is flat enough for a good fit and comfortable footing for your guests.

- *Does it suit the style of the wedding?* For formal weddings, that botanical garden may be the perfect background to set off your glamorous ball gowns and gentlemen in tuxedoes. A more informal wedding at a lavish outdoor site may not work as well.

- *Is there room for the caterer to set up?* Caterers often prefer a separate tent for their food preparation and tool area. Though you may think your kitchen or the site's standard kitchen is good enough, most caterers say that household kitchens do not have refrigerators or ovens wide enough for their trays, and the sometimes antiquated equipment of estate homes leaves them frustrated. So be sure to check out the cooking areas of established sites or measure out room for the caterer's tent.

- *Is there room for parking?* An established site such as a zoo, an arboretum, or even a beachside restaurant may already have a sizeable parking lot, but for some other locations you'll have to be sure there's room for your guests to park their cars comfortably and safely. Your backyard may be big enough for the tent, but if your street is a no-parking street, what will you do? Always check sites for their parking facilities. Some may have special arrangements with nearby parking garages or lots for bridal discounts.

- *Are there enough restrooms?* Check established sites' restrooms well. Though they're very often up to code for the amount of people you'll expect at your wedding, you'll need to make sure they are in good working order, clean, and well maintained. Ask if there will be a restroom attendant to keep track of paper towel and toilet supplies. (Note: If an attendant will be supplied, you should request a "no tipping" policy during the event from the management. You can arrange to provide the restroom attendants with suitable tips at the end of the night so that your guests do not feel pressured into handing over dollar bills). For off-site locations, it's time to think about portable toilets. Fear not, as you're no longer limited to the types of outdoor restrooms often found at desert-highway rest stops and construction sites—some of the new portable toilets are quite stylish and functional. You will have to consult with a portable toilet company and arrange for it to do the delivery, installation, and removal. The company can also tell you how many stalls you will need according to your guest list. (One more note: Be sure your restrooms are accessible for the elderly or handicapped.)

• *Where's the juice?* Be sure the site affords access to electricity. Everyone from the band to the bartender to the caterer may need to plug in. So consider your power sources, and talk to the site manager about outdoor power plugs. For an at-home wedding, think about generators as well.

• *Do we need a permit?* Most established sites such as parks and gardens will require you to buy a permit to reserve and use their grounds. For beach weddings, you will certainly need a permit from the town, and for backyard weddings you may need permits for parking (especially overnight), outdoor gatherings, liquor consumption, and noise-curfew exemptions. Ask the site manager or someone at the town hall for a list of required permits so that you're completely covered on your big day. Bring copies of the permits with you to the site in case you're questioned or hassled by police.

• *What's the fee?* Again, most sites will charge a fee for the use of their locations. Ask for a list of their fee schedule, as some sites charge one amount for use of their chapel, another amount for use of their ballroom, and another for use of their lawn area.

• *Are tents allowed?* See if the site manager allows tents to be set up on the grounds. Some gardens and parks have strict rules about holes being pierced in the lawn for tent poles. Same goes for portable toilets. See if there's a restriction or a rule about where (and for how long) those can remain.

- *Will we have any privacy?* Check out the spot for its privacy factor. Will other parkgoers be able to wander up and sample your buffet items? Will your beach wedding be effectively and attractively cordoned-off from onlookers? See if the grounds are surrounded by trees and bushes, so that your wedding doesn't overlook someone's unattractive backyard. Privacy is an important factor in outdoor weddings, as wedding experts report horror stories about wedding hecklers who thought they were being amusing as they loudly repeated the vows along with the bride and groom or yelled obscenities just to get attention. One bride broke down into tears when she saw her vindictive ex-boyfriend standing just beyond the fence as she was walking down the aisle. These may be extreme and unlikely scenarios, but you ought to be prepared for anything, as the nature of outdoor weddings is unpredictable.

- *What's the area like?* Some outdoor wedding sites look gorgeous in the advertisement photos, but when you visit you may find that they're right next to a factory, a superhighway, or an airport. Check out the site, certainly, but also check out the surrounding elements.

- *Is it a safe place?* Those plentiful ponds and waterfalls may be lovely, but are adequate safety measures in place at that perfect garden? Yes, small children will be supervised, but are there adequate rails for staircases or high enough walls on the sides of walkway bridges? A fall or injury should be prevented at all costs, even if it means choosing another location.

- *How loud can we get?* Outdoor weddings are especially vulnerable to noise-violation laws as set by the town and the site. Some establishments require that bands stop playing at a designated time of evening. You don't want your neighbors calling the police to bust up your reception as it rolls into the late-night hours, so be aware of official noise rules. Then you'll be able to make plans with the band for a turned-down–volume time.

• *Can we have that toast?* If you're planning on serving liquor at your reception, be sure that the site you choose allows you to do so. Some places do not allow drinking at all on their property, and that's a point best investigated ahead of time.

• *How's the ground?* Check for soggy or muddy patches, which would indicate a drainage problem, especially if it hasn't rained in four days. You'll want to avoid mud or puddles at your party site, so inspect well.

• *Is that the background we want?* You may have a certain idea in your head that you want to be married with a full view of the ocean or a great mountaintop behind you. During your on-site visit to the location, check out the vista to see if the skyline matches your dream backdrop.

• *What will be in bloom then?* This is a very important question. If you will be marrying outdoors at a location that's designed to be in bloom, such as an arboretum or garden, ask what plants will be in bloom at the time of your wedding. The site designer will be able to search her planting-time chart to tell you which kinds of flowers, and in which color schemes, will make up your actual surroundings on the big day. Established wedding sites often have their décor schedules planned out a year in advance, so ask for their bloom calendar to visualize the sea of daffodils or orchids that come with the site at that time.

• *Do we need to hire your professionals?* Some sites require you to work with their caterer, florist, or other wedding suppliers. For good reason, many official sites prefer to work with their own people, and you may not be allowed to hire your own. Ask what their vendor status is, and whether or not they will allow you to bring in your own supply of food or drinks, cake, or ethnic specialties.

• *How long do we get the site?* Established sites may have a time cap on the length of time that you can occupy their premises. Ask what time the clock strikes "party's over." Many sites have a five-hour limit, but the times may be different if you're booked on a Sunday or a Friday night.

FOR BEACH WEDDINGS

• *How hot will the sand be?* Try to visit the site during the same season as your wedding to assess the temperature of the sand at the time you'll be married. In some locations, the sand will be too hot for barefoot brides and guests.

• *Is the sand pristine?* Some beaches are known for their perfectly clean beaches, and some have more litter than others. Scout the site to see what the sand consistency is, and whether or not choosing this site will require you to assign friends to rake for debris before the ceremony. A bride recently reported that a guest stepped on a section of broken bottle, so keep the task of beach-cleaning in mind before choosing a particular site.

• *Does the site offer a foot hose?* The best beachside wedding sites have just at the edge of their premises a low-set hose or sprinkler system and drain that guests can use to rinse their feet of sand before slipping on their dancing shoes for the reception. Go the extra step, so to speak, by providing a tall stack of pretty paper guest towels for them to use to dry their feet.

• *Do we need wind blockage?* A very windy beachside site might require you to purchase a tent with netting sides that won't catch the force of air. See if the gusts are overwhelming, or if all of your favors might need to be anchored to the table. Some beach sites do have their own "wind blockers" in the form of pavilion design and special tree locations.

• *Is there any shade at all?* If there is no beach pavilion or shaded overlook for your more sun-sensitive guests, check on getting permission to set up a cluster of beach umbrellas that complement your site décor.

• *Where will the guests stay?* Beach weddings usually mean that the wedding party must travel to a seaside location. That may require finding lodging for your guests, so make sure there are blocks of rooms available close to your site, and that the hotels are not already booked up for tourist season. This is a very important step, as a lack of rooms could force you to move your wedding elsewhere!

For Boat Weddings

• *Is there a sheltered deck?* Most established boat and yacht companies offer boats that have several decks—an open-air deck on top and a lower enclosed deck for the reception. Be sure your chosen boat has a covered deck, as the enclosure offers protection from cool night air as well as rain.

• *How's the deck surface?* Check for some traction on the floor so that your guests will not have to worry about slipping if a wave should moisten the deck.

• *Is the galley big enough?* The chef will need room to cook and serve up meals, so be sure the boat you choose has an appropriately sized kitchen area.

• *How are the restrooms?* For obvious reasons, you'll need to take a close look at the types of toilets on board (but not too close!). Marine toilets need to be manually pumped with a big lever to the side of the toilet in order to move waste down into a septic-type tank. Electric toilets on boats are standard flush-types. Ask the boat captain for a tour of the restrooms as well, to be sure the facilities are in suitable and working order.

• *Is there climate control?* Be sure the inside of the boat has both air-conditioning and heating options to keep your guests comfortable.

• *Is there moisture damage?* Boats are, of course, exposed to the elements. Tour all parts of the boat to be sure there is no mildew smell in the lounges.

• *Will you hoist the sails?* If you will be holding your wedding aboard a schooner or a sailboat, which is a more intimate setting for smaller wedding parties, ask that the captain raise the sails for your inspection. A recent bride reports that she had booked a schooner for her most special cruise, but on the wedding day the captain wouldn't raise the sails for a beautiful and dramatic ride. He said the sails had been ripped, and so they putted around the bay, "powered" by a motor that the bride says "couldn't move a lawn mower."

• *Are the details up to par?* A true quality yacht will have polished brass, clean carpets, and suitable ropes and ladders. Be sure the boat is well maintained and attractive enough for your day.

• *What's the safety setup like?* All commercial and private boats must have an appropriate number of lifeboats and life preserver jackets on board to ensure guests' safety. Ask the captain for proof that he has his full safety certification, and look at his safety kit. All boats should have flares on board, as well as oxygen, a first-aid kit, and other safety measures.

• *How's the gangway?* You want to make sure that it's safe and easy for your guests to board the boat. A good yacht will have a sturdy metal gangway with handrails. If you have handicapped wedding guests, be sure that they will be able to access the boat. That may require measuring the width of the gangway to be sure that wheelchairs can be moved easily through.

- *We're staying in calm waters, right?* Always ask the captain where this boat will be sailing. You'll certainly want to stay in a calm bay where waves and wakes from other passing boats will not rock your vessel too much. If the captain says he's taking you right out to the deep waters of the ocean, consider another three-hour tour. Open ocean can translate into rougher water and more chances of seasickness.

- *Can we stay dockside?* Some couples prefer to avoid the open seas and the motion of the boat. Ask if the captain will allow you to hold your wedding on the boat while it's moored at pier.

- *What will we be seeing?* Ask for a description of the yacht's pathway scenery. Will you be passing old battle ruins and castles? Views of the city skyline? Or will there be a long stretch right at the beginning of your cruise where you're passing grim factories and commercial centers?

- *Are you and your crew commissioned?* Always ask for proof of a captain's training and commission to sail a boat, and ask about the training of the crew. Get in writing the number of crewmembers who will be working your crowd.

Of course, these are not the only criteria with which you'll concern yourself. Every location has its own strengths and weaknesses, and you will certainly want to investigate every possible element of each site you tour. Think about and discuss with each other what you most want from your wedding site, what logistics face you, and what you most want to avoid. Then you can make your choice according to your own standards and wishes.

FINDING THE PERFECT PLACE

Choosing an outdoor wedding location can be overwhelming when you've got the whole world available to you. There are so many beautiful spots that showcase unique and natural outdoor weddings that it

---

Be Prepared for More "Yes" RSVPs

Nationally, more guests respond that they will attend a boat or yacht wedding than a regular, landlocked affair. Perhaps it's the lure of the sea or simply that it's a completely different event than the same-old—same-old wedding at a banquet hall, but more of your guests are likely to accept your invitation when you're having a boat wedding.

---

would be a shame to limit yourself to the ones in your own hometown. Check out the following for special spots nearby and distant locations for getaway weddings:

• For general cities and locations across the country and the world, go to www.weddingspot.com for descriptions and links to prospective sites.

• If you want your wedding somewhere in the vicinity of New York's Hudson Valley through the ever-popular Newport, Rhode Island area and surrounding cities, check out the creative selections found through Charmed Places: www.charmedplaces.com, a company that scouts out wonderful, unique sites from beach coves to mountainous and scenic overlooks.

• For a wide range of national historic sites such as mayoral mansions, well-known landmarks, and famed social haunts of the elite, try www.nationaltrust.org.

• For national parks, such as the great outdoors of Yosemite, check out www.nps.gov.

These types of location services do the busywork for you, bringing you right to the details and necessities of booking various types of sites. Log in and look around. You may discover a little-known nearby historic villa that would be perfect for you.

A Conversation with a Wedding Locator

Sarah Stitham of Charmed Places has helped countless brides and grooms find their perfect wedding locations in New York's Hudson Valley, the estates of Newport, Rhode Island, and surrounding areas. "I work with creative clients who are looking for unique settings for their weddings," says Stitham. "We start off with a brief conversation in which I find out what the bride has in mind for her wedding, the size, the style, and her budget. If the bride has an image of her perfect setting—say, a view of the Catskill Mountains—we go from there, but if she's open to suggestions I ask her what she and her fiancé love to do together, where they love to go on vacation, whether they prefer more elegant, upscale things or a more homey country style. This way, I get a feel for who the couple is and I can help lead them to the perfect location."

Stitham does charge a fee for her services, as any customized site researcher would, and she accompanies couples at meetings with the owners of private vineyards and estates where she has relationships and experience at the site. A professional site locator can save you tons of time, focus your vision, and point out great places you may never have heard of before. So if you're stumped for a unique and beautiful place that's *you*, consider hiring a site-locator service for the most inside advice and help in locating your dream location.

When Your Wedding Is a Backyard Affair

Backyard outdoor weddings do adhere to the entire location criteria list. However, they present some special considerations you ought to keep in mind when opening up your home to the all-inclusive needs of a wedding day and night.

Here are your additional "something to think about" criteria questions for an at-home wedding:

- *Is there adequate area for each element of our wedding?* From where will you make your approach to the altar? Is there a separate area for the bridal party to spend a few moments alone for a toast before joining the guests? Be sure your home and backyard offer the kinds of layout options you prefer.

- *Can delivery trucks get close enough to our yard?* If your house is too close to a neighbor's, and if your yard doesn't allow enough access, you may have to take down a fence for the tent delivery guys to haul their gear into place.

- *Are there enough bathrooms?* Even if you have portable toilets in the side yard, don't be surprised if some guests insist upon going inside to use a "real" bathroom. Be sure that all of your bathrooms are well stocked with toilet paper (leave an extra roll on the toilet tank or counter), and supply guests with paper hand towels.

- *Has our septic system been pumped?* Wedding coordinators strongly suggest that you get your septic system checked and pumped a few weeks before the big day. You don't want to tempt fate on that account.

- *Should we hide our valuables?* There will be many people in the house on the day of the wedding, and a caterer's staff as well as guests you don't know will all have access while you're out in the backyard having a ball. So it's a good idea to protect your most precious possessions, even if it's just for your own peace of mind.

- *What about those Lladro figurines?* Anything breakable, particularly if children will be in the house, should be put away as well.

- *Is the kitchen set up for the caterer?* If you don't have room for a caterer's tent, clear some space in the kitchen for the caterer to work.

Put away smaller countertop appliances such as toasters or blenders, and leave plenty of room in the fridge for later courses and desserts.

• *Do we want to risk the rug?* If you've just gotten new cream-colored carpets, think hard about inviting 100 people to possibly run over it with muddy feet. If it starts raining and thundering, your guests may come inside for shelter, and then your rug is put to the Scotchgard test. It's a wise idea to invest in those clear plastic carpet runners for high-traffic areas in any situation, but consider this kind of valuable décor in your home before you make your final decision on a backyard wedding.

• *What will we need to rent?* We'll cover that more in chapter 11, but you will need to figure out your wedding date's weather requirements. Will you have to rent heaters or fans? Separate refrigeration units to keep food cold on hot days?

• *Can we make good use of the landscaping?* You've worked hard on that rock garden, and your Mom's prize roses may steal the blue ribbon for décor. So look at the existing décor of your backyard site, and see where you can play up strengths and avoid extra expenses. One couple planned their wedding around their in-ground pool, floating candles and lotus flowers in the pool for effect.

> ## Wedding Day Reflections
>
> There was something more special about holding the wedding around the pool. Everyone was dressed in their best, and the pool was glowing with its own underwater lights and the candles we set in the water. It was actually quite exotic, like we were marrying by a pool at Club Med.
>
> —Lena

• *How's the bug problem?* Some people's backyards are just havens for mosquitoes, especially at certain times of the year. Think about the insect factor and what steps you will have to take to rid yourselves of the hassle.

- *Will we need valets?* Even a home wedding makes good use of this great service for your guests. If your home's location is such that nearby parking isn't an option or that late-arriving guests will have to walk for blocks, think about your need for valet parking.

- *Will we need extra lighting?* Of course you will, unless you regularly light your backyard with strings of white lights, spotlights, and chandeliers. Lighting makes an outdoor wedding more ethereal, so think about what your site's light requirements are and what the cost is to meet them.

Always Have a Plan B!

Outdoor weddings, by nature, invite the unexpected, so you'll need to be sure you have a plan in mind for inclement weather. Think through the possibilities of moving your reception into your home, into your site's indoor ballroom, or to another site. Talk with all involved about what would happen should the need arise to move to the alternate location or change the existing one.

Couples who take the biggest gamble and do not have a plan B sometimes have to postpone their wedding when the worst comes to pass. That's a big loss on many levels, and it's one you really shouldn't risk. So sketch out your plan B and prepare yourself to be just as happy there!

6

Choosing Your Wedding Gown

NOW COMES the fun part, finding that perfect gown to rival the one in all of your previous wedding fantasies. This chapter explains the ins and outs of wedding gown shopping and selection, with special emphasis on outdoor wedding conditions that will affect your choice of outfit. For instance, what kind of dress is best for a beach wedding? Will your veil fly around in the breeze? How do you handle a train when you'll be walking through gardens and curved walkways?

Here, you'll begin your search for the perfect dress and all the accessories to complete your look for the big day under the sun or stars.

Choosing the Perfect Gown for Your Wedding's Formality Level

Of course, what matters most is how the gown feels to you, how your body wears it, and how it makes you glow, but a wedding gown always has to fit the formality level of your day. Although many elements of wedding etiquette have been swayed and bent to allow couples more freedom in planning what they want for the day, no doubt you'll agree that some level of tradition needs to remain when it comes to choosing a suitable gown.

The following are general guidelines for types for gowns according to formality level:

ULTRAFORMAL AND FORMAL

- *A full-length gown*
  Train at chapel length (1 yard) or cathedral length
     (longer than 1 yard)
  A long veil or tiara with veil
  Detailed or simple embellishments to the gown
  Gloves

SEMIFORMAL

- *A floor-length gown or cocktail-length dress*
  Sweep train
  Waist-length or fingertip veil

INFORMAL

- *A floor-length or cocktail-length dress*
  Suit dress
  Slipdress
  No veil
  Hair ornamentation, such as floral wreath, flower accents,
     jeweled clips

Choosing the Perfect Gown for the Weather

I spoke at length with Michelle and Henry Roth of Michelle Roth Bridal Designs in New York City about their suggested gown styles

Be a Smart "Material Girl"

It's going to be pretty hot outside on the day of my wedding. Which kinds of fabrics work best for warm-weather outdoor weddings?

Certain fabrics do hold up better in outdoor weather, as far as being light in weight and having some "breathing" capacity so that you don't perspire too much. As a general rule, fabrics with natural fiber content, such as cotton weaves, allow the dress to release heat from the bride's body. Synthetics stick to the body and trap heat and moisture.

Consider the following suggested fabrics for your gown:

- *Silk chiffon*
- *Silk organza*
- *Silk tulle*
- *Lightweight satin*
- *Shantung*
- *Linen*

Avoid overly encrusted appliqués or beading that add more weight and bulk to your dress as well.

and fabrics to suit the weather and mobility needs for the four different types of outdoor weddings. The following are their tips:

FOR OUTDOOR BACKYARD WEDDINGS

- "Choose gowns in a silk organza, chiffon, or silk crepe fabric that is most suitable for a less formal look that suits most backyard weddings."

- "Ball gowns, straight princess, or A-line gowns work well."
- "The train should be chapel length or a sweep train that can be bustled for easier movement."
- "The veil can be floor length or longer, but not too long (as in a cathedral length)."

FOR OUTDOOR ON-SITE WEDDINGS

- "A ball gown works nicely, something that allows you some movement as you walk down the aisle."
- "Great fabrics for this type of wedding are silks, satins, or a pure-silk weave called a 'mikado.'"
- "Incorporate hand embellishments on the veil and bodice for a more formal look."

FOR BEACH WEDDINGS

- "Wear a short lace dress without a train."
- "Show some skin with an open design, such as [with] strapless or thin straps."
- "Make sure your gown offers a feeling of lightness with its design. Use the element of wind as a part of your look, making sure that the dress and the train will look great when the wind moves it."
- "A fingertip or waist-length veil is suitable for a beach wedding."
- "Understand that beach weddings mean sand is going to get in your dress just from being out in the elements. Be sure your neckline and the folds of your dress allow for easy brushing away of sand."

FOR BOAT WEDDINGS

- "A floor-length gown is fine for a boat wedding, considering the added element of cool breezes and cooler temperatures out over the water."

A Professional Opinion

"Planning a wedding in the outdoors allows you to invite-in spontaneity. You'll need to feel great in your dress, allow for the elements of sun and wind, but prepare yourself to enjoy the unexpected! The weather is irrelevant to what you are trying to achieve with your wedding. After all, everyone at your wedding is experiencing the same conditions—it's a bonding experience for all, no matter what the weather brings. That said, the Forces of Nature bring people together, so know that whatever happens it will only add to the experience."

—HENRY ROTH, MICHELLE ROTH BRIDAL DESIGNS

- "Silk organza is lovely for a floor-length gown, as is an A-line cut with plenty of movement in it."
- "Be sure to pair your gown with a great complementary jacket for those cool night hours."

Gown Alternatives for Informal Outdoor Weddings

For an informal outdoor wedding, you might choose a wonderful cocktail or street-length dress in the traditional bridal colors of white, off-white, or blush hues. More and more designers offer a wider range of party-ready dresses, ranging from the office-to-club suit dress to the organza bohemian ankle-length dress. The options of turning regular dresses into bridal dresses are now limitless, as even some of the most famous brides in the world are choosing little white slipdresses for their informal beach weddings and shimmery sundresses for their garden weddings. An outdoor wedding always affords you a great deal more freedom in your plans than the standard indoor wedding, and that joyous freedom doesn't stop with informal wedding gowns.

Some outdoor brides look through department stores' formal departments, even through prom-gown racks. Those puffy-sleeved '80s dresses are long gone, and today's high-schooler has access to a more fashionable (and sexier!) look than ever before. So expand your search horizons, and check out what's just outside the wedding gown boundaries.

Finding the Perfect Gown for YOU!

You know what you look best in, what your strongest features are and what you might like to downplay. The gown you choose will make you look fabulous if you choose the right style and, perhaps, color for your features.

The following are some general rules about choosing the right gown for your shape:

- Princess gowns and A-lines are considered the most flattering styles, as they add height and length to the body.
- A bride with a slender, well-toned body might choose a sheath dress for a fitted line and a sexy look.
- V-line waists or basque cuts elongate the torso and make a short-waisted bride appear slimmer.
- Full skirts hide larger hips or bottoms.
- A sweetheart neckline flatters a busty bride.
- A square-cut neckline also flatters the busty bride.
- Brides with significant chests should avoid busy patterns above the waist or horizontal fabric lines across the chest.
- Brides with smaller chests can enhance their bustlines with a fitted corset that gives you some lift, or with some detail at the neckline that offers the impression of size.
- If you have great arms you're proud of, go sleeveless.

Add a Splash of Color!

Outdoor weddings are known for their beautiful colors, as seen in floral gardens, freshly cut green lawns, and the blue of the ocean, so bring the concept of color to your wedding day wardrobe as well! Add a dash of blush color (or even an eye-grabbing bright color) to the following:

• *Floral accents at the base of the back.* A white gown looks lovely with a cluster of pink flowers and greenery (formed out of fabric right at the base of a low-plunging backline). These florals can be added to the trims of trains, hems, even a neckline if it's done with simplicity.

• *Color in the embroidery.* Just a hint of gold in the stitching can have your guests doing a double take—in a good way. This unexpected stitch of color can add more drama to the flowing lines of your dress.

• *Color in your jewelry.* There's no rule that says your earrings or necklace have to be all-diamond or all-pearl. Brides with a penchant for color are now choosing jewelry and gemstone headpieces that bear their birthstones or complementary shades.

• *Color in your headpiece.* Aside from the colored gemstones that may add the "something blue" to your ensemble, you might choose to incorporate lovely flowers into your headpiece look, or just tuck a bright yellow daisy behind your ear. Sometimes it's the smallest burst of color that makes the entire white dress look better.

• Outdoor weddings mean that you can show more skin with your gown, so consider a dress that shows off your shoulders, back, or arms. Some brides even show off a flat abdomen by choosing a sexy, two-piece beach wedding dress.

These are just some of the well-known rules in the bridal gown industry. Every bride's body is different, and various styles may flatter her shape. Consider whether you want to go sexy or demure, traditional or trendy, and choose according to what you feel best in. You'll know when you slip into that great dress, twirl around in front of the mirror, and you get that *tingle*. This, you'll know, is "The One." (If only it were that easy to find the groom!)

Another element to consider is gown color. Sure, you may be set on wearing white, but did you know that there are various *shades* of white? Just as every bride has a different body, every bride also has her own skin tone, and certain shades of white look better according to the color of the bride's skin and hair. For instance, champagne or candlelight-white dresses look great on blondes and redheads, whereas bright whites flatter darker-haired and darker-skinned women such as full brunettes and women with black hair. Check your look in different shades of white; your sales professional will be able to help you tell the silk whites from the champagne whites. Just don't try to judge the color of a gown by the appearance of the store sample you're trying on. That gown may have been worn by a dozen or so brides before you, and it may have turned color a bit due to its time on the rack. Always ask to see a clean, fresh swatch of fabric when ordering a gown so that you can be sure it's the right color.

SMART GOWN-SHOPPING TIPS

No matter what your style or choice of wedding dress, no matter the thought you've given to the gown's suitability to your outdoor wedding, some universal gown-shopping tips still apply. After all, you may be spending a lot on your gown, and you have even more invested in how you'll ultimately look and feel on your wedding day. This is no time for shortcuts, and it's no time to ignore the most important rules of wedding-gown shopping. Here, then, are the top tips for finding and ordering your dream dress:

• *Do your homework.* Before you head to the bridal salons to pick that perfect dress off the rack and dazzle yourself in front of the mirror, you should spend some time doing research on the styles and types of gowns out there. Look through bridal magazines and surf the best wedding-planning Web sites to see their picks of what's hot for your season's weddings. You may discover a whole new look you hadn't thought of before, such as two-piece gowns and colored gowns.

• *Shop WAY in advance.* For the best selection of wedding gowns—and an assurance that you'll not only receive your gown by your wedding date but will also have time for fittings—start looking a year in advance. Order nine months ahead at the latest.

• *Don't bring too many critics along for the trip.* Wedding experts say they see it all the time. An excited bride brings her mother, her sisters, her bridesmaids, and probably a few women she's never met before to the bridal salon to search for the perfect gown. She then winds up a knotted wreck, as everyone's voicing their opinions and virtually throwing gowns at her to try on. Too many opinions means too much interference, and what should be a fun and exciting shopping trip becomes a circus. Avoid the temptation to share this big moment with everyone you know and just bring one trusted, objective friend along for the visit. What matters is what *you* want to wear, not what everyone else *thinks* you should wear, no matter how good their intentions.

• *Bring a Polaroid camera.* If you'll be trying on a lot of gowns at a lot of different shops, bring along an instant camera to capture you in that wedding-dress contender. Write the shop name on the bottom of

Simplify It

Several of the top wedding-planning Web sites offer great interactive tools that allow you to enter your gown criteria, budget, choice of neckline, etc., into a search engine and then view the top matching choices. These sites allow you to browse the different styles and dress elements, so that you can see for yourself just how that sweetheart neckline will look or how that fountain veil will go with your dress. You'll find great wedding gown "databases" at the following sites:

www.TheKnot.com
www.DavidsBridal.com
www.WeddingChannel.com

Gown Shopping for the Petite Bride

I'm only 5' 3", and when I tried on some wedding gowns, half of the gowns were on the floor! Nothing seemed to fit, and although the seamstress said she could "work wonders" with any gown for me, I'm still wondering if I should stop looking at traditional gowns and try to find a regular white dress that actually fits me. I don't want to spend a fortune on alterations, but I want a gown that looks great on me. What do I do?

Luckily, the wedding gown industry has heard this complaint enough times to have actually done something about it. Now you'll find that wedding gowns come in petite sizes that fit smaller brides better. Search wedding Web site engines for "petite gowns," or start your search with the bridal-gown company Priscilla of Boston, who does a sizable petite line. (See resource section at the end of this book.)

the picture so that you can locate the shop and the specific gown at the end of the day.

- *Skip Saturdays and Sundays.* Weekends are when all the other brides-to-be are shopping for their gowns, and some wedding shops can become quite busy. If you take a day—or an afternoon—off of work, you can make good use of that weekday by having the shop to yourself and enjoying the undivided attention of the shop's staff. Most brides say they loved the absence of the crowds, the unhurried expertise of the seamstresses and personal shoppers, and the more relaxed atmosphere. It made the whole event more enjoyable, and they were able to make smart, unhurried decisions.

• *Never shop tired.* This is an important job. One of the biggest mistakes some brides make is to go gown shopping when they really don't feel like it, just because the shopping trip is already on the calendar. It's never a good idea to shop for *anything* when you're wiped out, as you're more inclined to rush decisions and forget to ask important questions. Buying your gown shouldn't be something you have to suffer through. So hold off until you have the energy, and shop when you're fresh.

• *Always make an appointment.* Sure, you could wander in off the street and look around to your heart's content, but it's always best to go through official channels when shopping for your wedding gown. With an appointment set up, the shop will know you're coming, they'll have an assistant ready to help you, and you'll reserve a block of time that's devoted entirely to you. Plus, when you call a salon, they may be able to alert you to an upcoming trunk or clearance sale they're not advertising yet.

• *Don't limit yourself to one style.* Open up your options to include different styles of dresses, different necklines, different textures of fabric. Sometimes a gown looks completely different on your body than it does on a hanger, and you might be pleasantly surprised. (Or you might have to tackle your maid of honor to confiscate that Polaroid!)

• *Choose a shop that offers free alterations.* Great shops do provide this service, or else they have connections with quality seamstresses who don't charge a fortune. See if your shop offers a free or discounted alterations package, and study the details carefully. Does the shop offer one free fitting? Three? Unlimited, as long as the dress fits perfectly on the big day? Remember that alterations are what makes a great dress look perfect on you, so take this step seriously.

• *Don't guess at sizes, and don't order your regular size.* Wedding gowns generally do not adhere to your expected concept of the perfect size 8.

Always have a gown shop professional take all of your measurements and use those to order your gown in the correct size.

- *Always get a copy of the order!* Be sure the bridal salon gives you a copy of the gown order form, and that it includes—in writing—every detail imaginable about your gown and your payment for it. A style number for the gown should be on there, as well as size, delivery date, and a notation that your deposit has been paid in full. Have the salon salesperson sign the form, and you're all set to protect your investment and prevent delivery nightmares.

- *Research companies well.* Order from a reputable store that has been around for a long time, and ask recently married friends for referrals to gown shops they loved. If you'll be ordering your gown over the Internet, check the legitimacy of the gown site with the Better Business Bureau at www.bbbonline.org.

PINS AND TUCKS: YOUR FITTINGS

As I mentioned earlier, your fittings are going to make or break how you look in your gown. Most dresses need a significant amount of work when they come in, especially if you've ordered your gown over the Internet. Because every body is different, every gown is going to have to be tucked, pinned, and adjusted to fit your shape well.

Start your fitting process by allowing at least one month to conduct a number of fittings. Your first will be the "first shot" your seamstress has at conforming the lines and folds of your gown to make the most of your shape. A good seamstress knows how to pin the gown so that it fits your arms, chest, and waist well, and she'll create the perfect hemline. The most important part of the fitting process is to work *with* your seamstress. Tell her if the boning is cutting into your ribs, if your armholes are too low for your comfort, or if the neckline is just too plunging. Speak up now and allow the seamstress to do her job well. She wants to please you, so the best value you can get from your investment is to make your bride–seamstress relationship a partnership.

You might think that you can lessen your alteration needs by choosing a simpler gown. Not so, say the experts, as a simpler dress can be even more complicated to alter than a busier dress with a lot of design elements. Plain fabric will show the spots where stitches were added or taken out, whereas more textured fabrics will hide these tell-tale signs better. That detailed bustle can be easy for a talented seamstress to handle.

If it seems like I'm overstating the need for a good seamstress, you're right. I've heard too many horror stories of brides trying to save the $200–$300 a good seamstress charges by trying to choose a made-to-order gown or—gasp!—having a mother or aunt who knows how to sew try to take in the seams and complete the hem. On the wedding day, the dress falls apart, and the bride walks like a zombie trying not to bust out of the safety pins holding her gown together. Take no chances. Hire a professional.

During your fittings, conduct the "does it move with me?" test on your gown. A good dress not only looks great, but it moves well and allows you plenty of comfort. So after your first fitting, stand in front of a mirror, allowing yourself plenty of room, and try the following maneuvers to get a feel for how your dress handles the action:

• Can you sit in it? Sure, the bodice looks great when you're standing up, but does it cut into your stomach when you try to sit?

• Can you lift your arms? When dancing with your new husband, or hugging your loved ones during the receiving line, you'll need to be able to lift your arms. See if the shoulder straps pull, if the arm-holes reveal too much, or if the dress itself restrains your movement. Ask the seamstress to make the necessary adjustments so that you have a full range of motion.

• Can you bend over? That sexy neckline will earn your reception an R-rating if you spill out of your top.

- What's the view from above? Can taller guests get a look down the front of your dress when standing right in front of you?

- Can you breathe? Some celebrities and models may be willing to suck in their stomachs in supertight bodices and fitted waistlines during a 6-hour Oscar telecast, but you'd prefer to be more comfortable. Besides, if you can't breathe fully, you'll be more stressed out, oxygen-deprived, and a big fainting hazard. Loosen up those side seams a little and allow yourself to breathe.

Plan your fittings well in advance, and allow the seamstress to advise you on the best timetable for fittings before the wedding day. Some brides find that they're most comfortable with multiple fittings, ensuring them that, yes, the gown will fit.

Choosing the Right Shoes

More than at any other style of wedding, your shoes are extremely important at your outdoor wedding. After all, you may be spending a lot of time walking around on a lawn, where heels can sink into soft ground. Your chosen footwear will have to provide comfortable and *secure* footing on unlevel ground, while walking a cobblestone path, descending a marble staircase, or trying to stay upright on the slippery deck of a yacht.

Indoor brides usually don't have to give much thought to their heel width and traction while shopping for shoes, but you have a few more elements to deal with.

First of all, your shoes have to look great with your gown. Especially if you'll be wearing a shorter gown or a slipdress at a more informal outdoor or beach wedding, the shoes are going to garner some attention. Look for suitable styles that work with the formality of your look, and always consider the heel. "The best shoe for an outdoor wedding," says wedding-gown designer Michelle Roth, "is one with a wider, flatter heel. The Louis heel is one I recommend for its structure and function. A higher, thinner heel such as a stiletto is

There's Hope for Your Shoes!

White shoes almost always take a beating after outdoor weddings, whether from grass stains, mud stains, or just general wear from long hours of dancing. Rather than toss those great shoes out afterwards, take them to a shoe repair center or cobbler to have them cleaned well. Some fabrics need professional cleaning and won't respond well to homemade remedies. Consider having those shoes professionally dyed if you can't return them to their natural shade.

going to sink into the grass." Avoid the threat of awkward falls and sprained ankles right before the honeymoon and choose a more suitable heel size and shape.

For beach weddings, many brides decide to go barefoot for their beach ceremony. Some brides are adding the fun décor of toe jewelry for an unexpected accent, but if their reception will bring them indoors, they'll need to then slip into a pair of attractive, comfortable shoes for the inside portion of the event.

There are three things to think about when shopping for your shoes: first, the attractiveness of the design, then the function of the heel, and finally the shoes' traction. Scuff the bottoms of shoes well before the wedding day, especially if you'll be facing some tricky terrain as you approach your outdoor ceremony. Give the shoes a trial run over that stone pathway to see if you're tottering or otherwise off-balance. Your shoes are an important part of your look, but they also have to carry you through the day safely.

TOPPING IT OFF: CHOOSING FUNCTIONAL AND FABULOUS VEILS OR HEADPIECES

As with all other accessories, your veil or headpiece must match the formality of the gown and the event as a whole. Some veil lengths work better with different necklines and structures of gowns, and some formality levels lend themselves better to longer, more ornate veils. For a more sophisticated, almost royal look, your stunning gown may call for a full-length chapel veil. Romantic, floral gowns may call for a fingertip veil. Of course, you can always skip the veil completely. It all depends upon your chosen style and the designs you try out with your dress.

As an outdoor bride, you'll also have to take a few other factors into consideration. If your outdoor location is likely to be a bit breezy, such as at a park, on a cliff overlooking the ocean, at the beach, or on a boat, think about what the wind will do with your veil. Shorter veil styles are more likely to dance around above your head, although a good gust can whip your long, cathedral-length veil straight up into the air. You've seen the outtakes on those funniest-video shows, so consider the style of your veil against the potential influence of a stiff wind.

Another option besides the veil is the jeweled headpiece, such as the tiara or crown that tops your look with dazzling elegance. The diamonds or glass stones will glitter in the sun, transforming you into a regal beauty for your big day. Headpieces come in all manners of formality—and expense—such as those that incorporate sea-themed shells as minimal accents, for instance. Such additions may tie in with your look or give a splash of color to make your headpiece even more beautiful.

Outdoor weddings lend themselves as well to a complete *lack* of a headpiece. Perhaps you'd prefer your hair to be your crowning glory instead. We've all seen amazing photographs of hairstyles that are veritable sculptures of curls, twists, tucks, and turns, and such hair artistry may suit your wedding day style more than a traditional veil or tiara.

Simplify It

Check out the selection of veils at the following major wedding Web sites: www.WeddingChannel.com and www.DavidsBridal.com. Their search tools can help you pinpoint the perfect headpiece look for your gown in just a short amount of time.

Or, you might opt for a floral wreath, fresh flowers tucked into a French twist or braid, or even just a fully bloomed daisy perched behind your ear. Some brides choose a wide-brimmed hat that's perfect for a garden wedding, or go artsy with a feathered headband.

The choice, wonderfully and thankfully, is up to you.

Accent Your Look

If it's accessories we're talking about, of course we're going right to the jewelry first. You might want a dramatic, million-dollar look with a necklace that's just dripping with diamonds (or are they *really* diamonds?). Or you might prefer a simpler look with a single-stone drop necklace and dangle earrings. Whatever your preference, the choice is up to you. You can wear the new diamond-and-emerald earrings your handsome groom has given you as a wedding gift, or you can wear your mother's diamond posts.

Simplify It

Knowing that veils can experience some extra movement in outdoor settings, we insert tiny weights inside the hems of our veils. These weights are invisible to the eye, and they keep the veil more in place. With the addition of these weights, a bride can wear the veil she wants without worry.

—Henry Roth of
Michelle Roth Bridal Designs,
www.MichelleRoth.com

Whatever your choice, make sure you've spent some time "auditioning" the jewelry with your gown's neckline and how you'll be wearing your hair that day. The look should be complete, with your chosen jewelry accents working well with the rest of your look.

One of the most important accessories to remember for outdoor weddings is the stylish matching jacket or shawl. In the evenings, especially if you're at the oceanside or on a boat, the nighttime air can get a bit crisp. Plan ahead for a lovely coat designed to match or complement your dress, so that you're not left to shiver in bare shoulders or be hidden from view by the groom's overcoat.

Designers are showcasing wonderful styles such as the opera coat, the georgette coat, the shimmer-velvet coat (it shines in the light,

Turn Your "Something New" into a Keepsake

Your headpiece doesn't have to be a one-time-wear. Consider the new options of having your jeweled headpiece restrung into a string of pearls or a set of gemstone earrings that you can wear on all of your special occasions to come. The most recognizable name in the bridal industry when it comes to getting a second life out of that tiara is Winters and Rain, the Newport, Rhode Island company that creates custom headpieces from real gems—sapphires, rubies, cultured pearls, Swarovski crystals, and so on—and then allows you to return the headpiece after wearing to have it redesigned into stunning jewelry pieces. Check out their services—and their Oceania sea-themed tiara—at www.WintersandRain.com.

perfect for candlelight!), even a sheer-organza cover coat that doesn't hide the dress beneath. A satin shawl can also provide just the right amount of extra warmth and still look chic. Ask the wedding-gown staff for a selection of coats to match your dress and consider the look and feel of the styles. Yes, these may have to be altered as well as your gown, but you'll be grateful to have a beautiful cover-up that will allow you to continue the celebration in the night—regardless of those ocean breezes or nighttime chills.

Under It All

Choosing the right undergarments is crucial for making the most of your wedding-gown look. Though some brides have chosen the type of gown structure and material that will allow them to go braless, most women do not have that option. You'll need to be sure you choose the right bra and lingerie to enhance your look in the gown *and* thrill the groom at the end of the night.

Sheath dresses in particular require seamless panties or a thong to prevent panty lines, or a bodysuit underneath to prevent bra lines as well. Whatever the style of gown you choose, whatever the cut of the neckline or bodice, and whatever you have to show off in them, experiment with different styles of lingerie items. Some brides prefer the look of a push-up bra to make the most of that sweetheart neckline, or they have chosen a daring backless gown that requires a crisscross bra with straps that won't show. The world of lingerie now showcases a wide variety of underwear options, from secure tube-top bras to strapless-cup bras that do not slide down and out of place. Ask a personal shopper at a lingerie store to help you choose the best underthings for your gown's look, and try out a few styles.

One note of caution: Keep the weather in mind when you're slipping into that long-boned corset or the super-slimming Velcro slip. These new functional styles may make the most of your gown, but a hot day may make you wish you weren't wrapped up underneath that dress. Consider the price of underwear that cinches, slims, and smooths (and I'm not just talking about price tags!)

Wedding-Look Worksheet

Store name:

    Address:

    Contact name:

    Phone:

    Fax:

    E-mail:

    Contact's cell phone:

    Store hours:

Dress design number:

Dress designer's name:

Price for gown:

Gown delivery date:

Deposit amount and date paid:

Balance due date and amount:

Alterations fee:

Seamstress's name:

Seamstress's phone number:

Date of first fitting:

Date of second fitting:

Date of third fitting:

Date of final fitting:

Dress pickup date:

Accessories:

    Accessory store name:

    Accessory store address:

    Accessory store phone number:

    Contact:

List Accessories:

Accessory type	Date purchased	Price

Shoes:

Jewelry:

Undergarments:

Additional notes:

Your Bridesmaids' Dresses and Accessories

MOST BRIDES dread having to take all of their maids to the dress shop to agree upon a style and color of bridesmaids' dress. But fear not. Today's styles are a far cry from the outdated prom-gown styles of years past, and designers have created beautiful lines of maids' dresses to please your discerning honor attendants. In this section, you'll help mobilize your maids to find and order their wedding-day wardrobes, and you'll complete your bridal-party ensemble look so that all of your maids feel great on the big day.

The Hot Styles for Bridesmaids

Outdoor weddings usually mean that the bridal party can show more skin, go a little sexier, and wear the hottest new styles out there. Whatever your chosen wedding type, your maids will thank you for allowing them the freedom to wear more stylish designs that don't have to cover their shoulders and arms, as is often the case in a more traditional setting.

Take a look at the bridal magazines and department stores' bridal-style catalogs, and you'll see such outdoor-ready design elements as two-piece gowns that will let your maids show a little tummy and get some air in that satin dress. Embroidered camisole tops that pair up with long flare skirts, for instance, provide a sophisticated detail and an article they'll surely wear again with a more trendy skirt or pants.

Look also for sleeveless or spaghetti-strap gowns or bustier ball gowns that match up with a jacket, plunging backlines with delicate strings of pearls sashed across the straps for a more elegant nighttime look, and simpler satin ball gowns with flowing sheer wraps for accents. Georgette-draped fronts add some fabric molding to simpler styles, and even the more informal bridal party can jazz up swishy satin skirts with classic, white or pale-colored button-down shirts in matching fabrics— unbuttoned at the top for a bit of sex appeal—and tied at the waist for a peek at the midriff. Laser cutouts at the waist and the small of the back add another fun element.

The new designs offer such great imagination and sexy styling, your maids will know this is not just another bridesmaid's gown to hang *way* in the back of their closet.

Colors range from pales to brights, with sleek styling and detail, and the current trend of allowing your maids to choose their own

---

Simplify It

Begin your search for your bridesmaids' gowns at a wedding-fashion Web site such as www.Davids Bridal.com. At this type of site, you can mix and match different styles of tops, skirts, and wraps, then view them in a wide range of colors to discover a look that's perfect for your wedding. Invite your faraway maids to visit this site as well as to prescreen your choice and perhaps choose their own favored neckline and skirt type. This type of tool is priceless and a big time-saver when it comes to bringing your group of maids to reaching personal decisions, as well as ensuring a smooth ordering process.

necklines and skirt styles in the agreed-upon color means that all your maids will find the perfect cut for them. Such individuality is important to any bridal-party member, and you'll make the "most considerate bride ever" list when you break the news that your maids will not all be stuffed into the one prescribed gown. Designers are aware of maids' preferences, and they're tailoring their collections to reflect the changing nature of the bridal-party look. Petite gowns abound, as do plus-size and maternity-gown options that— finally!—honor women of all shapes and sizes.

A Word About Formality

Just as your gown has to adhere to the rules of etiquette, suiting the level of formality and the style of your wedding, so too do your maids' gowns. Their style should complement yours, with the elements of their dresses matching the same criteria you used on your shopping trip. Look back at the formality list in chapter 6, and read over the gown style suggestions from Michelle and Henry Roth to get a feel for the type of gowns you should consider for your maids.

Sizing Up Your Maids

Once the style and color of gown is chosen, it's time to gather up your maids and get their sizes. Notice I didn't say to ask them their sizes, as the gown fashion world doesn't adhere to the normal sizes of regular clothing. If you're a size 6 in street clothing, you may be a 10 in gown sizing. Now, I realize that your maid may be traumatized by the idea that she'll be wearing (oh my Gosh!) a size 14 at your wedding when she is always bemoaning the fact that she's now a size 10. Luckily, the wedding world is aware that the bridge between real-life sizes and wedding-wear sizes can be quite off-putting to their clients. In any bridal salon, the seamstress will assure her client that the sizes "run differently," and she'll produce a tape measure to capture the only numbers that count: the client's true body measurements. That's why the maids are measured at the chest, waist, hips, arms, and height with measuring tapes, and the results written on size cards, so that the right dimensions for the ordering of each gown are correctly received. And your traumatized maid might feel better about her size label when she sees that her hips haven't grown two sizes overnight.

Faraway bridesmaids should be instructed to go to a seamstress to have their measurements professionally taken and recorded on standard tailoring size cards, with those cards sent to you or to whomever is placing the dress order. If a maid is reluctant to show you her size card, allow her to send it to you in a sealed envelope for the shop manager's eyes only. This sounds petty and trivial, but it really does take some of the heat off the maid, and you're not in the awkward position of having to ask your maid—or worse, your pregnant maid—how big her chest is.

Use the following sample size card and information chart to understand exactly what the seamstress is looking for during the sizing portion of the order process:

One of my bridesmaids is pregnant now, and we have no idea what size she will be in six months when the wedding is taking place. How do we order a dress for her?

Pregnant bridesmaids do present a challenge when it comes to ordering gowns. To be on the safe side, talk to the shop manager and the seamstress to get their input on just how large a gown to order. The maid should agree to ordering a gown with a dropped waist that naturally gives her room to grow. Any fitted side seams would certainly become a major headache, so the style of dress itself can allow for an expanding maid. Order large and allow the seamstress to work her magic right before the wedding day.

Bridesmaids' Size Cards

Name:

Address:

Phone:

E-mail:

Cell phone:

Chest:

Waist:

Hips:

Height:

Shoe size:

Glove size:

Head measurement (for floral wreaths):

Fitting appointments:

    1.

    2.

    3.

Deposit payment made:

Final payment made:

Fittings payments made:

Dress picked up on:

Ordering The Maids' Gowns

Perhaps you all live in separate states. Or, you live in the same town but hardly ever see each other due to conflicting work and family schedules. How do you organize your maids' gown orders when all your girls are in different places? Does everyone place their own orders? Absolutely not. All the gowns should be ordered in one group placement at the same location. It takes a bit of work, but you should have one person—be it yourself or your maid of honor—take on the job of collecting size cards and deposit checks from each of the maids and then placing the group order with one call or visit. It's important to order all of the gowns at the same place, because different regions have their own production sites where their individual dyeing processes can mean slight (or major) differences in the hues of the dresses. Your one maid could be standing in her pale pink dress next to another maid in a brighter pink dress and then again next to another in a dusty-rose dress.

For the bridesmaids' gown order, be sure you see and receive a copy of the order form. Each order should include the maid's name, size, style of gown (since each person may each be ordering different necklines or cuts), price, deposit amount marked *paid*, and the date of delivery. Keep a copy of this order form as proof of payment and purchase, and use it in case there is a discrepancy when the order does come in.

Deliver your maids' gowns in person, or via a well-known delivery service such as

Simplify It

Some brides and maids do prefer to make their fittings a group event. If you need to contact all of your maids with the date, time, and place of their fittings, send a confirmation e-mail rather than calling each one after work. Or, try a new phone service called 800-SOUNDBITE. Dial that number, record your message of up to two minutes of duration, enter your bridesmaids' phone numbers, and the job is done. This service will automatically dial all of your numbers and play the message to them at the same time, getting the word out about a changed appointment or the real address of the shop in minutes flat. If no one answers, the service will either dial again or leave a message on voice mail. How much does this service cost? Nothing for the first month of your membership, and just a modest fee afterward. Call 800-SOUNDBITE for current details and package plans.

Federal Express, making sure to opt for insurance and proof of receipt. This is an important parcel, in price and in meaning, and you'll want to protect it to the best of your ability. Have your maids let you know when they receive their dresses, and instruct them to go get their first fittings right away. The gowns may come in five months before the wedding, but they should be inspected and tried on in case of any major problems with the style or condition of the dress.

Fittings for Maids

Your maids will have to schedule their own fittings according to their own time constraints. For best results, let them know that several fittings will be in order throughout the months preceding the wedding, with the final fitting taking place a week or two before the deadline.

Let them know about the "can this dress move?" test that you've taken with your gown, so that they can "test" their gowns for the same kind of movements they'll need to be able to make on the wedding day: sitting, standing, bending over, breathing, raising their arms. Encourage them to be open with the seamstress, so that their gowns are fit to make them look good *and* feel good.

You should also tell them to wear the exact same shoes and undergarments they will be wearing on the wedding day. The seamstress needs to know the precise heel height in order to get all of your maids' hems to line up, and the fit and lift of a bra can affect the way the gown holds across the chest. Encourage your maids to choose the right kind of bra, perhaps one with crisscross straps or a high-quality strapless number, in order to make the most of their backless or more revealing dresses. Going braless may save money, but I've heard complaints about maids whose obvious lack of support took way too much attention away from the bride.

You do not have to attend their fittings, and they do not all have to be done together. It would take a great deal of coordinating for all six of your maids to be able to spend several hours at the seamstress's place, each waiting an hour or so for all of the other honor attendants to be pinned and tucked. So make this an individual effort, and ask the maid of honor to keep all of the women on track with their fittings and payments.

Slip into Some Shoes

Just as your shoes have to allow for some rough or soggy terrain, so do your maids' shoes. Although many brides allow their maids to purchase their own preferred styles of shoes—in keeping with the trend of individuality and the promise of future use for the shoes—you should tell your maids that wide, flat, lower heels would be an advantage during the wedding day. Tell them about how their heels might sink into the ground, how there is a cobblestone walkway leading up to the reception area, and how the deck of the boat will call for some suitable footwear. Your maids will thank you for the heads-up, and you won't have to worry about twisted ankles or falls.

If the maids will be wearing shoes that match their gowns, again, have all of the shoes purchased and dyed at the same shop so that their hues will match. Your maids can provide their shoe sizes without having to get their feet professionally measured, as most sizes do run according to a standard.

If you're having a beach wedding where you'll be barefoot during the ceremony and your maids and guests will be barefoot as well, be

Wedding Day Reflections

I surprised my maids on the morning of my beach wedding by scheduling pedicures for each of them at the beauty salon while I got my massage. They all had their feet massaged and their toenails done in matching pink shades, with their heels pumiced and moisturized for a great, healthy-foot look.

—Anita

sure to tell your maids that shoes *will* be needed for the indoor reception. Your maids should definitely be made aware of this so that they have time to select appropriate footwear for later in the day. (Brides commonly forget to tell their maids that the entire wedding is not a barefoot event.) For fun, encourage your maids to adorn their feet with toe rings, ankle bracelets, and a great shade of matching toenail polish. Just be sure to have them all wear the same shade of polish— or have their toes French manicured to match their fingers—and alert them to the fact that their feet will be on view.

Accessories for Your Maids

Shop early to find the best earrings and necklaces for your maids' wedding-day look. You might be able to find simple silver-heart lockets or gemstone pieces that match their gowns, and you can assure yourself that their accessories will suit—and not overpower— their gowns.

Most brides do give their maids their wedding-day jewelry as a gift at the rehearsal dinner, providing both a heartfelt present and the assurance that their maids will have matching accessories. You'd be surprised at how many brides face the nerve-shattering task of having to ask a maid to remove a clunky necklace or inappropriate earrings right before the ceremony. Though everyone's personal tastes may be different, it may be important to you for your maids to have a unifying look right down to their earrings.

Another popular wedding-wardrobe accessory is the hat. For garden weddings, having your maids top off their floral sundress look with a wide-brimmed straw hat—perhaps with a delicate matching ribbon—makes for a very polished look, and the hat will also keep the sun out of their eyes. Most brides planning informal outdoor weddings love the novelty of having their maids wear hats, and they say it makes for great, unique pictures during the day.

Can I Make Her Cover That Thing?

One of my maids has a very large and very obvious tattoo on her shoulder blade. I support her decision to express herself however she'd like, but the appearance of her tattoo makes me want to choose a more conservative gown for my maids just so her entire back will be covered. Am I being ridiculous, or do I have a right to ask her to cover the tattoo with makeup or something?

This is a topic that affects a lot of outdoor brides, as many women do have tattoos of all sizes and taste levels on their backs, shoulder blades, ankles, and elsewhere. The kinds of skin-baring gowns that are often chosen for outdoor weddings do mean that body art becomes a thing within view. It's a tricky situation to ask your friend to cover her tattoo but, handled well, you can strike an agreement. Remember that some people do get tattoos so that they will be seen, and the maid might be offended if you ask her to cover her mark of individuality. But it is your wedding, and you have a right to ask her to cover the tattoo. Just be sure you see her in her dress when judging the appearance of the tattoo before you make a hard-and-fast rule. If the look is not garish, then perhaps you can just remove yourself from the issue and allow your maid to choose her own appearance for the day. If her entire back is covered with a Japanese dragon that's spitting blood and driving a knife into the heart of her ex-boyfriend, then go with the full-coverage dress. The same discernment applies when it comes time to ask your maids to remove their eyebrow rings and tongue studs. Hopefully, your maids will know the difference between a nose-ring—appropriate event and a wedding, but you do have the right to ask, diplomatically, for the removal of such distracting items.

Don't forget about jackets or wraps for the evening hours, especially if you'll be beachside or on a boat. Your maids should agree upon a style and weight of their chosen wrap so that everyone keeps that bridal-party look even as the temperature falls. Designers offer great lines of shawls, wraps, and jackets in matching satin or silk fabrics, and you can also find more fitted jackets to be worn over the more bare corset and camisole tops your maids will be anxious to show off. Make the jacket a must-order, no matter how sure the maids are that they'll just be too hot from dancing during the night. Some sites are very breezy, and a good chill can take the party spirit out of any reveler.

If your wedding will be a formal outdoor affair, you might choose to have your maids finish off their wedding-day look by wearing elbow-length gloves. Have the maids try on several pairs at the bridal shop, just to get a look at how the styles complement their gowns. Some gloves are full-fingered, and others attach at the middle finger with a loop to allow for full use of the hands. Research your options, and assure your maids that they can remove the gloves once the ceremony is over, if they'd like. Again, order gloves in one shot at one place, especially if they will be dyed-to-order as well.

Dressing Flower Girls

You've had some fun choosing the bridesmaids' dresses, making them sexy and skin-baring, perhaps going with playful floral sundresses or summery slipdresses for the beach. Now, you get to exercise your creative mind in order to outfit your flower girls.

Brides who are planning outdoor weddings find that dressing their flower girls becomes an enjoyable task. They're not just looking at the standard lineup of flower-girl dresses in the bridal salon or at discount kids' clothing stores. They're opting for fun outfits that show a level of playfulness and a tie-in to the theme of the wedding. Flower girls at traditional weddings are often dressed like minibrides,

---

Professionally Speaking

"Since the flower girl is the first one you see to walk down the aisle in the procession, she sets the tone as far as the style and elegance of the occasion. So you'll need to be sure that her outfit is a suitable design that matches the formality of your day. Yet even with the bounds of etiquette, you can have more fun with the clothing and accessories of a flower girl at an outdoor wedding. Have her stand out as the adorable child she is, but have her blend in with her surroundings."

—MARCIA PETERS, FOUNDER OF CHILDREN'S CLOTHING
WEB SITE FINETICA CHILD, WWW.FINETICACHILD.COM

---

poufed out in white dresses with multiple layers of fluff. It's an understood concept that flower girls are not to be dressed like minibridesmaids in sophisticated, adult, even sexy styles, so brides often dress their flower girls in white, add a colored sash and a floral wreath on their head, and voilá! You have the perfect flower-girl look.

While it's most common for the parent to choose and purchase the child's wedding-day wardrobe—with special thought to it serving another future purpose as a party or first communion dress—you, as an outdoor bride, can help create a more suitable look for your little ones that not only impresses the guests but allows the child some comfort and movement on the wedding day. Because all kids run around at weddings, they'll run around even more so at an outdoor wedding. So some thought must be put into the child's activity level and the terrain on which they'll be playing. Long sashes and bows will almost certainly be dragged behind a running child, and grass and mud stains are a certainty for young ones who will sit and play in the grass. The temperature, too, will make a difference, as heavier materials will cause the child to become overheated and perhaps cranky. So choose your flower-girl outfits with the weather and the surroundings in mind just as strongly as the appearance of the dress.

Remember that children in wedding parties are often placed in what is an uncomfortable situation for them. They are the center of attention (perhaps of hundreds of people), they have to stand through a long ceremony, be quiet, pose politely for pictures, and sit through hours of music they've never heard before and probably don't like. Such discomfort can cause tantrums and fidgeting, so don't add to their discomfort level by dressing them in something uncomfortable, itchy, or otherwise displeasing. Always consider the comfort factor when dressing flower girls.

The best way to ensure comfort is to avoid lacy collars and a complicated structure to the dress. Go with something simple, and leave off the sashes and bows that curious children can play with and destroy. "Be sure to choose high-quality fabrics that have some body to them," says Marcia Peters of Finetica Child. "Always choose a dress with a cotton lining rather than a polyester lining, which can be too warm for most children."

For more informal outdoor weddings, a flower girl may be allowed to skip the frilly dress and wear a simple sundress or linen dress. You'll find a wide variety of suitable dresses for informal backyard events and beach weddings at a number of stores and Web sites. Another fun option is to go with a nautical theme, especially if your wedding will be held at the beach or on a boat. An adorable navy sailor dress will make your flower girl look her best and be a perfect style-setter for the day.

Don't forget the appropriate accessories for kids! Be sure their shoes are comfortable and durable for the surfaces on which they'll be

Simplify It

If you love the idea of dressing your little ones in seafaring outfits, don't waste time hitting every shop at the mall to find the right style. Go right to the source. Children's outfitter Katie and Co. offers a special line of kids' nautical outfits and accessories, with tons of options to choose from for both girls and boys. Check them out at www.KatieCo.com.

walking (or running). Beach flower girls can wear pretty floral-accented sandals, for instance, and there are many types of appropriate footwear out there for kids. Though ballet slippers may make for a pretty look at indoor weddings, they may not offer the kind of foot protection you'll want kids to have on the big day. All it takes is one sharp rock or a piece of broken glass on the lawn from an earlier dropped champagne glass, and the child has an injury that could have been prevented.

Wide-brimmed straw hats, decorated with flowers or a ribbon, make for a festive outdoor look, and sunglasses will protect kids' eyes from the sun. Kid-friendly jewelry will complete the look for your outdoor wedding, and even the smallest flower girl at a barefoot beach wedding can wear a tiny ankle bracelet to match the rest of the women in the bridal party.

The most important thing is to have fun with the dress selection for your flower girls. Outdoor weddings, again, offer a lot of freedom of expression, and the unique quality of such an event allows you to break with tradition and allow the children's personalities to shine through as well.

Bridesmaids' Dresses Worksheet

Bridesmaids' dress shop name:

Address:

Phone number:

Fax number:

E-mail:

Contact name:

Store hours:

Gown designer:

Model number:

Alternate style number in case of two-piece gown ensemble:

Price:

Deposit amount:

Deposit date:

Payment schedule:

Payment method:

Delivery date:

Alterations shop:

Seamstress name:

Price:

Fitting schedule:

1.

2.

3.

FedEx pickup # (if dress to be mailed to attendant):

Shoe shop name:

Address:

Phone number:

Shoe shop contact name:

Model number for shoes:

Dye color:

Price:

Delivery date:

Shoes to be picked up by:

Final payment made:

Jewelry:

Stockings:

Other accessories:

Notes:

Dressing the Men

ANOTHER PLUS to planning an outdoor wedding is that the men have some freedom to wear great, stylish getups that don't make them look like a lineup of maître d's. Depending upon your wedding's style and formality (of course), the accepted wedding wear for men can range from those classic tuxedoes with a dash of color in the tie or vest to a smart, casual look of khaki pants, a crisp white button-down shirt, and a navy print tie. Your men will want to look great and feel comfortable at the wedding, especially if they'll be out in the sun or facing some warm weather throughout the day. So keep their comfort level in mind as you team up with the groom to select the formalwear (or informalwear) for your dashing groom and his buddies.

Choosing Men's Wardrobes Based on Formality

The men, of course, do need to suit their look to the formality of the wedding so that they match the occasion and the bridesmaids' dresses. Etiquette still reigns here, but you'll be glad to know that even with the traditional requirements, you can add some spark to the classic tux, suit, or informal ensemble for your guys. Here are general guidelines as to what your formality level prescribes for the men's attire:

ULTRAFORMAL EVENING

- Black coat with tails
- White wing-collared shirt
- White vest
- White bow tie
- Black patent-leather shoes
- Shiny cuff links for accents

ULTRAFORMAL DAYTIME

- Black or gray waistcoat
- Gray pants
- White wing-collar shirt
- Striped tie
- Black patent-leather shoes

FORMAL EVENING

- Black tuxedo
- White shirt (or off-white shirt, to match bride)
- Black tie
- Black cummerbund or vest
- Black patent-leather shoes
- Cuff links and other classy accents

OR ...

- Black tuxedo pants
- White or off-white dinner or cutaway jacket
- Black tie
- Black patent-leather shoes
- Cuff links and other classy accents

FORMAL DAYTIME

- Gray cutaway suit or gray jacket with gray pinstriped pants
- Light-colored or white jacket
- Tie or vest in color or coordinating print
- Formal, long ties are an option in place of bow ties
- Black shoes. NO WHITE SHOES, PLEASE!!!

SEMIFORMAL EVENING

- Black tuxedo or suit
- White or slightly hued shirt
- Black or color-coordinated bow tie and vest
- Black shoes

SEMIFORMAL DAYTIME

- Navy, gray, or white-linen suit
- White shirt
- Color-coordinated tie
- Dark-colored dress shoes for dark suits and light-colored dress shoes for lighter suits

INFORMAL DAYTIME

- Khaki pants
- White button-down shirt
- Solid or patterned tie in coordinating color

The Weather Factor

You'll certainly want to keep in mind the many weather factors of the day. Even though you will be providing shade via a tent or a cluster of trees, there is always a chance that a hot spell could slide over your day, raising the temperatures and the sweat quotient for all of your

Simplify It

Find a great tuxedo or formalwear shop that is registered with the International Formalwear Association. This certification means that the shop is legitimate and the consultants well trained, and that you'll have guaranteed access to many of the top designers and styles. Talk to your formalwear consultant about your plans for the day, where and when your wedding will be, and the formality of the event. Then allow the expert to present a lineup of suitable suits and wearable formalwear for the day. Remember, experienced experts know what will work for your style of outdoor wedding. Ask plenty of questions, see fabric samples, and research well.

guests. So be sure to keep your men in lighter-weight fabrics whenever possible. You may love the look of your men strolling about the garden in their full tuxedoes, but I can guarantee you that those jackets and ties are going to come off as soon as the last picture is snapped.

Talk to your menswear expert, whether it's a tuxedo-shop consultant or the suit guy at Macy's, about finding the right type of outfit in the right weight and fabric to make your men look and feel more comfortable. The higher the thread count of a tuxedo fabric, like super 110s and 120s, the lighter the weight of the garment and the better the fit. You may pay a bit more for this kind of quality, but it will be worth the investment to have your men in clothes that work for the elements of the day.

If you're going informal, such as at a beach wedding, your men can follow the general guidelines I mentioned and go with the popular styles of khaki pants, even khaki shorts, and smart white shirts or polo shirts. As long as the style matches the women's style and the formality of the day, this dressed-down look often comes off great and sets the tone for a relaxed occasion.

Sizing Up Your Guys

Your men will also need to be professionally measured for their wedding-day wardrobes. That means going into the shop to have their dimensions taken and the results recorded on size cards. If you have groomsmen that live out of the area, they can simply visit a tuxedo shop near them for an official size-measurement session. These sizing appointments are generally free at the shop where you're placing the order, but faraway groomsmen may have to pay a nominal fee to a shop near them to complete this simple task. Though most shops use standard sizing cards, the following sample size card shows you the required measurements and info:

Men's Size Card

Name:

Shirt size:

Neck size:

Sleeve length:

Waist:

Inseam:

Shoe size:

A quality formalwear shop will offer the services of a well-trained professional who knows the correct length of sleeves (the end of the jacket just hits the top of the hand, for instance) and who will ensure a fit that allows for good range of movement. Your men should be able to sit, stand, even squat comfortably (for that lunge after the garter!).

The tuxedo should be ordered in the size that fits the grooms-man's biggest dimension, be it the waist or the length of the pants. Order large, as tailoring can fix the fit. A too-small suit will make your groomsman look and feel terrible, and any mistakes discovered at delivery date may make for a tremendous headache when a better-fitting tux cannot be found in time.

When you have the correct sizes for all of your men, including the faraway ones, it's time to put in your order and reserve those great tuxes or suits for the big day.

The Ordering Process

The first and most important rule when ordering tuxes or arranging for your men's wedding-day wardrobes is to allow plenty of time. Complete this job months in advance, as you may be competing with lots of other summertime-wedding bridal parties and promgoers. Part of planning early includes choosing the right formalwear store. You always want to go with high quality, the store with the long track record in your area and the most referrals from your friends. Comparison shop as a couple before you bring the men into the mix, and choose the store that offers the most in terms of price quality, range of options, and customer service.

Once you've made your shop and tuxedo-style selections, inform your groomsmen of the style and of your need for their size cards, and put your dibs on those great tuxes before anyone else.

Using the size cards, place one order at the tuxedo shop. Do not allow your men to call and individually order their tuxedoes. This kind of "bulk" purchase affords you control over the process, the assurance that the job has been done, and perhaps a group-rate discount or a free tux for the groom. With the help of the consultant, you will complete the order form and contract to include the following information:

- The name of the groom as "ordering customer"
- The wedding date
- The time of the wedding
- The names of all the groomsmen

- Individual sizes for all of the groomsmen
- The name of the tuxedo designer
- The style number for the tuxedo
- The fabric of the tuxedo
- Specific style names or numbers of all accessories, such as ties, vests, etc.
- Specific color names of all colored items, such as ties, vests, etc.
- The style name and number of rented shoes
- All shoe sizes
- Specific style names and numbers of all accessories
- Deposit amount marked *paid*
- Final payment amount and due date
- Pickup date
- Return date
- Late-return fee
- Cancellation policy and refund rules
- Signature of formalwear consultant
- Contact information for shop and consultant

Simplify It

For referrals to formalwear shops that are registered with the International Formalwear Association, check in at www.MarryingMan .com as well as at the major wedding-planning Web sites. This fun site provides helpful tips and buying smarts just for the men, and it delivers a list of the recommended shops in your area. Be sure to research all recommended companies well, and do your homework.

A few days before the wedding, the men should go together for their final fittings and garment pickups. In many cases, this will be the first time the faraway groomsmen try on their suits, so some alterations will likely be needed. The formalwear shop, again, has plenty of experience with last-minute fittings, but you should allow as much time as possible for alterations to be made. Never leave this job for the day before the wedding; allow two or three days for such work to be done. You'll avoid rush fees and frantic running around when you all have other things you need to do.

Be sure that the men know what they're picking up—that they also have to get their shoes, cuff links, ties, even socks that work with their wardrobes. Never send a groomsman to the shop without the basic info, such as whose name the order is under, the specifics of the order, and how much needs to be paid that day. A well-informed bridal party is always an organized bridal party, and you won't have the hassle of rescheduling pickup times because the usher couldn't get through to you on your cell phone.

Also, designate a "return man" who will gather up all of the tuxedos and shoes the day after the wedding and return them to the shop. It's always best to have one person—the best man, perhaps—take on this responsibility so that the job is completed by someone you know (or hope!) will be reliable. Late fees could be charged to your credit card if you've placed and paid for the order, so be sure this job is done in your absence.

If you're not going the rental route but are instead having your men dress in more informal attire such as khaki pants and matching white, button-down shirts, then the group shopping trip is a must. Gather your men on a mutually agreeable day— and this includes the fathers of the bride and groom and the ring bearer—and hit the stores in search of a single style of khaki pants and white shirt. Do *not* simply tell your guys to go to the mall and get a pair of khakis, as colors can vary wildly.

Everyone chooses their size of the same khaki pants, and everyone chooses their size of the same style of white, button-down shirt. Then head off to the shoe store so that the men can use the color of their pants to select appropriate footwear. Don't skip this step either, as some of your men may be perfectly comfortable showing up at the wedding in the same ratty sneakers they've had since high school. Uniform footwear is a must, even at an informal wedding.

Wedding Day Reflections

I almost had a stroke when the men showed up on the wedding day. They all had khaki pants on, but the colors ranged from a pale, pale beige to almost a brownish-green. The guys didn't match at all, and we had to send one to a department store to find another pair. Since it was an informal look, we wanted the guys to match well. We made a terrible mistake in skipping the work it takes to coordinate the men's clothes.

—Deanna

Don't be afraid to lay down the law with your male attendants, giving them specific instructions on all aspects of their wedding-day look. If you want them in Oxfords with black socks, say that. Leave nothing to chance and go along with the men on their shopping spree so that you can see what they're planning to wear. If you're there, then the men can't choose the Hawaiian shirts or the joke-imprinted T-shirts that show through their classic, white button-downs. (What they do after you leave is another story!)

Dressing the Little Guys

It's not just the flower girls who comprise the "Oh, how cute!" factor at a wedding. The ring bearers also draw their share of attention in their smart little tuxes and minicummerbunds. At an outdoor wedding, your options are even more widespread, and the cuteness quotient can go up even further if you're planning a more informal affair.

I spoke to Marcia Peters of Finetica Child (see resources) about dressing up the little guys for the big day. Your options are not limited to putting the ring bearer in a minigroomsman getup and sending him down the aisle. Couples are now having some fun with kids' clothing for their weddings, and nowhere is the creativity element more in play than at an outdoor wedding. Peters says that although kids also have to fit in with the formality level of the wedding and coordinate with the rest of the bridal party, their wardrobe choices are enormous.

Again, as with the flower girls, comfort is key. If your little guys are buttoned-up into a starchy collar and jacket, there's going to be a lot of fidgeting and cranky behavior. "That jacket is going to come off," says Peters. It's important that you take the weather into consideration, as even the kids who are happy to play out in the hot sun all day will not want to do so in a restrictive outfit. Kids love to run around, even at a wedding, so the clothing they wear is going to be facing some wear and tear.

Choose high-quality children's clothing for the boys. Look for solid construction and a good fit, secure hems and seams, and breathable cotton linings or fabrics. Just the same, avoid a cotton blend that is too light and too casual, one that doesn't hold its shape when worn.

Here are some style ideas for the little guys so that you can blend the formality rules with a bit of fun and playfulness for kids:

OUTDOOR BACKYARD WEDDING

- If the wedding is formal, put your little guy in dark suit pants and a white, button-down short-sleeve shirt with a tie to match the men's.
- For a great look, go with a European-style look of navy blue gabardine pants and a high-quality cotton short with slight weave in the texture.

MORE INFORMAL OUTDOOR WEDDING

- A suit to match the men's style, with a color-coordinated tie (the jacket can come off later)
- Suit pants with a white, short-sleeve dress shirt and coordinating tie
- Khaki pants and crisp, white, button-down shirt

BEACH OR BOAT WEDDINGS

- Khaki or navy shorts (Peters suggests the new well-styled cargo pants that unzip at a later time in the day to become shorts—very fun, and very functional)
- Plain, cotton polo shirts
- Button-front shirts in white
- Nautical-themed casualwear
- Boat shoes

Part of the fun of dressing kids for outdoor weddings lies in all of the ways you can incorporate color and patterns. Add a dash of color with the boys' ties, and go ahead and use that navy-and-white sailor's theme for appropriate wedding celebrations. A dash of color can come from the children's accessories as well. Many brides and grooms find great sunglasses for their child attendants in tinted shades (see the resources section at the end of this book). One couple even had their ring bearers carry brightly colored beach balls down the aisle to set the stage for their beach-party wedding. Another put a dab of pink zinc oxide on the ring bearer's nose to have him match the bridal

> ## *Simplify It*
>
> F*or a good look at the types of nautical wear available for boys of all ages, visit www.KatieCo.com, a company that runs a special line of seafaring clothing for kids.*

party's colors *and* to protect his little nose from the blaring sun. Creativity abounds when dressing the most junior members of your bridal party, and today's fun styles suit outdoor-wedding kids to a T.

Men's Wardrobe Ordering Worksheet

Name:

Address:

Phone:

Cell phone:

E-mail:

Tuxedo designer and style number:

Size:

Shoe size:

Accessories:

- Tie
- Cummerbund
- Vest
- Cuff links

Other:

Deposit payment amount and date:

Size card received:

Final payment amount and date:

Pickup date:

Drop-off date:

Wedding Rings

YOU'VE PROBABLY already heard about the famous four C's of diamond selection: cut, color, clarity, and carat. If your groom has gone the traditional route of selecting your engagement ring without your input, he's already delved into the world of diamonds. Now, even as you're wading through your own four C's of caterer, cake, credit cards, and checks, it's time for the two of you to learn more about wedding-ring selection, shopping, and handling.

The most important thing to keep in mind when choosing your wedding rings is the idea that these will be your everyday jewelry pieces. The style and fit are going to have to suit your personality, your tastes, your personal sense of style, and your lifestyle. These rings are the symbol of your vows, a declaration to the world that you belong to one another, but let's face it—the ring has to look perfect on your finger.

A great many aspects of ring shopping must be addressed before you plunk down a sizeable amount of money for your bands. You'll need to consider various styles and colors, whether or not you want plain bands or ones holding diamonds or gemstones, and you'll need to think about the durability of the rings you choose. After all, your rings will last forever. They are the one truly everlasting piece of your big day that you take with you, the only item that lasts forever along with your vows and your love for one another. So choose well.

Ring Trends

Platinum is the band of choice for its strength and durability, its shine, and its everyday practicality. Though platinum is also one of the priciest metals, most couples find that the investment is worth the benefit; they would rather spend more for a ring that will not get nicked, dented, or worn after time. Platinum never tarnishes, and its natural state makes it 100% hypoallergenic and kind to the skin. You'll find a wide range of rings in valuable platinum, and in other metals as described in the sidebar, and your selection begins with the width of the bands in question. Do you want a narrow band, or a thicker one? A plain band, or one with ridges? Jewelry designers can now laser-cut bands to give the appearance of lacy cutouts and engraved designs.

No More Plain Gold Bands?

Whereas men usually go for the more plain bands, many women are now choosing diamond-inset bands to coordinate with their engagement rings. Another popular choice, especially among older brides and brides marrying for the second or more times, is the gemstone ring, either in a precious stone such as a ruby or an emerald, or in a birthstone. A bride may choose to incorporate both her and her fiancé's gemstones, if the particular colors go well together. Research your gemstones well, as some stones are more durable than others.

Are you more the simple elegant type, or do you favor a more detailed look?

Many past brides and grooms advise couples to consider the future implications of choosing rings with ridges and cutouts. These grooves do catch a good amount of dirt from daily wear, and they'll certainly become encrusted with any kind of messier materials with which you come in contact on a regular basis. Cleaning your rings, then, becomes a more difficult chore. So if your line of work or your hobbies would expose you to materials that might threaten the well-being of your rings, think hard about the designs you're considering.

Ring-Shopping Advice

The most successful ring-shopping trip starts with a bit of research way before the visit to the store. You'll need to look up those four C's again if you'll be using diamonds in your band settings. You'll also need to learn more about ring metals to narrow down your scope and make your selection easier.

PLATINUM

If you've decided on platinum, keep the following in mind: For top-quality platinum, which is usually 95% platinum and 5% alloys of iridium or palladium, look on your rings for the markings of 900 Pt, 950 Plat, or Plat.

GOLD

Whether you're choosing yellow gold or white gold (which looks like platinum), remember that the higher the gold percentage, the softer the band! Gold does not tarnish or rust, but it isn't as durable as platinum. You may think that your 24-karat gold ring is top-notch, but 24-karat in its pure form is the most malleable form of gold there is. Designers do incorporate alloys into golds, bringing the strength up the lower the numbers go. Most jewelers will recommend 18-karat gold for its added strength; 14 karat is acceptable according to jewelers' standards, but they maintain that such a level is not practical enough for fine jewelry such as a wedding ring. White gold is also more fragile than yellow gold, due to the combination of alloys used. Price is dependent upon the amount of pure gold used in the mix, but as with everything else in the wedding, the cost goes up when more design or work is needed.

Silver

Sterling silver is a fine choice for wedding rings, and it is sometimes the only choice for brides and grooms who may be allergic to gold. Pure silver is also a very soft metal, so again alloys are used to strengthen the material. Sterling silver brings the mixture up to 92.5% silver and 7.5% alloy. Jewelers recommend choosing a silver with a copper alloy, as copper adds durability without any effect on the color of the silver. When looking at silver jewelry, check for grading marks such as "sterling," "ster," and ".925." Those marks attest to the quality of the metal, and most fine-jewelry designers will notch their works with such grades. (Please note: Silver jewelry must be protected from strong household cleaners and chlorinated water such as swimming pools and hot tubs, as these liquids do deteriorate silver's quality.)

Now that you've chosen your band material, it's time to decide if you want diamonds or gemstones. The groom could probably use a little reminder of the four C's (hopefully, he followed them when he chose your engagement ring!). A diamond may last forever, but a high ranking on the four C's scale will make your ring look like it's brand-new every day. All diamonds and diamond rings are certified according to a universal scale of colors, cut, clarity, and carat. Gemologists inspect these rings under high-powered microscopes and assign grading numbers or letters to "stamp" on the ring. The ranking affects the pricing, and it also indicates the level of perfection in each piece. Always ask to see the grading certificate of any ring you're considering, and learn to read the charts that explain the ranks. A good jeweler should be able to present you with a grading chart and a fine-printed explanation of your ring's particular "DNA."

COLOR

Diamonds come in colors ranging from pure white to yellow. The pure-white ones, the ones with almost no color at all, are considered the most valuable, in all senses of the word. Colorless diamonds are graded as D, and the variations from there are indicated with letters continuing down the alphabet from that point.

CUT

You'll certainly want your diamond to sparkle brilliantly on your hand all the days of your life, and the cut of your diamond can affect its radiance. The cut of the diamond depends upon the skill and vision of the artisan who creates the diamond's shape and is therefore the only artificial aspect of a diamond's natural value. Look at diamonds cut in princess (square-cut), round (the most popular choice), marquis, emerald, pear, and a selection of other shapes to see which cut allows the greatest amount of light to hit the surfaces and ridges of your diamond. Even the highest-quality diamond can be dulled by poor cut and poor placement in a setting, so inspect various shapes of diamond cuts in a variety of settings before making your purchase.

Wedding Day Reflections

I knew ahead of time that I didn't want a big diamond. I have small hands, and a big rock like a 2-carat would look like a golf ball on my hand. So I limited myself to quarter-carats or half-carats, which looked better on my hand and didn't cost us a fortune. Now that I have it on, I'm finding that I'm not knocking it against anything like I did when I tried on the bigger diamonds for fun.

—Amanda

CLARITY

Tiny flaws inside your diamond are graded as well. You may not be able to see a tiny chip or carbon spot with your eye, but a look through the jeweler's viewfinder can point out a world of defects. Flaws may be internal (called "inclusions") or external (called "blemishes"), and it's best to know these terms so that you understand the jeweler's explanations of your diamond's quality.

You might be able to live with a ring that has tiny marks within, especially if no one can see them, and those less-perfect diamonds will be priced lower. Some flaws, however, can be seen with the eye, and those rings should be avoided. Very few diamonds are flawless, and those are most likely to be in a museum and not on someone's hand. So use your best judgment when presented with a stone that has barely detectable flaws.

CARAT

This is the one you've heard about most often. The size of the diamond reflects the carat weight. Larger diamonds are, of course, more expensive than smaller ones, but the other three C's affect the pricing as well.

For any ring-shopping trip, always go to a reputable jewelry store with an established reputation for fine service. Be sure the jeweler is a registered member of the American Gem Society (www.ags.org or 800-346-8485), a national organization that requires its members to complete rigorous training, accumulate years of high-quality service, and provide ethical service. Ask your recently married friends where they bought their rings, and get the name of the salesperson who helped them out. Especially in the jewelry business, word-of-mouth means everything. A good shop has a reputation for fine service, high-quality rings, and fair pricing. As with anything else, taking shortcuts and seeking deals that are too good to be true will only get you ripped off in the end. So go to the best to get the best.

As you both may be ordering rings, your groom should choose a style of ring that works best for him. Do not limit yourselves to ring sets, thinking your rings have to match. Individual tastes and preferences matter greatly, and your rings do have to suit your lifestyles and activity levels as well. So encourage the groom to look at his own collection of rings, try them on, and select the style he likes.

Because fit is very important, be sure that you both get your ring fingers professionally measured and sized. You may know that you wear a size 6 ring—and always have—but designs can vary in size. You'll want to get the best fit right off the bat so that you do not have to pay for extra sizing once the rings come in.

Be sure that the salesperson completes the order form with all pertinent information, records your payment, and states a delivery date. Get a copy of this agreement and keep it someplace safe. You will certainly need a record of this sizeable purchase, and being organized can save you from some of the biggest ring-related nightmares in the wedding industry. For instance, one couple returned to the jewelry store only to find that the ring they had chosen and paid for was not the same ring they received. That gorgeous, nearly-perfect, 3-carat stone they selected after much scrutiny and budget-crunching had been secretly replaced with a same-size, more flawed, less valuable stone by a bad-apple unscrupulous vendor. They didn't notice until weeks later during the ring appraisal.

Simplify It

To begin your ring deliberations, visit www.BlueNile.com for a fun trip through its "Build Your Own Ring" interactive tool. You'll be able to "try out" different diamond cuts and sizes in a wide range of settings in order to find the best style for you. Or, look at www.adiamondisforever.com in order to truly design your own ring, and then print out or e-mail the design to others for their opin-

INSCRIPTIONS

Personalizing your rings is a wonderful gesture for adding even more significance to them. Some couples surprise each other by trading

Don't Risk It

Always have your rings appraised at a site other than the shop where you bought them. Get a valid appraisal certificate that states the value and specifics of the ring. While you're at it, have your rings insured by a reputable insurance agency to protect your investment and save you a fortune in case the rings are lost or damaged in the future.

rings before the wedding and then taking them to the jeweler to have a special saying engraved on the inside of the bands. The following are some popular choices:

- The bride and groom's names
- The wedding date
- *Forever*
- *My True Love*
- *My Best Friend*
- *Always Yours*
- *Je T'aime* (or *I Love You* translated in any language)
- The couple's nicknames for one another

Engraving usually takes only a few days, but it's best to get this job completed well before the wedding. During busy wedding seasons, the jeweler may be extremely busy, and delays might ensue.

Handling the Rings on the Wedding Day

Besides the wedding license, your rings are the must-haves on the wedding day. It's a good idea to hand the wedding rings off to the best man and the maid of honor on the morning of the wedding, not the night before at the rehearsal. With so much activity at the rehearsal, at the rehearsal dinner, and at any more festive activities after the rehearsal dinner, the ring could get lost. In addition, the trusted honor attendant might forget the rings on the morning of the wedding, or otherwise misplace them between destinations. Anything could happen, so it's best to keep them within your sight until the last possible moment. For security purposes, keep them in a family safe or lockbox until the trip to the ceremony site, and have them transported in a separate box or velvet bag. Never allow the carrier to put the rings in his or her pocket, as they may slip through any holes in the pocket lining and be lost inside a jacket—or truly lost forever. Also, do not allow your maid of honor to put the ring inside her change purse, as the ring may get scratched or damaged.

> ## Wedding Day Reflections
>
> My maid of honor put my ring in a little bag along with the rest of her wedding-day jewelry. Apparently, some of her diamond pieces knocked against my diamond ring and chipped off a corner of it. And then she wouldn't pay to have my stone recut.
>
> —Eileen

Be sure that the best man and maid of honor actually have the rings on them right before you depart for the ceremony. This last-minute check will avoid any unfortunate, though understandable, lapses by the maid or best man, who accidentally left the ring in the velvet bag back in the house.

Jewelry for Kids

If you or your groom have children, it's a wonderful idea to include them in the ceremony by giving them a gift of a diamond-chip ring or necklace. Groom Anthony Padovano presented his new stepdaughter Leigha with a diamond-pendant necklace during the vows he took with his new wife Patricia, symbolizing his promise of loyalty and love to her. Such a gesture is always remembered and always appreciated.

Ring Ordering Worksheet

Store name:

Address:

Phone number:

E-mail:

Web site:

Contact name:

Bride's ring style number:

Bride's ring specifics:

Bride's ring size:

Price:

Engraving:

Groom's ring style number:

Groom's ring specifics:

Groom's ring size:

Price:

Engraving:

Bride's ring appraisal:

Bride's ring insurance-policy number:

Groom's ring appraisal:

Groom's ring insurance-policy number:

Child's jewelry information:

Store:

Style:

Size:

Price:

Engraving:

Notes:

10

The Ceremony

As IMPORTANT as you may find the flowers, the gown, and the cake to be, the real crucial part of the day is the ceremony. It is the public declaration of your promises, the ritual that bonds you, and the legal binding of your marriage. So consider this the most important step in all of your wedding planning. In this chapter, you'll learn how to choose the right officiant for your style of wedding and which questions you need to ask, as well as how to select the elements that will comprise your ceremony. Will you include religious components? Will you include a musical interlude? Or will you keep it short and simple so that you can get to the reception more quickly? The choices are up to you, as outdoor weddings—due to their lack of the kinds of rules imposed by many houses of worship—afford you a great deal of freedom in selecting only the elements you wish to include. Plus, they allow you to incorporate a great deal more personal expression and extraspecial elements into your ceremony.

Religious or Nonreligious?

This becomes the big question at the outset of planning a ceremony. You will not be married in a church or synagogue, so what are the rules about including the various religious elements in your outdoor service? Basically, that will be determined by the agreements made between you and your officiant. Some priests, ministers, and rabbis will not perform outdoor ceremonies, as the rules of their houses of worship state that marriage ceremonies must be held within their own walls. Other religious officiants will come to an off-site location such as a banquet hall, a personal home, or an estate home. When you do find a religiously affiliated officiant who will come perform a ceremony at an outdoor location, you will have to discuss his or her requirements. Some priests, for example, may agree to come perform a ceremony in your backyard, but they may not offer a mass. In the case of a dual-faith ceremony, the officiant from both of your houses of worship will have to work with you as a team to create a ceremony that suits your ritual needs and their allowances.

> ### Simplify It
>
> Many established wedding locations do require the use of their own officiants. Or, they may supply a list of accredited officiants whom they favor. Ask the site manager for a list of recommended outdoor-wedding officiants, then continue your research with that list in hand. To be on the safe side, once you select your officiant, call the site manager to get the final okay on using an "outside" officiant to conduct your ceremony.

That said, your first step is deciding what kind of religious service you desire for your wedding. If you have your heart set on a mass, you might consider having your ceremony in a church or chapel and your reception outdoors. If the presence of a religious officiant, plus the wording of the mass, would be enough to suit your needs, then the next step is to meet with an officiant to discuss the religious components of your ceremony.

By far, the average outdoor wedding is less religious and more secular, less bound to the requirements of the traditional ceremony, and more open to interpretation of your own level of faith. So talk with your fiancé about what style of ceremony you wish to have, and how much religious inclusion you desire.

Informal Ceremonies

If the two of you do not have strong ties to any house of worship, or if your personal beliefs are such that a nonreligious ceremony would be preferable, then your ceremony will follow the more informal route that is highly popular among outdoor-wedding couples. In instances where religion is not a factor, a secular officiant may be chosen to lead a short ceremony that includes a processional, readings or music, the vows, the exchanging of rings, the kiss, and the recessional. These outdoor weddings are short in duration—which is a plus when Mother Nature has given you a sweltering day—and they include only the elements the bride and groom prefer.

Again, because all couples have individual wishes for their ceremonies, the creation of your ceremony will have to begin with an in-depth discussion about what you both want. Then you will be ready to choose the officiant who can make it happen for you.

Choosing the Officiant

A religious officiant may be willing to conduct a ceremony that does not include Scripture or other religious elements, but more often than not a secular ceremony will be conducted by any of the following, according to your state's certification rules:

- Town mayor
- Town deputy mayor
- Town committee chairperson
- Federal district court judge
- United States magistrate
- Municipal court judge

- Superior court judge
- Tax court judge
- Retired superior or tax court judge
- County clerk
- Minister in any religion

To locate a certified officiant who is recognized by your state as being qualified to perform marriage ceremonies, just call your town hall or county courthouse to get a list of the judges, magistrates, or mayor, and their phone numbers. Conduct this step as early as possible in order to make sure the officiant will be available on the date of your wedding. Ask about required documentation, fees, preceremony meetings, ceremony rules and regulations, and any other steps necessary for that officiant to conduct your ceremony.

INTERVIEWING OFFICIANTS

As with all other steps of the wedding, you will need to do your research when looking for an officiant, which means you will have to interview potential officiants to find out their accreditation, their experience level, and their personal style. One couple learned the hard way that this step is not to be taken lightly: The officiant they found through the phone book and hired after only a phone consultation showed up at the wedding in an old purple choir robe and rambled on about how the trees and the birds around them were blessing the couple with "their songs in the breeze." The guests had a good chuckle, but the bride and groom were mortified. So, interview your potential officiants in person, and get the full story on what you can expect from each person. The following are the main questions you should ask:

THE BASICS

- Do you conduct outdoor weddings?
- Would you be willing to come to our location at our home/ garden/beach to conduct our wedding?

- Do you have a current, valid license to conduct wedding ceremonies in this state? (Always ask to see a copy of the license, and remember: Not all boat captains are licensed to perform ceremonies.)
- How many weddings have you conducted?
- How many outdoor weddings have you conducted?
- Are you available on our wedding date?
- Are you available at the time of our wedding?
- How many other weddings are you doing that day?
- How much time do you allow between ceremony appointments?
- Do you have the amount of time we require open in your schedule?

The Particulars

- Do you perform nonreligious ceremonies?
- Do you perform interfaith ceremonies?
- Will you perform the ceremony with another religious leader, as we require?
- Do you offer bilingual services?
- Will you allow us to choose our own ceremony elements?
- Will we have the chance to review the wording you plan to use?
- Will you allow us to write our own vows?
- Will you allow our children to participate in the ceremony?
- What will you be wearing to the ceremony?

The "Vibe"

- Does the officiant speak articulately and present him- or herself well?
- Does the officiant allow you to express what you want in your ceremony?
- Does the officiant make you feel at ease?
- Does the officiant grill you about your personal relationship— or lack thereof—to the church? Many brides report that some

officiants are reluctant to handle their wedding if the couple is not affiliated to a great degree with the officiant's house of worship.

THE BUSINESS END

- What are your fees?
- Do we have to make a donation to your church?
- Do we have to pay for your travel expenses to our location?
- What documentation do you require of us?
- Do we have to attend counseling with you?
- How many meetings must we have with you?

Using the Location to Make Your Ceremony Special

You may have chosen a particular outdoor site for its great view, its beautiful gardens, or even a beautiful marble staircase leading down to a pool and terrace. Use those elements to accentuate your ceremony! At Callaway Gardens in Pine Mountain, Georgia, one of its outdoor wedding sites offers a beautiful rock altar that is the focal point for ceremonies. At a beach wedding, perhaps a dune on a slight rise would be the perfect place to take your vows. At a botanical garden, you'll find gorgeous flower-lined pathways that would make a great walkway for your approach to the ceremony site.

Make the most of your location's natural surroundings, using your imagination to create great processional surroundings and select the focal point at which you'll take your vows.

Ceremony Elements

Here comes the fun part: creating your ceremony from scratch. Most couples who marry within a traditional setting such as a church are bound by the prescribed elements of a wedding ceremony, but you're free to include or eliminate whichever elements you choose. In this section, you'll choose your music, your readings, and your vows, and you'll decide how to make your ceremony reflect your own promises and personalities.

Length of the Ceremony

As was previously mentioned, it's always a good idea to keep the ceremony short when it's held outdoors. You really can't tell ahead of time what the weather will be like, so it's best to keep the official portion of the wedding day to a limited duration. Most guests do dread having to sit through an hour-long ceremony, and their discomfort will be evident on the big day (and on the videotape!) if they have to sit through several musical performances and lengthy readings while the temperature soars and the sun beats down on them.

The average outdoor wedding ceremony runs for about fifteen to twenty minutes, although some may be as short as ten minutes. The choice is up to you. By no means should you rush through your ceremony—or leave out anything you truly want—for the sake of saving time. Just keep the duration factor in your mind as you move through the next steps of planning your ceremony.

> ## Wedding Day Reflections
>
> Our chosen wedding site had a pretty waterfall right next to the main house. We set up our ceremony site so that we would have that waterfall as our backdrop, and the guests would be seated in a half-circle facing us. It couldn't have been more gorgeous, especially when the sun came out stronger and created a double rainbow within the mist from the falls.
>
> —Nancy and Steve

Music

Music is always a lovely part of a ceremony, whether you have it piped in through a sound system at your location or have live musicians announcing your arrival with the unmistakable sounds of a violin concerto or flutes announcing your approach as if you were in a Shakespearean play on the green. An outdoor wedding, free from the musical restrictions of a church, might open up your options a bit. Many outdoor couples have chosen to place bagpipe players at the front of their processional, keeping in tune with their ethnic pride. Beachside weddings might call for a fun rendition of "Here Comes the Bride" played on a collection of steel drums.

For the musical interludes within your ceremony, you might choose to have a soloist or musician play one of the following popular wedding songs:

For the Guest Seating

"Matrimonial Benediction," Camille Saint-Saens
"Flower Waltz," Peter Tchaikovsky
"String Quartet Menuett No. 8," Luigi Boccherini
"Menuett in D Major," Wolfgang Amadeus Mozart
"Jesu, Joy of Man's Desiring," Johann Sebastian Bach
"Air" (from *Watermusic*), G.F. Handel
"Benediction Nuptiale," Camille Saint-Saens

For the Processional

"Bridal Chorus" (from *Lohengrin*), Richard Wagner
   (also known as "Here Comes the Bride")
"Rhapsody on a Theme," Niccolo Paganini
"The Four Seasons," Antonio Vivaldi
"Wedding March" (from *The Marriage of Figaro*),
   Wolfgang Amadeus Mozart
"Ode to Joy," Ludwig van Beethoven
"Canon in D Minor," Johann Pachelbel

Standard Performance Songs

"At Last," Etta James
"Beautiful in My Eyes," Joshua Kadison
"True Love," Elton John and Kiki Dee

"It Had to Be You," Harry Connick Jr.

"You Are So Beautiful," Joe Cocker

"I Cross My Heart," George Strait

"Amazed," Lonestar

"What a Wonderful World," Louis
  Armstrong

"I Swear," All-4-One

FOR THE RECESSIONAL

"Wedding March" (from *A Midsummer Night's
  Dream*), Felix Mendelssohn Bartoldy

"Wedding Chorus" (from *Lohengrin*),
  Richard Wagner

"The Four Seasons," Antonio Vivaldi

The choice of music to be included in your wedding is up to you. One couple from Florida asked a musician friend to compose a song especially for them and to surprise them with it on the wedding day. "Their song" was a song they had never heard before, and it was perfect for them. It became the musician friend's gift to the couple, presented to them on a CD after the wedding.

> ### Simplify It
>
> Complete your wedding music search in record time (get it?) with a visit to www.wedalert.com, where you'll find extensive lists of songs for all segments of your ceremony and reception, plus the options of either listening to or reading the lyrics for a better sense of which songs are right for you. This site also shows you which songs are the most downloaded, and therefore the most popular, among other brides and grooms.

READINGS

If you choose to include readings in your ceremony, you might select from any number of timeless wedding standards, such as Elizabeth Barrett Browning's "How do I love thee? Let me count the ways?" or her devoted Robert Browning's "Grow old along with me! The best is yet to be . . ."

Or, you might choose writings from today's most often-quoted writers: Marianne Williamson, Pema Chodron, Anne Morrow Lindbergh, the Dalai Lama, Maya Angelou, and others. If you and your partner have

Simplify It

A great many books on the market contain poetry, essays, and quotes that make for great ceremony readings. Check your local library for the ones that speak to you. Or, use the Internet to find great quotes and poetry that you can include in your day.

made a practice of writing love letters to each other over the years, why not read excerpts of your most swooning notes, sharing your personal thoughts with your loved ones?

A reading may be performed by the officiant, yourselves, your best man or maid of honor, your parents, your godparents, or even your children. Many couples enjoy including their loved ones in this part of the ceremony, as it makes the experience more memorable and more a statement of family love. Ask your loved ones if they'd be willing to participate, provide them with a copy of what they'll be reading, and allow them plenty of time to practice. Of course you'll need to include your readers in the rehearsal so that they may give their reading a first public run.

VOWS

For vows, you may choose to go with the old standard of "to love, to honor, to cherish, etc." This does the job well, but many couples wish to personalize their vows more. After all, they are individuals. Their expressions of love and the promises they wish to make are highly individual as well. Writing your own vows will offer you the chance to express your true feelings to your partner and to make a verbal commitment that suits your relationship well.

If you will be writing your own vows, keep the following simple rules in mind:

• *Take your time writing them.* Go through several drafts, and see which words come to you and just feel "right."

• *Write your vows in private.* Don't share this job with your partner, as a tag-team approach will make your vows sound very similar and will not include as much of your own expressions.

- *Keep it short and sweet.* You'll be nervous, your intended will be nervous, and you may get emotional. So don't overwhelm yourself with a long speech. Just a few sentences are fine.

- *Don't bother trying to memorize all of it.* Or, if you think you must come prepared with the vows all set in your head, have them printed on a card held by the officiant in case you need a little coaching.

- *Don't wing it.* Some couples actually go to the altar without their vows written, saying that they want to just speak what's in their hearts at the time. Bad move. Though spontaneous expressions are always wonderful, you may be too nervous, emotional, or overwhelmed to say what you really feel. It would be terrible to regret later on that you didn't say something you should have said—or that you clammed up and didn't say much at all.

- *Agree on a timed length of speech.* It sounds petty, but you might be bothered by the fact that your partner had a lot more to say than you did.

- *Get personal.* Don't just rattle off a list of what you promise to do for the rest of your life. Though it's always important to say you'll love and respect your partner and be faithful to one another, your vows also present the opportunity to share how special your partner is to you, what you felt the first time you met, your favorite moment with your partner, or the moment you knew that he was "The One."

- *Don't be afraid to be funny!* A little humor is always a great part of any vows, especially if you're getting teary-eyed.

- *Include your children in the vows.* If you have kids, and if your partner has kids, add a short section after you take your own vows in which you both promise to love and comfort the children as you join your families together. You might choose to give your new stepdaughter a ring or necklace of her own at this point as a gesture of that love.

I can't hear you!

One of the most common complaints at outdoor weddings is that the guests can't hear the vows. Inside a church or enclosed location, the acoustics of the building will carry your voices to all parts of the room. Out in the elements, however, sound has a tendency to be carried away by the wind. So arrange to be fitted with minimicrophones (the videographer will probably have a set on you anyway) and to have your words played through a speaker system. This option works well if you'll have a large gathering of guests, or if your location is subject to lots of outside noises, such as that gorgeous waterfall, the crashing of the surf at the beach, or even the occasional airplane flying overhead.

Grand Finales

One of the great things about outdoor weddings is the freedom you have to add special elements at the end of the ceremony. You might choose to release doves or butterflies to symbolize your marriage taking flight. Just be sure to hire a reputable company that regularly releases these animals in your area. Animal-rights groups have complained recently that many species of butterflies cannot survive in the regions where they're shipped and released. Trained doves are not to be released in inclement weather or when it's getting dark. Research dove- or butterfly-release companies well, and always be sure a certified handler will be on site for the dove release. Ask plenty of questions, share detailed information about your wedding site, and consider the expense and risks of including such an impressive grand finale to your wedding. Some sites just are not right for the release of birds, either for the safety of the animals themselves (such as having them fly over an airport on their way home) or for the complexity of the legal liabilities involved in your district. Plus, the expense of a live dove release—quite lofty in some areas—may not be a worthy drain to your budget.

Speaking of grand finales, I include here the option of fireworks only with strict, strict warnings. Some couples—and not just celebrities or the fabulously wealthy—do hire professional, licensed fireworks companies to set off a few rounds of fireworks in the night sky right after the couple's first kiss as husband and wife. If this option is for you, be sure to check out the fireworks company well. Make sure that it's licensed and legal in the state, that you have the required permits from your state and wedding site, and that the weather conditions will be right. According to fireworks experts, you'll need to make sure that there aren't drought conditions in effect, leaving the ground under the fireworks susceptible to fires, and that there is no wind advisory where breezes can blow the fallout onto roofs or tents, starting blazes. Though fireworks are always a dramatic ending to an outdoor wedding ceremony, there is a lot to

Simplify It

A *receiving line is not a necessity with an outdoor wedding. After all, you will be mingling with your guests throughout the reception, making introductions as the opportunities arise. So unless you have your heart set on standing in a lineup and shaking hands with all of your guests before you get your first sip of champagne, skip the formal line and just proceed to the reception.*

consider as far as legality and safety are concerned. Research well and get all permissions, and be aware that you will be assuming all responsibility for this choice. Better yet, just plan your outdoor wedding for the Fourth of July and enjoy the fireworks over the town or river for free.

11

Planning the Reception

Outdoor weddings provide a wonderful opportunity to create a unique, memorable, and thoroughly enjoyable reception. With the open-air environment, your wedding takes on a more original tone compared with the same old receptions your guests have attended in banquet halls, and your guests will enjoy the elements of your reception even more in such a new and beautiful environment. Most guests I spoke to said they loved being in the outdoors; they loved strolling the beautiful grounds with a champagne flute in one hand and a canapé in the other; and they loved enjoying gorgeous sunsets and starry night skies as the night progressed. Here, you will design the reception of your dreams, according to your wishes and the boundless opportunities afforded by your chosen location.

The Chat with the Caterer

It all begins with a sit-down chat with your caterer. When you first begin this process, you will need to find a reputable caterer who has

Questions to Ask Your Potential Caterer

1. Do you belong to a professional association?

2. At which culinary institute did you receive your degree or certification?

3. For how many years have you been a caterer?

4. How many outdoor wedding receptions have you catered?

5. How many weddings will you be catering on the weekend of our wedding?

6. Do you have any other weddings to cater on our scheduled wedding day?

7. Can you provide the types and style of food that we desire?

8. Do you have a fixed menu, or are you willing to add new dishes to your lineup according to our requests?

9. Do you charge extra to bring your own cooking equipment to the site?

10. How many assistants and servers will you provide on the wedding day?

11. Do you offer a refund or cancellation clause in your contract?

12. Do you have insurance?

13. Can we come in and sample your menu offerings?

14. Can we see pictures or a portfolio of some of your buffet or food presentations?

15. Can you provide letters of referral?

16. Will you come view the site ahead of time in order for us to discuss your needs on the wedding day?

17. What are your fees, including extra fees or overtime?

18. What will you and your staff be wearing on the big day?

experience in planning menus and service at outdoor weddings. Many established wedding sites do require or recommend their own caterers, and this is an advantage. After all, these caterers are used to working at that particular site, they are used to the kitchen environment at that site, and they have a working system already in place. In most instances, you will just have to select the items on your menu and plan serving times.

If you are not bound to using the on-site chef but are free to hire your own caterer, you will need to be quite careful in your interviewing process. Not all caterers are adept at taking their usual working methods and bringing them out to an outdoor wedding site. Some caterers will not accept outdoor wedding assignments, and some charge extra for the burden of setting up their own cooking tent. So interview well, ask if the caterer has experience with outdoor receptions, and always do a taste test of the caterer's culinary offerings. Secure a complete contract, including all agreements—from the number of shrimp cocktails to the uniforms of the serving staff— and keep careful track of your budget and payment information. A quality caterer will be a member of a professional chef's association and will have had training at a culinary institute.

Just as you assessed your wedding coordinator for her enthusiasm, her pleasant demeanor, and her willingness to listen to your

> ## Simplify It
>
> Ask recently married friends for referrals to the caterers that they loved. And, don't forget that caterers also serve corporate and charity events, so if you have any friends or relatives who plan conferences or special dinners for their corporations or clubs, ask for the names and numbers of the caterers they favor as well. This kind of road-tested recommendation saves you time and ensures that the people you know and trust have found that caterer to be well worth the investment.

ideas, so too will you subject your caterer to the same subjective criteria. It's important to find a caterer with whom you have a positive rapport, as you will be working as a team for quite some time. A great caterer will be open to your requests, will happily make any changes to the menu that you'd like, and will help you create a top-notch menu according to your budget. As it is the food that makes or breaks any wedding reception, hiring an outstanding caterer is one of the most important parts of the entire wedding-planning process.

TALK ABOUT STYLE!

Once you select and contract the caterer who will turn your reception into an unforgettable event, it's time to talk about how the menu will reflect the style of your wedding. Your caterer, if chosen well, will be able to suggest suitable appetizers and entrées for your upscale garden reception, your beach clambake, or your informal backyard cookout. Discuss in detail the images you have for your day, the menu you have in mind, what *must* be on the buffet table, and what you can live without. If at all possible, take the caterer for a quick tour of the reception site, whether it's the terrace of a mansion by the shore, a dune by the ocean, or the garden at your grandparents' house. The caterer will get a feel for the layout, the wind and sun conditions, and more of a visualization of what you want your wedding to be. Some caterers will ask to see a picture of the bride's gown, judging from that the true level of formality.

The first question you'll need to answer is, What kind of reception do you want? You'll need to choose according to the style and formality of your wedding. Will you plan a full lineup of courses, from passed hors d'oeuvres at the cocktail hour to the five-course sit-down dinner and full dessert course? Or would your garden wedding call for food stations and passed hors d'oeuvres only? Don't forget about outdoor brunches set up as buffet spreads. Know what kind of reception you want, whether your formal plans require a sit-down dinner or your informal tastes allow for a more relaxed setup. The caterer needs to know this basic, fundamental information in order to plan the menu in its entirety.

Obviously, the menu for a New England clambake will vary wildly from the classic English tea at a gazebo behind an estate home. Work with your caterer to list the kinds of menu elements that interest you, and ask the caterer for her own suggestions. Very often, no matter how much as you've watched the Food Network and think you know a great deal about culinary arts, the caterer can suggest a novel way of preparing a salmon steak. Her ideas will often come right from her own genius, her own training at the top institutes in the country, or from caterers' conferences where the newest trends in event menus are born. So be open to new ideas. Your flexibility can help you create an extraordinary menu elaborately presented, which will go a long way toward making your wedding a complete success.

Talk About Money!

An important part of the menu-creation process is being honest with your caterer about your budget restraints. A good caterer will stay within the bounds of your stated budget, working magic with the menu to offer a variety of delectable foods in a cost-effective way. The caterer, too, will be honest with you, letting you know just what your stated budget will buy you. Some couples walk into the initial meeting with the caterer carrying an unrealistic expectation of what catering expenses are. For some, it's quite a wake-up call when the price list comes out and the price-per-guest figure is seen for the first time.

There are a great many ways to get more menu for your money. I spoke with one of my favorite caterers, Jerome Louie of The Bernards Inn in Bernardsville, New Jersey, and he assured me that it's quite common for brides and grooms to work with the chef to save money on the reception menu without sacrificing quality. The following are some of his hints:

• Have hors d'oeuvres passed by the wait staff, instead of arranged on a buffet table. Guests will naturally consume fewer pieces of shrimp cocktail or bacon-wrapped scallops than they would if they sidled up to a buffet table and mindlessly picked as they talked. This is one of the top ways for caterers to control portion sizes and therefore expense.

• Create combination platters. Instead of surf-and-turf, provide three grilled jumbo shrimp and a few flavorful beef medallions as an entrée. Avoiding the lobster tails and filet mignon will save money per head, and the expertly prepared combo plate will still please the taste buds.

• Have fewer food stations at the cocktail hour. Stick with pasta or seafood stations, which are less expensive than carved-meat stations. Think about it. Do your guests really need a slab of prime rib as an *appetizer*? Talk with your caterer about original ways to present pasta dishes. Find a unique recipe that will please your guests.

• Go with in-season seafood. Depending upon where you live, various seafood will be available at lower prices at certain times of the year. Granted, seafood is subject to the current market prices, but your caterer will be able to advise you right up until a few days before the wedding as to the most economical and suitable seafood for your reception. Go with what's coming in at a reasonable price.

• Consider a different meat dish than prime rib or filet mignon. Your guests may love the fresh new choice, making your reception a welcome departure from the usual wedding fare they're used to. Try a loin chop, a pork dish, a lamb chop, even ostrich or buffalo for some new flavor.

• Limit the meat dishes. Your vegetarian and health-conscious guests will love you for the meatless lasagna and vegetable dishes.

• For a more informal wedding, provide a wide array of appetizers.

For more ideas on budget-savvy menu options, plus many ways to save on all other areas of your wedding, consult my book *1001 Ways to Save Money and Still Have a Dazzling Wedding.*

TALK ABOUT LOCATION AND WEATHER FACTORS!

The caterer will have to take into consideration the weather and location conditions at your wedding site. After all, a cheese platter should never be left to warm up in the sun, and hot weather can melt some of your dishes right to the ground. So let the caterer know about your weather concerns, and ask for her suggestions about choosing the right foods for the day's temperature and humidity factors. A good caterer can assure you that foods on the buffet table can be set upon hidden platters of dry ice, so there will be no cause for concern about food spoilage. Still, there are some menu selections that do not handle warm weather well, and your caterer will warn you about true dangers or options to avoid.

Think about serving lighter fares and more cold foods if your wedding day is likely to be steamy. Your guests will find a chilled gazpacho to be more refreshing than a hot seafood bisque. A fondue will sit untouched as the guests hover around the chilled seafood bar. Think also, however, about how your salads will hold up to the heat. Green salads may wilt in the sun, and mayonnaise-based salads will certainly need to be chilled to prevent food spoilage. Though these are additional worries that indoor brides and grooms do not have to suffer, your outdoor-wedding menu should provide foods that will hold their color and presentation in even the most tropical temperatures.

> ## Simplify It
>
> If you know the weather is likely to be hot on your wedding day, skip the ice sculpture. Those doves or that arrow-pierced heart will melt away in a heartbeat.

Sample Menu
Provided by Callaway Gardens in Pine Mountain, Georgia

Heavy Hors d'Oeuvres
Garden Display and Assorted Dips

Seasonal Fresh Fruit and Berry Display

International Cheese Tray with Assorted Bread and Crackers

Assorted Mini-Quiches

Crab Cakes with Tomato-Basil Fondue

Roast of Chicken Kebob with Pineapple Glaze

Shrimp and Andouille Sausage Kebob with Cajun Sauce

Carved New York Strip Steak

Pasta Station

Penne with Whole-Roasted Garlic and Goat-Cheese
 Roasted Peppers

Three-Cheese Tortellini with Prosciutto, Basil,
 and Sun-Dried Tomatoes

Assorted Mini Pastries

Coffee, Decaffeinated Coffee, and Iced Tea

Tray-Passed Cold Hors d'Oeuvres

Selected Cold Canapés

Brie en Croute with Raspberries

Crab Rangoon with Soy-Ginger Dipping Sauce

Mini Deep-Dish Sausage Pizzas

Coconut Shrimp with Muscadine Marmalade

Plated Dinner

French Onion Soup with Gruyere Crouton

Caesar Salad

Grilled Filet Mignon and Jumbo Prawn with Beaujolais au Jus and
 Lemon-Citrus Sauce

Callaway Basil-Potato Duchesse

Fresh Garden-Mix Vegetables

Grand Marnier Chocolate Devil Cake

Assorted Rolls and Butter

Coffee, Decaffeinated Coffee, and Iced Tea

Of course, you will find any number of suitable appetizers, carving-station options, entrées, and desserts at your caterer's hand. You may prefer your menu to reflect your wedding to an even greater degree, such as with a classic seafood menu for a beach, boat, or even a backyard wedding:

Assorted Fresh Tropical-Fruit Platter

Crackers or Breads with Caviar Cream-Cheese Spread

Lobster Bisque with Oyster Crackers

Shrimp Cocktail

Coconut Shrimp

Bacon-Wrapped Scallops

Clams on the Half Shell

Oysters Rockefeller

King Crab Legs

Devilled Soft-Shell Crabs

Lobster Tails or Marinated Lobster Meat

Fire-Pit–Cooked Baked Potato with Scallion Sour Cream

Mixed Green or Mesclun Salad

Cake and Desserts

Drink Up!

Your guests will be lined up at the bar for drinks to either cool down or get into a partying mood, so give some thought to the beverage menu for your reception. Because receptions take up the biggest chunk of your wedding budget, you may be looking at a high price tag if you want an unlimited alcohol supply of top-shelf liquors and high-priced vintages. Though you do want to make sure your guests have wonderful drinks to carry them through the day and night, you don't have to go overboard by stocking up on thousands of dollars worth of booze.

The Perfect Bar

Bartenders who work outdoor weddings say that the following are the most popular bar options:

- Specialty drink stations, such as one bar at which you can get martinis, one where you get champagne, etc.
- Chilled vodka shots, or flavored vodka shots in attractive shot glasses
- Serving top-shelf liquors at the beginning of the evening, and then serving call bar, or less prestigious, liquors the rest of the night to save on the bar tab
- Giving the drinks a new name, such as "Mandy's Martini," named after the bride
- Limiting the drinks menu, but making those chosen few really stand out
- Serving drinks in real crystal glasses and not plastic cups
- Offering microbrew beers instead of the old standbys
- Having after-dinner drinks served by a strolling waiter in tuxedo, who pours the cognac or Grand Marnier right from the bottle with a white-gloved hand
- International coffee bars, including espresso, cappuccino, lattes, chai tea, and flavored coffees

Instead, practice smart bar arrangement and limit your alcohol supply to the most common wedding standards. Bartenders and caterers say that for more formal outdoor weddings, the "usuals" are wine, champagne, beer, vodka, rum, gin and tonics, Whiskey Sours, Martinis, and soft drinks. Though Cosmopolitans, Long Island Iced Teas, and Martinis are always a big hit at parties, the alcohol content of those drinks means that more money is likely to be spent. Those kinds of drinks, as well as shots, are best left off your drinks menu.

If you will be having a less-formal wedding, such as a backyard informal or a beach wedding, then your drink menu might reflect a more casual style. Piña coladas, Mudslides, Rum Runners, and

Daiquiris are well suited to those kinds of events. Think hard, though, about having blender drinks served at your wedding. How would you feel about the screeching sound of a blender interrupting your romantic first dance? At several outdoor weddings I've been to, multiple blenders whirring made the place sound like a construction site.

Try to the best of your ability to accurately estimate how much your guests will be drinking so that you can arrange to purchase the correct number of bottles. At one recent outdoor wedding, the maid of honor had to make two extra runs to the liquor store in the middle of the reception to bring back more alcohol. Seems that the guests at that wedding had quite a thirst for Jack Daniels and Coke and the poor maid of honor couldn't join in, as she was the official designated alcohol-run driver. Remember that any unused liquor or wine bottles can usually be kept for later consumption, so instruct your bartenders to open bottles only as needed.

Some established wedding locations have their own rules about liquor at weddings, and they may only supply certain kinds of drinks at certain rates. Ask the site manager about his or her rules for the alcohol supply and whether you would be allowed to bring in your own stock.

A very popular option among brides and grooms is holding a wine-tasting party at their home a few weeks before the wedding. The bridal party is invited for the event, with the sole purpose of taste-testing new vintages and liquors in order to choose the favorites that will be served at the wedding. To choose the selection of drinks to be tested, check out the rankings and mentions of new hot vintages at www.winespectator.com.

How Many Bartenders?

This is a tricky question. Ask a banquet-hall manager, and he or she will say that two or three bartenders are fine for a wedding of any size. Ask a real bartender, though, and the answer will be closer to one bartender per seventy-five guests. If your guest list tops out at 100, it would be best to hire two bartenders to keep the drink line from wrapping all the way around the dance floor.

Most weddings do have open bars, as it is now considered crass to offer a cash bar at your reception. Your guests shouldn't have to pay for their drinks. It is your judgment call, however, as to whether or not you will allow the bartenders to put out a tip cup. If you feel strongly that your guests shouldn't feel pressured to slip bills into the snifter upon each trip to the bar, then instruct the bartenders to remove the tip cup, and assure them that they will receive their tip at the end of the evening.

DRINKS FOR KIDS

Smart couples set up a separate drink table for kids. It may just be a table upon which you've set bottles of soda, a bucket of ice, and kid-friendly cups, but it's always a good idea to make the soft drinks more accessible to kids and guests who want to avoid alcohol.

Whatever your preferences for alcoholic and nonalcoholic drinks, whatever the setup will be, there is one drink that should always be in ample supply at any outdoor wedding: water. Particularly in warmer weather, your guests will be happy to sip on an ice-cold water with a slice of lemon floating in the cup. Pregnant guests will find this option to be their best choice, and even your drinking guests will like to take a break and get rehydrated from time to time. So include several gallons of water on your drink order, and find a way to keep them really, really cold.

> ## *Wedding Day Reflections*
>
> We didn't want all the kids to stand in line at the bar, so we set up the soda table to the side. Our original intention was to make the line shorter for us, so that we could get our drinks faster, but we found an unexpected benefit. Several of our guests had recently given up alcohol, and they thanked us for having the soft drinks away from the bar where they wouldn't be tempted to have a beer. They said it made the night easier for them, and we were so happy about that.
>
> —Marisa and Dan

Speaking of cold, be sure to have enough ice on hand. Most established wedding locations with outdoor facilities do offer the use of industrial ice machines, but if you're setting up your own location in your backyard, on a beach, or in a park, find a way to supply a large amount of ice cubes throughout the night. Some liquor stores, convenience stores, and grocery stores do offer big bags of ice cubes or ice chips, but you might be best served by renting a hotel-strength ice-making machine for a steady supply. Some couples borrow a large freezer and set it up around the corner of the house or in the garage, and they store bags of ice and extra beverage bottles in there. Freezers too can be rented, but see if the borrowing arrangement will work out for you.

Choosing a Cake and Desserts

Choosing the cake is always one of the most enjoyable parts of planning a wedding. You get to visit a bakery, taste a few samples of the kinds of cakes and fillings it has to offer, and flip through albums filled with hundreds of pictures of cakes too pretty to eat. This is one of the glamour jobs, but again, having an outdoor wedding does throw a little curve into the process.

At a recent wedding, the sun was setting just as the cake was about to be cut. By the time the guests were served their slices of delectable carrot cake with cream-cheese frosting, the evening population of gnats exploded, and they went right for the sweet, sticky icing. Guests were picking dead bugs out of their frosting and disgustedly placing down their plates and walking away from dessert. Although you can't prevent bugs from crashing your outdoor party, you can make some smart decisions when it comes to choosing and serving your reception desserts. With regard to the gnat infestation, the couple could have planned to have their cake served earlier during the event before the nighttime critters came out of hiding.

Gail Watson of Gail Watson Custom Cakes suggests avoiding any cake fillings that are custard-based when you know your cake is going to be out in the sun. Such fillings will go bad in the heat, and your cake will be inedible. The same goes for icing. Buttercream icing does hold up better than whipped-cream icing, but even buttercream has its limits. To solve the melting and spoiling problem when it comes to wedding cakes, Gail Watson sets dry-ice packets around the bottom of the cake to keep the entire confection cool. You must take this step if you plan to display your wedding cake for any length of time out in the elements. Some couples display a single, highly decorated layer of wedding cake, slice into that for the cake-cutting portion of the evening, and then have the guests served from a separate sheet cake that has been stored indoors the whole time.

Another option for smart, outdoor wedding-cake serving is to avoid separating the layers of your cake by columns. As talented as your baker may be, and as structurally sound as your columns and cake weights are, there is no telling what effect the weather will have. Intense heat, even if the cake is in the shade, has been known to melt the icing right off the cake and cause the layers to slip to the ground. A good gust of wind by the seaside can blow your cake right over. For better stability, arrange your cake layers right on top of each other to eliminate the risk of loss.

> ## Simplify It
>
> Serving the guests from a separate sheet cake is a great way to save money. Because the true expense of a wedding cake comes not from the frosting or the filling, but from the labor and skill it takes to pipe on all the lacy designs and weaving, you'll save a bundle by having one cake layer for show and using a separate cake to serve.

FILLINGS AND FLAVORS

You're not just limited to the old standard of white cake with strawberry filling anymore. Cake designers now feature exciting flavors, and they will gladly provide a different cake flavor for each layer of your cake. Consider the following highly popular flavors:

CAKE FLAVORS

- Yellow
- Lemon
- Almond
- Chocolate
- Carrot
- Coconut
- Banana
- Hazelnut

FILLING FLAVORS

- Vanilla butter
- Lemon
- Strawberry
- Raspberry
- Peach
- Banana
- Apricot

The most popular cake-filling flavors right now are chocolate mousse, cannoli cream, and cappuccino cream. For an outdoor wedding, you'll have to be *very* careful when including cream-based fillings or fillings that include raw egg, such as the chocolate mousse. If you have your heart set on these choices, then keep the cake refrigerated until the moment before you cut it, and serve it cold. You don't want to risk illness in your guests due to spoilage of the cake.

ADDITIONAL DESSERT OPTIONS

Few couples leave it at just "let them eat cake." These days, the dessert buffet, or Viennese table, is the big thing, with row upon row of cheesecakes, mousses, pies, chocolate-dipped fruits, and tarts. At an outdoor wedding, these options are open to you as well, but they should be brought out from refrigeration right before serving. Chocolate desserts

Simplify It

Because the greatest expense with wedding cakes stems from the time it takes to decorate them, why not order a plainer cake and do the decorating yourself? Or join in with your bridesmaids or groom to adorn the cake as a team project? Gail Watson Custom Cakes offers easy-to-use "cake kits" that offer any number of cake accents and design materials. Check out the packages at www.gailwatsoncake.com.

may melt, and custard creams may go bad. So last-minute presentation is the best way to ensure the desserts' best appearance, taste, and safety.

At less formal receptions, you might choose to provide a fresh tropical-fruit salad with mangos and kiwis. Some couples even match the fruit colors to their wedding-décor colors, serving apricot flambé to match the pale apricot of the bridesmaids' dresses. Though fashion isn't going to be the biggest determining factor of your dessert menu, such personalizations do make the selection process more fun.

As always, talk with your cake baker or dessert professional about the fact that you're planning an outdoor wedding and that weather may be a factor. These experts may be able to suggest more appropriate options for your dessert lineup, and they'll be better able to deliver and serve them at the right time during the reception.

Planning the Reception Location

Some established wedding sites do take care of the entire setup of tents, tables, chairs, and dance floors, but if your chosen location doesn't offer such an advantage, you will have to do the measuring, planning, renting, and set up yourselves. The arrangement of a tent and tables does give an outdoor setting a dreamy, attractive look, so you'll have to be sure that you choose all of your items with the ultimate picture in mind.

TENTS

Times have changed since the days when you could only rent one kind of tent for your outdoor wedding. Now, you'll be amazed at the variety of tents available to you in any size, in any configuration. Some have support poles underneath the tent, and others are self-supporting with only poles at the outer edges. Basically, there are three kinds of tents available:

- Push-pole, which is supported by poles at various places underneath the tent
- Tension, which structurally does not require as many poles
- Frame, which does not require the use of poles and can be assembled in multiple directions, even around corners

Of course, your first concern is going to be appearance. You'll want your tent to be clean, relatively new, and in good condition. Next, you'll want it to be functional: sturdy, with solid anchoring poles and good support structure, and resistant to wind and rain. The newest tent systems, such as Anchor Industries' amazing interchangeable tent-element setups, allow you to design your own tent right down to the placement of supports and the peaks in the roofs. Web-tensioning devices keep the tent in place, and a special lining system keeps the rain out. An even better advantage to these new mix-and-match tent systems is that they can be adjusted to suit any landscape situation. If you have a hill at the far end of your yard, the tent can be arranged to allow for that hill's slope.

Be sure that the tent you choose has sides, or flap walls. These sides can be used to block breezes, provide shade, and afford privacy. In most cases, the sides can be rolled up and stored out of view. For more formal weddings, consider a tent with sturdy, in-place sides. Some designs offer window cutouts to let in more light.

In most cases, you will find tents made out of vinyl or canvas. Experts say that vinyl is more sturdy than canvas, and because it is easy to clean is very often more attractive. If you want a tent with a bit of color to it, you'll find more color options in the vinyl types.

On the less functional side, you may have a picture in mind of a tent with draped fabric entrances and walls, a cathedral-type ceiling, even support beams for the hanging of chandeliers. The sky is the limit, especially when you can now rent tents with clear roofs for the viewing of the night sky! I could go on forever about the new innovations in rental tents, but I'll leave it to you to research the offerings at your own local rental agency. Just be sure to ask for the agency's top-quality tents. If you scrimp on this crucial piece of equipment, your wedding as a whole will suffer. It is, after all, a visual centerpiece of your wedding, the shelter you will depend upon in case of weather elements, and the backdrop for many of the priceless memories you'll make that day. So keep the following tent-rental advice in mind:

• Visit several rental agencies as recommended by the American Rental Association, www.ararental.org.

• Ask to see the agency's catalog of available tents.

• Know your needed dimensions ahead of time, keeping in mind that the tent professional will come out to measure your site as well.

• Ask to see the agency's tents in an installed state. That might mean taking a trip out to a reception site before the reception begins in order to look at the true condition of the tent.

• Ask the tent professional to come visit your site to measure and assess the surroundings and access to your location. This service should be provided for free.

• Find out how far in advance your tent will be assembled. Some agencies like to erect the tent and lay the dance floor three to four days ahead of the wedding in order to allow time for all of the other professionals to get in and do their own set up. If you're having an at-home wedding, this option may be fine. If your wedding will be at an established wedding site such as a garden or park, you may have to arrange for same-day set up, which would require an early start for the assembly team.

Think also about the extras you desire for your tent, such as tent liners, which are installed under the inside of the tent top to hide the circus-like ceiling and connections of the poles and brackets. The new liners create the appearance of a smooth or gathered ceiling, and they can be set with lights according to a professional's setup. These liners provide a great finishing touch, and they hide a multitude of flaws such as a water-stained roof, special-effects lighting, and wires and cables.

Also available are tent skirts, which are lengths of fabric that hang from the outside edges of your tent. They may be left to hang freely, or they may be draped and gathered with color-coordinated cords to provide entryways or a simple design accent to the tent. Tent skirts are often 100% polyester and flame-retardant, which is a necessity if you will be decorating your site with candles or torches. If you desire to make a grand entrance, consider having the tent agency create a canopied foyer at the front of your tent.

Lighting Systems

The rental agency can also create a wonderful lighting system for inside your tent. Structural beams can be set up to hold dramatic chandeliers, light globes, and track lighting that can send down pin lights to illuminate the center of each table. Freestanding patio lights in clusters or with a single light attachment also make great lighting fixtures within the tent and along the walkway leading to it.

Strings of white lights always make the interior of a tent look more magical, so ask the rental agency about its string-light rentals. The most common strings of white lights are called "twinkle," "fairy," or "bee" lights, and are most often used not in a Christmas-y sort of way, but in far more creative arrangements. Look at sample books to see what the lighting pro can do for you, and choose your accent lighting well.

Often, the lighting expert is quite skilled at hanging these stringed white lights across the tops of tents, around support beams, and in spirals down fabric-draped tent poles. They might also string the surrounding trees and shrubs with beautiful white lights to extend the design around your tent or out to your ceremony site. Lighting is an important part of an outdoor wedding, so do leave it to the professionals to handle the intricacies and requirements of such a task.

How should lighting be used? Consider the following areas of your tent that will need any degree of light, from spotlights to pin lights to dramatic shaded lighting:

- The entrance to your tent and surrounding landscape features, such as ponds, fountains, or waterfalls
- The walkway to your tent
- The head table, where you will be seated
- Guests' tables (candle centerpieces may not be enough)
- The buffet table
- The dance floor
- The DJ area
- The bar area
- The restrooms
- The walkway to the restrooms
- The caterer's tent

Simplify It

If your rental agency does not have a lighting specialist, you can find one through a theatrical lighting company—look in the Yellow Pages under "lighting consultants and contractors," or at www.ntech.net /theater/lighting.html, to find specialty-lighting companies near you.

Lighting experts recommend the use of diffused-color lights, such as pale amber, pinks, and lavender, rather than bright white light. The effect is very subtle, hardly noticeable, but extremely complementary to the ambience and the skin tones of all of your guests. If you will be lighting water features, such as pools, fountains, or ponds, ask for a bluer lighting tone, and avoid green gels unless you are lighting trees

Project Your Love

Rather than decorating the walls of your tent with hanging flower arrangements, art-work, or other accents, ask the lighting technician to provide "light décor" by project-ing images or interesting light flows onto the walls of your tent. The lighting technician will place a "gobo" or stenciled plate over the light fixture to project a shape or im-age onto a surface. This trend, known as "projection," is the hot new thing in lighting design, and is used at lavish Hollywood parties and celebrity weddings. Best of all, the light projections can be designed to change throughout the evening, providing a vari-ety of images and suitable mood setters.

and landscaping. Green undertone lights do not flatter the skin tone of people, and you may look ill in your pictures. White light can be harsh, especially under a tent, so ask your lighting expert about using "gels" or color slides over the lights according to the setup of your location.

Outdoor weddings especially need good lighting, as you are deal-ing with the changing light of the setting sun, nighttime, and full-blaring daylight. Have your lighting specialist on hand to change the lighting throughout the event, offering more romantic illumination during the dancing hours and more functional, brighter light during the dining hours.

Good lighting can create a marvelous ambience, making your tent look even bigger and more elegant. It sets the tone, the mood, and the feeling of your reception.

Obviously, lighting is a very important part of planning your re-ception, so do not scrimp on this very crucial element. Wedding coor-dinators say that at least 10% of your reception budget should be allocated for adequate and attractive lighting for an outdoor wedding. When you consider the effect, you'll find it's well worth your money.

How Big?

So how do you figure out how much tent space you'll need before you go to the pros to see their tents? First, you'll need to figure out how many tents you'll need. Obviously, you will have one for the reception, but you would be wise to provide a second, smaller one for the caterer. Some couples even rent a third smaller one in which to house the portable toilets in a more attractive and inviting way.

Although your tent-rental specialist will be able to measure the amount of space needed when you tell him your number of guests and explain the setup of your desired dance floor, bandstand, and buffet area, you also should know that the industry standards usually just figure in the number of tables, chairs, platforms, dance floors, and serving tables. Too often, the tent ordered is too small, because uninformed professionals forget to add in mingling room and enough space for guests to occupy. Especially when the weather is warm, you'll want to provide plenty of space for your guests and for your décor to take center stage. To better gauge your own space needs—*keeping in mind that these are estimations only, and that your rental professional can assess your needs in the best manner possible*—consider the following:

Seating Space

Square tables: 10 square feet per person
Round tables seating 6, 8, 10, or 12: 14 square feet per person

Industry professionals suggest allowing 60 inches between tables for ease of movement and chair-maneuvering space. Remember that chairs will take up 18 inches of this space, so that leaves even less moving room between tables. Always allow for plenty of space, so that your guests don't feel trapped and your conga line can weave through the reception area!

COCKTAIL PARTIES

With all guests standing and mingling: 8 square feet per person

With some guests standing and some seated at assorted tables: 10 square feet per person

RECEPTION-AREA STRUCTURAL NEEDS

Dance floor: 3–4 square feet per person

Band area: 15 square feet per instrument

DJ area: 65 square feet

Piano: 100 square feet

Buffet area: 100 square feet

Bar area: 100 square feet

Restroom area: 100 square feet

With the help of your tent-rental professional, you will be able to create a layout of your reception area, often with the help of a computerized-imaging system. You can expand the size of your dance floor, if needed, move the band to the other side of the tent, then finalize your finished image so the ordering process can begin. Take your time on this step and take it seriously, as you will want to be sure you're creating the perfect setting for your outdoor reception.

Next, you will have to contract with the company for its assembly workers to deliver the tent, tables, chairs, and other rental items; set up the tent in the area where you specify; anchor it, and hang the lights and chandeliers; set down the dance floor; and arrange the air-conditioning system. Some couples try to save money by arranging to do this part themselves, but this is often a big mistake. Allow the professionals to work their magic on your site and watch your backyard or beach spot turn into your dream setting right before your eyes. Professionals know best how to anchor and arrange a tent in order to avoid any number of mishaps, so their involvement is a very wise use of your money.

Questions to Ask About Your Tent

1. What size tent do we need?
2. What fabric is the material made from?
3. Is the fabric flame-retardant?
4. Do you have tensioning devices to keep it in place?
5. Will poles have to be inserted into the ground? (Very important, as some sites will not allow pole insertion into their lawn!)
6. What is the wind load? (As in, does this tent withstand winds up to 70 miles per hour? Very important if you're having a breezy beach wedding.)
7. Are there wind meshes at the top of the tent?
8. Are tent skirts available? In what style and colors?
9. Are tent liners available? In what style and colors?
10. Can you add support beams for chandeliers and lighting fixtures?
11. What tent fabric colors are available?
12. Do you offer tents with gabled ends and walls? (Curve allows rain to roll off easier.)
13. Do you have tents with see-through windows or roof?
14. Does your tent come with latching devices to keep attachments in place?
15. At what time of day will your assembly team set up the tent?
16. How long will assembly take?
17. When will the team return to take the tent down?

The professionals too will disassemble and remove all of your rental items after the party or the next day, so that's one less thing to worry about. Your family and bridal party will have better things to do during that twenty-four hours anyway.

TABLE SETUP

You will also have to choose the various tables you will need for your outdoor wedding site. The following is what your order might look like:

- Small, round main table for bride and groom
- Fifteen ten-seater round tables
- Two 10-foot rectangular buffet tables
- One 10-foot rectangular table for the gifts
- One 10-foot rectangular table for the DJ
- One 10-foot rectangular table for the cake and desserts

Think about what you might need tables for: the guest book, a small table outside of the restroom area to use as a vanity table, tables for an informal bar. Visualize your table needs, and then work with your rental agent to arrange the individual table setup.

The task of making your seating arrangements, as far as where each guest will sit, is then up to you.

Laying Down the Dance Floor

If your site allows the laying down of parquet dance-floor tiles—some sites do not, so ask first!—have your rental professional measure out the required dance-floor space. Then choose your style and color of dance-floor segments, and ask about the anchoring system. Some tiles are fastened into the ground in much the same manner as the new breakaway baseball-field plates, with a latching system that is nailed into the ground and then attached with a system of ridges. Others are not staked into the ground and lay flat. These latter styles are very often a headache, if not a downright hazard. Poorly

I have a relative who is wheelchair-bound. We're concerned that the ground may be a little too soggy for his wheelchair to make it out to the tent area. What do we do?

In special cases like this, arrange to have a ramp system installed. One enterprising couple I spoke to had thick wooden walkways staked into their yard, leading from the front driveway to the entrance and front portion of the tent where the disabled guest was to sit. This wooden floorboard was then covered with a high-quality artificial turf that not only fit in with the green and white of the outdoor surroundings, but also served as a great procession walkway to the reception tent. They lined this walkway with potted topiaries and candles, turning their functional rampway into an attractive entrance element.

Wedding Day Reflections

We actually had a pole in the middle of our dance floor. We had it strung with white lights so people could see it, but we were shocked when some of our more inebriated guests starting using it as a sort of pole that you'd find in a strip club. And these were 50-year-old women! It was funny then, but now I cringe when I see my aunts gyrating next to a stripper pole on my wedding video.

—Lauren

installed dance-floor tiles will come loose and possibly trip your celebrating guests. So be specific when asking about dance-floor installation, and see what new innovations have come to pass there as well.

Be sure to allow for plenty of dancing room for your guests, and try to arrange for the dance floor to be far away from support poles. Having a pole in the middle of your dance floor can take up valuable space, and your waltzing guests might run into it and disturb the sturdiness of your tent.

EXTRAS

Your rental agent will best be able to arrange the placement of air conditioners or heaters in hidden spots around the tent space. Even if you're expecting moderate temperatures that day, rent the air conditioner anyway. You never know how hot it's going to get with so many guests and lights under that tent, so it's best to be safe and supply yourself with a source of cool air.

As mentioned earlier, you can camouflage the portable-toilet area by surrounding the units with a pretty tent with a draped-fabric entrance. For even better service to your guests, set up a small vanity table and mirror right outside the portable toilets, set out a candle that is encased in a protective glass holder, and provide a basket of minitoiletries such as disposable hand wipes, oil-blotting papers for shiny noses, refreshing wrist spray, and breath mints.

RENTAL ADVICE

We've been talking mainly about tents, tables, chairs, and dance floors, but the list of items you'll need to rent goes on and on from there.

Even more important than the list of what you'll be renting is the reputation of the rental agency. Always choose a highly respected company that is recommended by the American Rental Association (800-334-2177), ask your friends for referrals, and see the items in person. Inspect all merchandise at the time of your order, at the time of delivery, and before it's all returned to the company after the wedding. A good rental agency will offer a wide range of items in a wide range of colors and styles, and you will be free to select the perfect accents and equipment for your day.

As always, be sure to get a complete contract and itemized order list, and keep careful track of your payments and receipts. Ask to see a copy of the agency's license and its liability-insurance certificate.

What Do You Need?

Every wedding will be different, and each couple has various items at its disposal. Your wedding location may come stocked with its own tables and chairs, thereby saving you the rental fees for those items, and your backyard may already have a tented shelter for your small guest list. So I provide this list as a general guideline for standard wedding-rental needs. Look through it and mark what you'll need for your wedding. Obviously, you won't need the dance floor if you're having a boat wedding, but you may need a reminder about the table linens and the coffee urns. Take all suggestions into consideration, and be sure to think about your own individual needs to add to your own list:

- Tent for reception
- Tent for caterer

> ### Simplify It
>
> If you will be picking up and dropping off the rental items yourselves—or having someone in your family or bridal party do it—be sure to find out the date and time by which all of the items must be returned. Missing a cutoff time by returning the items an hour or two after the noon deadline could cost you another day's rental time, which adds up to a fortune when you consider how much you may be renting!

- Tent for portable toilets
- Chuppah
- Bridal arch
- Pedestals for floral arrangements
- Chairs for ceremony
- Chairs for reception
- Bride and groom head table
- Guest tables
- Buffet tables
- Table for DJ
- Table for gifts
- Table for guest book
- Portable bar
- Bandstand
- Dance floor
- Lighting fixtures
- Table linens
- Table skirts
- China
- Silverware
- Glassware
- Serving dishes
- Serving silverware
- Butler-style silver platters for appetizer serving
- Punch bowls
- Coffee urns (several, including one for decaf)
- Espresso machine
- High chairs
- Booster seats
- Candelabras
- Ramps
- Walkways
- Fountains

- Special-effects machines, such as laser lights, video-display unit, bubble machines, etc.
- Air conditioner/fans
- Heaters

Talk with your helpful friends and family and assign someone to supervise the setup of your wedding location on the morning of the event. You will certainly be busy with your brunch and salon visit, as will your groom with his intended plans (perhaps a round of golf with the boys), so it's best to assign a responsible relative to observation detail. This person should be asked to inspect all delivered items to see if they're in perfect order or if anything is broken or needs to be replaced.

Entertainment

The musical entertainment for your reception does more than just give your guests a great lineup of songs to dance to. It sets the tone, determines the atmosphere during dining, and enhances the entire affair. In this section, you'll consider the types of entertainment you want, whether you want a band or a DJ, what your outdoor environment will dictate for the entertainers you choose, and whether you'd consider additional live performances at your open-air party.

OUTDOOR WEDDING RULES

One of the main concerns when planning entertainment for an outdoor wedding is whether or not the DJ or band can or will agree to work in an outdoor setting. Some entertainers do not want to subject their instruments or equipment to the elements, and the whole issue of powering their equipment becomes a major concern when your event is not held at an established banquet location.

When you begin your search for the perfect entertainers, you will need to start your questioning by asking if the performers in question will agree to working in outdoor conditions. Explain that you'll have a tent set up, so they know they will not be in complete open air, and ask whether that arrangement suits them. Outdoor weddings are extremely popular now, so you probably will not meet the resistance you might have encountered several years ago. Many entertainers have adapted their business acumen to allow for outdoor locations. In any case, you will save a lot of time and begin an effective dialogue with the entertainers when you're clear from the start about your special circumstances.

The next issue is the weather factor. Talk to the entertainers about the location of your wedding. Some may be fine with performing under a tent in your backyard or at a botanical garden, but they just won't do a beach wedding for fear of moisture and sand wreaking havoc with their sound systems.

These important issues must be discussed so that you can create a perfect fit with the entertainers you have chosen.

The Basics of Choosing Entertainers

The #1 issue facing you is deciding what kind of entertainment you want for your style and formality of wedding. Your garden cocktail hour may be well suited for strolling violinists, rather than a pianist, and your informal backyard bash may call out for more of a free-spirited DJ than a six-piece orchestra. Decide now if you want separate cocktail-hour musicians, or if you will just let your DJ play easy-listening or classical music while your guests enjoy the prereception food and drinks.

When deciding between DJs and bands, remember the following:

• It is often cheaper to hire a DJ than a band.

• A DJ takes up less space in the tent than a full band.

• With a DJ, you only have to pay for one meal at the reception, rather than ten meals for a full band.

- DJs can offer original recordings of the songs you love so that there is no question about the quality or performance of those titles.

- DJ packages now offer the option of live performances by professional singers. For just a slight raise in fees, the singer can come out for a few numbers and then turn the floor back over to the DJ. This option provides the fun of a live performance, or a personalization of a favorite song, without the expense of hiring a full band.

- A full band has its advantages as well. When you find a good one, there's nothing like the live music, great sounds of a talented vocalist, personalization of songs, and audience interaction. If you have the space and the budget, go for it!

- Think about the musical tastes of your guests. If you have a large number of teenagers who'll want to hear pop tunes, the middle ground that is happy with Top 40 and '80s music, and then the old-timers who prefer to do the Lindy to Glenn Miller tunes, then think about a DJ's ability to meet everyone's needs throughout the night. A band may not have that full range.

Your search for a quality entertainer will begin with asking your recently married friends which entertainment companies they loved, which treated them well, and which provided the kinds of music they requested. When you look at entertainers' advertisements in your local newspaper, regional bridal magazines, or through Web sites, you will find an endless list of bands, DJs, and specialty-entertainment companies, and the ones that interest you will have to be subjected to the same scrutiny you would use when hiring a caterer. After all, the entertainers are going to set the stage for the enjoyable party atmosphere of your wedding. The quality of their sound, the rapport they have with the audience, and even their appearance will make or break your reception, so much care should go into the selection process.

Allow plenty of time for interviewing, and *always* arrange to hear a live performance by the group or DJ before you sign any contract. A

Questions to Ask When Interviewing Entertainers

1. Are you willing to play at our style and location of outdoor wedding?

2. Are you available on our wedding date?

3. How many weddings have you worked?

4. How many outdoor weddings have you worked?

5. What's your style of music? Do you specialize in Top 40 only, or do you have a wide range of styles, from jazz to rock?

6. Can we hear you perform live at a scheduled audition?

7. Are you familiar with the kinds of music we'd like played at our reception?

8. Can we see a list of the songs you have in your repertoire?

9. Can we request the addition of songs you do not have included on your playlist?

10. For how many hours will you be playing?

11. How many breaks do you plan to take, and what will the duration of the breaks be?

12. What will you be wearing during the reception? Tuxedoes?

13. What are the special elements of your performance? (We don't want any surprises, so let us know if you plan to break out the sequined dinner jacket and the fog machine.)

sample videotape can be edited to mask a multitude of flaws, and that recorded performance may have taken place a year ago when the band had different lead singers. A live audition is always necessary for the best assurance of quality for your big day.

If you are hiring a band, be sure to get the names of the band members and specify that you'd like to be notified with any changes in the band's makeup. As you will be booking them a long way in advance, and because band members are free to leave their groups at any time, you'll need to be sure that the band you hired is the same one that shows up on your wedding day. Just stipulate that you'd like a phone call if the band is changing their lineup or the type of music they play.

14. Do you include props in your performance, such as inflated guitars? If so, is that included in the price, or do we have to pay extra?

15. How much space will you need for your equipment and movement area?

16. Will you need us to supply a table to hold your equipment? (If so, get the measurements of the table and a specification of how sturdy the table should be. Find out the weight of the equipment and talk to your rental agent about it.)

17. How long will it take you to set up?

18. How much time do you need before the wedding to be fully prepared?

19. Are you willing to stay later than contracted if the party's still going strong? (Very important, as you don't want the band to be inflexible and strand your guests on the dance floor because the big hand hit twelve.)

20. What are your package rates?

21. What are the differences between your low-end packages and your high-end packages?

22. What extras can we purchase with the package, e.g., live singer, special lighting effects, etc.?

23. What are your overtime rates?

24. Do you charge overtime by the hour or by the half-hour?

25. Do you have a cancellation refund policy?

Once you have the performers hired, create a playlist. Talk with the performers about the kinds of songs you'd like to hear at your reception. You'll need to decide if you will be doing the special spotlight dances, such as the father-daughter dance, and if you'd rather die than hear any cheesy line dances.

Specify any ethnic dances you'd like to hear. Weddings are more personalized these days, and couples are incorporating their own ethnic pride into the celebration. If the DJ has never heard of the Ukrainian songs you'd like played, supply him with your own CD, labeled for return to you. You might be surprised at the lineup of ethnic songs available through most entertainers. And many are willing to work with singers or musicians you hire to play traditional songs at your wedding. So consider the options, check with the national organizations affiliated with your particular heritage, and find out what an individual performance would take out of your budget and thus add to the quality of your day.

If the DJ will be acting as emcee for the reception, be sure to supply him with a complete list of names to be announced, special toasts or presentations you have planned, and any other pertinent info.

After the details are arranged, create a solid contract with the professionals, including everything from the wedding date, time, and place, to the exact time when they should arrive to start setting up. Make sure the details of their playing time have been put in writing, along with any extras that you've purchased. Record the overtime-fee agreement, as well as a payment schedule for deposits and final checks. Get the musician to sign the contract and keep a copy for yourselves.

ENTERTAINMENT FOR KIDS

If you will include children in your festivities—as many outdoor weddings lend themselves well to large gatherings of complete extended family and friends—you will need to provide some sort of entertainment for the kids. It's doubtful that the little ones and the middle-graders will sit politely through a five-hour reception, and you're tempting fate and inviting wild behavior if you do not plan activities and diversion for them.

I spoke to Dr. Stevanne Auerbach (also known as "Dr. Toy"), noted play expert and author of *Smart Play: How to Raise a Child with*

Simplify It

Rather than go through your entire CD collection or the DJ's list of thousands of available titles, check out the collection of most popular wedding songs at www.weddingtips .com. This site offers a lineup of the thirty most popular "first dance" songs, plus suggestions for the spotlight dances and best party songs favored by wedding guests. With one click, you can listen to a sampling of each song and choose your playlist from there.

Eliminate Humiliation

To avoid mispronunciations of your bridal-party-members' names, or the wrongful introduction of your divorced parents as a still-married couple (ouch!), be very specific on the emcee's announcement cards as to the correct announcements. If names are tricky, write them out phonetically and explain to the emcee that you were playing it safe. Include exact wording, such as "the bride's father Mr. Henry Sheldon and his fiancée Elaine Reynolds" rather than ". . . and Elaine Reynolds." Talk with everyone involved and see how they'd like to be announced. This preplanning prevents major social faux pas and fragile ego injuries.

a Smart P.Q. (Play Quotient) for her suggestions on providing age-appropriate entertainment for children at outdoor weddings. She suggests hiring several child-care providers to watch over the children during the day, freeing the parents to enjoy themselves throughout the event (see page 198 for a list of tips from her). Quality, licensed child-care providers should be interviewed and screened carefully to ensure the children's well-being. Once you have your sitters hired, plan activities for the kids according to their ages and tastes. For instance, if you're having a backyard wedding, perhaps the kids could be corralled and brought inside the house for a supervised screening of a children's movie. A craft table could be set up to the side of the wedding location so that kids can make floral leis, painted pasta necklaces, or other items.

Another option with kids is using or renting yard toys, such as a giant inflated "bouncer" ride (the commonly known Moonwalk for instance); other inflated bouncers (giant slides, giant animal shapes, or cushioned laser-tagmazes); or a pit filled with colorful plastic balls. (Just be sure the kids are well-supervised for all of these attractions.) Always popular are coloring books, small handheld video games, and

Dr. Toy's Advice for Hiring Child-Care Workers on the Wedding Day

- Hire a sitter whom you have used before. This isn't a good time to try out someone new.
- Ask friends who have kids if they would recommend their sitter.
- Check on the sitter's experience and references.
- Observe the sitter caring for other children before the event and gauge the sitter's interactions with children, protective instincts, and reliability.
- Plan the activity list and meal list for the kids ahead of time, and talk with the sitter about your wishes.
- Be sure the sitter knows the location's layout, particularly where the restrooms are.
- If the sitter will take the children off-site or simply to another area of the grounds, be sure she has a cell phone and can contact you or the parents if needed.
- Ask parents to provide extra clothing for the kids for changes during the day
- Ask parents to write down kids' food allergies and other allergies.
- Ask parents to provide all equipment kids will need, such as inhalers, etc.
- Provide safe and adequate transportation for the sitters to and from the wedding site.
- Pay the sitters well.

Visit Dr. Toy's Web site at www.drtoy.com

a supply of fun dress-up items such as feather boas, tiaras, ballerina tutus, and masks and capes for the kids to wear.

If your budget allows, why not hire a children's entertainer, such as a magician or themed character, to make the day more special?

Whatever you decide to go with, be sure the activities are safe, that they keep the kids quiet, and that they are not a major distraction to your reception.

Special Performances

At a recent wedding, the couple celebrated their heritage by inviting an ethnic dance troupe to perform a lavish and colorful number at the beginning of the reception. The guests were thrilled, exclaiming, "We didn't know we were going to be treated to a show as well!"

One couple I spoke to actually called a local ballet company and hired its lead dancers to perform a lovely *Swan Lake* pas de deux for their guests. This special feature set the tone for a beautiful, classical reception, and the flower girls were enraptured by the beauty of the costumes and grace of the performance.

Of course, you could always hire a steel-drum band to play during your beach wedding, setting a tropical atmosphere, or ask your local Irish heritage group to send over some bagpipers or an adorable children's dance troupe. One couple who was crazy about drum and bugle corps invited the trumpet soloists of a professional corps to come perform a voluntary as they were announced into their reception. The trumpeters played the regal announcement, then broke into a showstopping portion of "Malaguena," the couple's favorite song.

Toasts and Tributes

Weddings are all about the public announcement of your vows, but during the reception, what becomes public is how much your loved ones care about you and wish you well. The best man's toast, as emotional or as humorous as it may be, has always been the standard, but now the maid of honor, the bride's parents, the groom's parents, and even the couple who introduced the bride and groom are stopping the music and lifting their glasses to pay tribute to the happy couple. Toasts and tributes have always been a special part of the reception, but lately a most wonderful trend has been growing. Brides and grooms are now proposing toasts to one another and to their parents.

Wedding Day Reflections

We knew we had a powder keg at our reception. My cousin Rob always gets a little too drunk and then wants to be the center of attention. He had been joking about making a "big announcement" at the wedding, but we ignored him. It turns out that he was drunk out of his mind, stood up on stage, and said some very inappropriate things. If we could do it again, we would tell the emcee that no guests are to take the stage without our permission. Just find us on the dance floor, and ask if it's okay.

—Jim and Tania

The couple's children are proposing toasts to their parents. And departed parents and grandparents are being remembered with bittersweet tributes.

Let your loved ones know your wishes about toasts and tributes during your reception. Invite special people in your life to say a few words—whatever's in their hearts. And consider taking the microphone yourself to express your feelings to your new spouse in a much more relaxed atmosphere and state than you were in during your vows.

Let your emcee know that you've invited several people to speak during your reception, and provide a list of the tributes to be offered. A warning, though, is offered by a couple who learned the hard way that some control ought to be kept over who gets to grab the microphone (see sidebar on this page).

12

Stems and Blooms

W HAT WOULD any wedding be without beautiful, fragrant flowers? As part of your ideal wedding image, you may see a bouquet of white calla lilies and roses, elegant centerpieces of tightly bunched white and pink tulips, or fresh, exotic gardenias floating in a crystal, water-filled bowl. You might be thinking about having your maids carry nosegays of lilies or lavender. Whatever your vision, the simple truth remains: Choosing your flowers is going to be one of the most enjoyable parts of the wedding plans, one where you can use your creativity to design a floral theme that only makes your day more exquisite. Flowers help set the mood for your wedding, and they'll certainly give your guests something else to rave about. Even better, outdoor weddings offer so many more opportunities for unique floral décor. So, let's get started on painting this lovely portion of your wedding-day picture.

Using an Outdoor Location's Natural Floral Décor

One of the factors you may have considered when selecting a site for your outdoor wedding was its natural greenery, gardens, and land-scaping accents. If you've chosen to hold your wedding at a botanical garden, for instance, then you're assured a vast array of beautiful flowers and trees in bloom. Such bountiful surroundings provide in-stant décor—included in the price of your site-booking fee—and you will then not have to spend a fortune at the florist. Some sites offer great eye-catching features such as waterfalls, wishing wells, swan ponds, and brooks that wind throughout the grounds and under foot-bridges. In the presence of such highlights, more than half of your floral decorating task is already completed.

If you will hold your wedding at a garden, estate home, or other location where the grounds are guaranteed to be professionally de-signed and manicured, then you should ask the site manager for a copy of the site's bloom chart. This chart is a record of which types of flowers and plants will be featured on the grounds at the time of your wedding. A sample from The Sibley Center of Callaway Gardens in Georgia reads as follows:

Time of year	Indoor flowers	Outdoor flowers
April, May	Forced azaleas, fuchsias, snap-dragons, hydrangeas, Easter lilies, hybrid lilies, begonias, geraniums, forced caladiums	Caladiums, impatiens, tropical plants (bromeliads), coleus, variegated tropical foliage plants
June, July, August	Pansies, spring bulbs, snap-dragons, delphiniums, di-anthus, foxglove, geraniums, springtime flowering shrubs	Assorted summer annuals, perennials, tropical flowering plants
September, October	Fall mums	Fall mums, fall annual

Please keep in mind that the chart is a sample from one floral center in one region of the country. Because flowering times and seasonable temperatures vary throughout the country (and internationally), be sure to consult with the site manager of your particular location in order to find out exactly what will be in bloom on the day of your wedding.

Make the most of the natural surroundings, even if your at-home wedding will feature the new rock garden your father just installed or your mother's prize rose bushes. A wedding at the beach needs very little floral décor when set against the dramatic setting sun over the horizon.

Floral Décor Tips for Special Outdoor Touches

Some of the most beautiful outdoor weddings incorporate special décor touches that make the most of an open-air setting. I surveyed many wedding coordinators, brides and grooms, and bridal professionals for their best decorating ideas:

- Hang baskets of flowers and ivy cuttings from tree limbs.

- Use collections of fruit in baskets and bowls to give more "flavor" to the décor.

- For more color, cut open some of the fruits, such as pomegranates, star fruit, kiwis, oranges, and lemons.

- For an original look, use fruit-bearing potted plants or topiaries as centerpieces and buffet table markers.

- Use greenery or herbs tucked into napkin holders.

- Float floral arrangements in bodies of water, such as pools, lakes, ponds, even fountains. For added pizzazz as the sun goes down, light safely embedded candles in these arrangements.

- Suspend floral pomanders from tree limbs and tent support beams.

- Use bowls of flower petals in place of full floral centerpieces. For added bonus points, use unique flower petals with unusual colors or shapes to them.

- Use floral wreaths as decoration.

- Tie mini-pomanders to the backs of guests' chairs.

- Use plenty of greenery garland to wrap around columns, support beams, handrails, even the cake table.

- Use butterfly bushes and butterfly-friendly flowers to keep those butterflies you released in the area.

- If you're on a beach or overlooking the ocean, incorporate the sea theme as much as possible. Use conch shells as place-setting holders, a real sand sculpture as décor (artists can work wonders with wet sand), and starfish and shells as centerpieces.

- Place a potted flowering plant on the outer edge of each step of an outdoor walkway.

- Hang floral arrangements from lampposts leading up to your wedding site.

- Use the color scheme of the location. If you're on the beach, use the natural earth tones. If you're in a bright green garden, go with brights.

- Use fabric to enhance your floral arrangements. Layers of chiffon or tulle in different shades of pink and draped or laid stylishly around the floral centerpiece extend the color outward.

- Always use fresh flowers on the cake. Sugar flowers may melt in the heat.

- Use flowers in the chandelier. Arrange for the floral designer to affix floral arrangements to make the chandeliers more attractive.

• Decorate the ceremony site with tons of white flowers to symbolize the purity of your love. If the ceremony will be held at sunset, use white pillar candles to further enhance the mood.

• Place a single white rose on every guest's seat at the ceremony. (Just remember to remove the thorns—it's bad luck to have thorns on any of your wedding roses!)

• Use ice sculptures to keep appetizers or bottles of champagne cold. They're going to melt anyway, so you might as well use them in a decorative and functional way during the event.

• Use the floral theme for your favors as well. Consider handing out seedlings or a selection of flower-seed packets to your guests. For added creativity, choose flowers or plants that coordinate with your color scheme, your birth-month flower, or a flower or plant that suits your ancestry such as heather or tulips. And if your name happens to be Rose, Lily, Jasmine, or Calla, why not hand out flowering plants that share your name?

• One very important point: Consider aromas from the flowers you will use. It might be wise to use a large amount of one or two different flowers so that the rose scent is not competing with the gardenia scent and thirty other scents. Unify the aroma theme and allow your location to smell just glorious. For an added aroma perk, choose delicately scented candles as well.

• Wear the flowers as well! At an outdoor wedding, the bride and the maids will look ravishing with tiny flowers tucked into their loosely flowing or upswept hair. Some brides even pin small flowers to their dresses at the small of the back for an added accent.

• *Have the bee-sting kit ready and waiting. With all of those wonderful flowers, someone may get a sting from a little yellow party crasher. The odds are increased with all of those blooms and all of those people.*

The Complete Floral-Shopping List

YOUR FLOWERS

❏ Your bouquet
❏ Flowers for your hair

THE BRIDAL PARTY (WOMEN)

❏ Maid/matron of honor's bouquet
❏ Bridesmaids' bouquets
❏ Flower-girls' bouquets
❏ Rose petals for flower girls to sprinkle along your path
❏ Flowers for the maids' hair
❏ Flowers for the flower-girls' hair

THE BRIDAL PARTY (MEN)

❏ Groom's boutonniere
❏ Best man's boutonniere
❏ Ushers' boutonnieres
❏ Ring bearer's boutonniere

PERSONAL FLOWERS

❏ Bride's mother's corsage
❏ Bride's grandmothers' corsages
❏ Groom's mother's corsage
❏ Groom's grandmothers' corsages
❏ Corsages for godparents
❏ Corsages for readers, candle lighters, performers, wedding coordinator, other special female guests
❏ Boutonnieres for readers, candle lighters, performers, other special male guests
❏ Flowers for new stepchildren
❏ Memory flowers

CEREMONY-SITE FLOWERS AND DÉCOR

- ❏ Pew bows
- ❏ Floral bunches for backs of each chair
- ❏ Altar décor
- ❏ Candles
- ❏ Floral arch
- ❏ Chuppah
- ❏ Aisle runner (optional)
- ❏ Floral arrangements on pedestals
- ❏ Flowers on guest-book signing table
- ❏ Greenery garlands
- ❏ Tree-hanging flowers

RECEPTION DÉCOR

- ❏ Centerpieces for head table
- ❏ Centerpieces for all guests' tables
- ❏ Centerpieces for buffet tables
- ❏ Centerpieces for gift tables
- ❏ Centerpieces for guest-book table
- ❏ Centerpieces for name-card table
- ❏ Centerpieces for favors table
- ❏ Centerpieces for bar
- ❏ Floral arrangements for restrooms (if indoor restrooms are used)
- ❏ Flowers to decorate the cake
- ❏ Flowers to "sprinkle" around candle centerpieces
- ❏ Flowers for the getaway car
- ❏ Throwaway bouquet
- ❏ Tree-hanging flowers
- ❏ Potted plants to line walkways
- ❏ Accent potted plants
- ❏ Floral garlands to wind around stairway handrails, deck railings, ship masts, etc.
- ❏ Other flowers

Choosing and Hiring a Florist

The florist you hire will be the one who creates the entire floral and décor design for your wedding. Floristry is an art, and as such should always be handled by a well-trained, experienced, and reputable professional. The best in the field can create veritable English-countryside gardens out of a wheat field, and they can transform your backyard into a magazine-cover spread. So take your time and follow all the steps to hire the perfect professional for your style, budget, and extravagance level, and then work with this expert to design your own dream floral creations.

Simplify It

Get top-notch referrals from The Society of American Florists at (703) 836-8700 or the American Institute of Floral Design at (410) 752-3320. A recommendation of a local floral designer from either of these sources means the professional is well rated and is in good standing in the industry. Consider it a nod from a knowing source and take the interview process from there.

WHERE TO START

Ask recently married friends who they hired to do their flowers, and check referrals from corporate-event planners within your social circle. Very often, the most talented floral craftspersons also do the centerpieces and decorating for company conferences, charity events, and political black-tie galas. Don't count these specialists out, as they very often can create just the look you want for your wedding. Be sure the florist is licensed, insured, and a card-carrying member of a professional association, and be sure that she has plenty of experience with outdoor weddings. She'll really need to know her stuff when it comes to outdoor floral design, as the weather and site requirements can be a factor in determining the kinds of blooms you'll use. Experience is key here, so keep that in mind when you begin your interviews.

Before you start making those calls, however, you must know the specifics of the floral order you desire—not necessarily the exact number of delphiniums you want in your centerpieces, but the basics. Designers can help you much better if they have all of the details they need. Angela Lanzafame of Potted Germanium in East Hanover, New Jersey, suggests that brides come in to the meeting with the floral designer with all of the following major decisions and details already made:

1. Know your exact wedding date, so that the florist can tell you if she's available that day.
2. Know the formality of your wedding, so that the florist knows what styles of arrangements and décor will be most suitable.
3. Know the setting of your wedding, so that the florist will know what kind of space she has to work with, the size of the layout, what existing floral décor is in place there, and what new and exciting floral designs she can envision for that space.
4. Know the size of your wedding, so that the designer knows how many centerpieces and bouquets you're looking at.
5. Know the size of your bridal party.
6. Know what your gown looks like, so that the florist can create a bouquet to complement the cut and style of your dress.
7. Know what your bridesmaids' gowns look like, so that the florist can create appropriate bouquets and hair wreaths for them as well.
8. Know your colors, so that you can suggest to the floral designer a few different varieties of flowers that may coordinate well in a bouquet or matching centerpiece.
9. Know what you want and be able to describe it or show it in pictures, so that the floral designer can assess your personal style.
10. Know your budget, so that the designer knows just how elaborate or just how budget-conscious to go.

Only by your providing all of this information can a florist accurately assess your needs and the scope of the job, and can you accurately assess whether or not she is the florist for the job. Even if you don't have the minor points worked out yet, it's still crucial that you're able to provide an accurate picture of the design job ahead of you. And just as you're providing information to the florist, so too will you have to collect information *from* the florists you're considering in order to make the important decision of whom you will be handing the magic wand to. Ask the following questions of all of the experts you're interviewing for the job, take good notes, and make your decision based both on the answers *and* the gut feeling you get while talking with her.

QUESTIONS TO ASK FLORISTS

1. Are you available on our wedding date?
2. Do you do outdoor weddings?
3. How many outdoor weddings have you done?
4. Have you designed any weddings at our particular location before? Similar locations?
5. How many weddings are you working that weekend?
6. Are you working another wedding on that same day?
7. How long have you been in business?
8. To which professional associations do you belong?
9. Can I see pictures or reviews of your work?
10. Can I see live examples of your work? (Hint: Visit the shop on a Friday when the floral expert's staff is putting the finishing touches on the next-day's bridal bouquets and centerpieces.)
11. Can you work within my budget?

Simplify It

Remember, *this working relationship is a partnership, so you'll need to be sure you feel free to discuss your wishes with the designer and that the designer is open to your ideas and wants to please you above all. Though artistic vision is always a wonderful thing to behold, a stubborn artiste with an attitude will be a nightmare for all involved. So assess the florist not only for her credits on paper and the beauty of her portfolio, but for your comfort level and ease of conversation with her.*

12. Will my flowers be arranged by you, a trained member of your staff, or an assistant?
13. Can I rent other items from you, such as aisle runners, a Chuppah, columns, or pedestals?
14. Can I rent additional potted plants or live potted trees from you?
15. Do you deliver, or will we have to pick up our order? (It's best not to assume.)
16. What is your delivery fee?
17. Will you be present at the wedding site to set up the floral décor? Or will a member of your staff be assigned that role?
18. Do you have insurance?
19. Do you offer a cancellation or refund policy?

Get More for Your Wedding Budget

• Use flowers that are in-season. Consult the florist's charts of floral bloom times in order to determine which types of flowers will be in season at the time of your wedding.

• Expect higher prices during times of popular flower-giving holidays such as Valentine's Day and Mother's Day. Flower prices go up at this time of year, and you'll pay the price in your wedding budget.

• Use flowers that are grown locally, rather than exotic blooms that have to be imported at greater expense.

• Consider different varieties of flowers rather than the traditional "bridal" ones such as white roses, orchids, tulips, and gardenias. These styles are often more expensive, especially during the most popular wedding months. Get a little creative and use more original types of flowers in your arrangements. No doubt your search will reveal flowers you've never seen before, and they just may become your favorites.

- Use more expensive flowers, such as your favorite bird of paradise, only as accents to larger, more economical arrangements.

- Use larger flowers for centerpieces and decorative arrangements. You'll need fewer per collection.

- Add some color to your arrangements. A grouping of all-white roses will require more flowers per bunch in order to make an impression. A splash of color will make your bouquets and arrangements look better at a lower price.

- Use smaller bouquets and arrangements. Today's trends favor smaller floral pieces, so that the bride can be seen behind her bouquet and the guests can see each other across the table.

- Use simpler floral arrangements and bouquets. A great amount of the florist's bill is related to the amount of labor required to wire together your bouquets and assemble your intricate centerpieces. Instead of choosing the most difficult-to-design styles, consider using flowers for your bouquet that are tightly bunched and tied at the stem, and tightly bound, low-sitting flowers as your centerpieces.

- Rent potted flowers and plants to decorate your reception and ceremony areas. For a lower price, you can fill your location with a larger number of atmosphere-setting plants, create walkways, and even provide centerpieces for your buffet table.

- Don't use flowers in your centerpieces. Choose pillar candles or other creative, inexpensive centerpiece ideas instead.

- Have your maids set their bouquets in front of them at the head table to eliminate one centerpiece, or get a two-for-one from your investment by having your maids place each of their bouquets in the centers of a guest table (if there are enough to suit your guest list).

- Skip some nice but unnecessary floral expenses, such as having a small floral arrangement on the back of each guest's chair, decorating the getaway car with floral swags, placing floral arrangements in the restrooms or on the gift table, and using fresh flowers to decorate the cake.

• Shop for candles in craft stores where you can buy inexpensive brands in bulk.

• Freeze the candles before lighting them so that they will burn longer.

Creating Wedding-Day Bouquets

Together with your floral designer, you will select and create the bouquet that will set you apart as the bride and complete your look on the wedding day. Today's bride has a world of options when it comes to the bouquet, as the trends are moving toward adding color to the

Green Ideas for a White Wedding

If you're of the ecological mind-set, or even if you simply want your floral investment to last more than just a day, consider these earth-friendly options for your wedding-day flowers:

• Use small potted flowering plants or tree seedlings for your table centerpieces, and then—after the wedding—take them home and plant them in your yard for an everlasting reminder of your big day.

• Use potted trees to line the path to your reception tent, and then take them home after the wedding and plant them in your yard.

• Allow your guests to take home their potted-plant centerpieces for planting in their yards, spreading the memories of your day to other neighborhoods.

• Use petals from leftover flowers to make potpourri.

bouquet. You're no longer limited to the all-white bouquet but are instead free to add some pastels or even some brights to the mix. Again, a little color will go a long way toward making your bouquet look larger and more dramatic, so consider the palette and make your selections according to your wishes.

Bouquets for yourself and for your maids come in several general styles:

• The nosegay: A small, round gathering of blooms tied together with ribbons or lace. Although popular for decades as the style for the "throwaway" bouquets, the nosegay is now one of the most popular styles chosen by brides who favor a smaller collection.

• The Biedermeier: A more formal arrangement, and also a more expensive one, the Biedermeier is a formation of tightly clustered flowers formed in a circular pattern. As this is a detailed design, it takes more labor and more flowers to create.

• Hand-tied: A gentle cluster of long-stemmed flowers tied at the stems with a beautiful, wide ribbon.

• Hand-wired: In this more detailed bouquet, each flower's stem is individually wrapped with florist tape before the group is bound together as a whole.

• Cascade: Though larger, draped floral bouquets are "out," you can design a smaller style of this design, whereby the flowers are lined up to hang down together in a graceful spill.

• Pomander: Formerly the arrangement of choice for flower girls, brides are now wearing this small, ball-shaped floral piece suspended from their wrist with a ribbon loop. Small and unobtrusive, this design works well for the bride who doesn't want to lug a heavy bouquet around.

• Breakaway: This trend is *hot* right now. With one pull of a ribbon, a separate section of the bride's bouquet comes apart from the rest of the arrangement for use as the throwaway bouquet. This concept allows a more meaningful part of the bridal bouquet to sail through the air to the waiting arms of the single ladies. More ingenious floral designers can rig the bride's bouquet so that it comes apart into several individually bound clusters, which comes as a big surprise and added treat to the several single ladies who catch a portion.

Have the floral designer take a look at a picture of your gown, assess your shape, and consider the style and formality of your wedding, and then you can discuss and order the preferred bouquet style for you.

Flowers for the Men

You might think that ordering boutonnieres is a simple task. These days, however, the increase in floral creativity at weddings means that the men's flowers are also more unique and eye-catching. Instead of the standard white rose or stephanotis sprigs and a few tufts of baby's breath, try different types of blooms. Some couples are taking the individuality thing to the next level and allowing each of the men to wear a different type of flower in his lapel. Some popular men's lapel flowers are rosebuds, gerbera daisies, chrysanthemum, beargrass, chincherinchee (check this one out—it's great for a beach wedding!), gloriosa orchids, ranunculus, and double lisianthus with camellia leaves.

The Floral Contract

As this will be a very involved order, complete with numerous purchases of a certain type of bouquet, color specifications for the maid of honor's bouquet and yours, and any number of other details, it's extremely important to include in your contract a copy of the detailed, itemized order form that you have devised with your designer.

Nonfloral Centerpiece Ideas

Rather than decking out your tables with floral arrangements—which can cost you upwards of $100 each, depending upon the style and region where the wedding will be held—consider some of the following options for inexpensive, nonfloral center-pieces. Many of these items can be found at craft shops for just dollars apiece:

- Pillar candles of varying heights
- Single, wide, scented pillar candles
- Clusters of individual votive candles in pretty little holders
- Clear or colored glass bowls filled with water and a single floating candle or gardenia
- Collections of wedding-day favors
- Framed photographs of the two of you
- Framed photographs of other family brides and grooms: your parents, grand-parents, siblings, etc.
- A lavish bread basket filled with different types of breads and spreads, tapenade, garlic butter, olive oil decanters
- A basket filled with exotic and colorful fruits such as star fruit, kiwis, pineapples, and mangoes.
- A basket filled with lemons or limes (great if pale yellow is the "color" for your wedding, and it's cheap too!)
- Beautiful rented crystal decanters filled with sangria, iced tea, water with lemon, and other noncarbonated beverages
- A mini-wedding cake for the guests to dig into on their own time
- For seaside weddings: a glass fishbowl filled with sand, seashells, starfish, and a miniature beach ball
- For the kids' table: a collection of toys and games

Include also the date and exact street location of the wedding site, a phone number there if there is one, the delivery time and location, the deposit and payment amounts, a refund and cancellation clause, and the designer's signature on the contract.

As an extra precaution, name the "fallback" flowers that will be used in case the flowers you've selected are wiped out during a freak frost in the Netherlands. Naming the backups now removes one "what if" and sets up a safety net in case of trouble down the road.

Be sure to also note when the delivery will take place, and state in writing that the floral designer you hired will be the one to deliver and set up your floral accents, centerpieces, and pew bows. Get every detail into this crucial document, so that in the event of nondelivery or delivery of the wrong items you can receive your refund with little fuss.

So what happens if the wedding is called off because of rain? Discuss this feared possibility with the floral designer ahead of time. Different shops have different policies for rain-outs, and though few will guarantee a complete re-do of your order two weeks later, you may be able to negotiate a lower price for future wedding-related purchases. It's up to the shopkeeper's discretion, but it definitely warrants a chat ahead of time.

13

Photography and Videography

Other than your memories of the big day, it's your pictures and wedding video that are going to last forever.

Capture the beautiful images of your wedding by hiring the *right* professionals for your event and making smart decisions when choosing your prints and video elements. Pictures and film are the only lasting physical mementos of your day, becoming even more valuable as time passes, so this is one area of your planning that should definitely not be taken lightly. Yes, the fees may shock you at first. And you might be tempted to shave a few thousand off your wedding budget by asking a friend to take your photos, but I would advise against taking any shortcuts. Even if you're having a simple, informal affair at home, it's a wise idea to hire true professionals for those unmistakably expert shots and footage.

Now, let's get started building your photography and videography plans.

Outdoor-Wedding Special Concerns

I spoke to several professional photographers and videographers about their special concerns when working outdoor weddings. They pointed out the differences between the average indoor wedding and an outdoor wedding as being all about "the elements." At an indoor wedding, they're dealing with predictable and manageable indoor lighting. Outside, there's glare, shade, and an ever-changing amount of natural light throughout the day and evening. Indoors, the temperature is controlled. Outdoors, the temperature can soar to blistering heat. The wind can cause sound problems for the videographer, and blowing sand at a beach wedding can cause damage to equipment.

Good photographers and videographers are aware of all of the dangers associated with the outdoor elements, and they also know how to handle them. They know how to protect their equipment and their film, they know how to avoid potential disasters, and they know how to use the natural light of the sun and shade for optimum effect. Without a doubt, outdoor weddings do present unique challenges to these professionals, but all of the experts declare that they are manageable. The greatest advantage your outdoor wedding offers is the opportunity for wonderful, one-of-a-kind photographs and footage.

Preparing your photographer and videographer for the outdoor elements is one of the most important things you can do. Make clear that it will be an *outdoor* wedding at the beach, in a garden, or at your home. Sometimes they can't tell from the address you give them or the reception site's name, and they will need this valuable information in order to prepare their equipment and plan their methods. In some cases, it's wise to bring the photographer and videographer out to the site just for a scouting visit. The experts can tour the grounds, look for attractive landscaping or structural features that might be used as backdrops, and consider the various challenges of the weather. A videographer, for instance, will appreciate having advance warning about the breeze at your beach wedding. A photographer may choose

Professionally Speaking

"Shooting an outdoor wedding is always exciting. I can always find great settings for wedding portraits, whether it's a dramatic willow tree for the couple to stand under, a multilevel jetty by the ocean, a great stone wall along a garden border for the bridal party to sit on, or the misty backdrop of a waterfall in full effect. Outdoor weddings give you more options for great pictures, and the technical concerns don't even compare to how beautiful the photos come out."

—RICH PENROSE, PHOTOGRAPHER, DEAN MICHAELS STUDIO, MADISON, NEW JERSEY

to attach a safety strap to his camera for that boat wedding, avoiding a disastrous loss of equipment and already-taken, irreplaceable photos when the boat shifts with a wake.

Your professionals may also assess the patterns of the sun's movement so that the level of shade is known ahead of time for weddings that will progress into sunset. Your picture professionals will then know what kinds of extra equipment to bring, from reflector sheets to additional lights to color gels.

They may need to check the grounds for power sources, particularly the videographer. Although a good video pro will bring plenty of batteries for his equipment, you never, ever know what might happen. His battery pack might suffer some unforeseen damage from the sun, causing him to pull out the emergency power cord. He'll need to have someplace to plug it in. If there is no power source near your wedding location, he'll know that ahead of time and bring extra battery packs, batteries, and equipment to your site.

Although it may seem excessive, you'll find that once your wedding plans are in full swing that even the smallest detail holds great importance. An outdoor wedding—with all of its special concerns— requires that you take *every* little detail into account. The beauty of the day will make it well worth your while. Understand this, and allow your picture professionals to tailor their own plans and preparations to meet the special conditions of your day. With the right advance steps, your photos and video are going to be wonderful.

Hiring a Photographer

Your pictures are only going to be as good as the photographer you hire. It's his eye that spots the priceless moment, the great setting, and

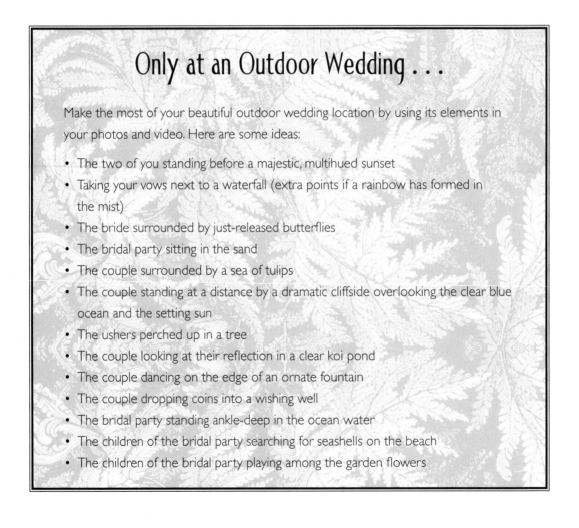

Only at an Outdoor Wedding . . .

Make the most of your beautiful outdoor wedding location by using its elements in your photos and video. Here are some ideas:

- The two of you standing before a majestic, multihued sunset
- Taking your vows next to a waterfall (extra points if a rainbow has formed in the mist)
- The bride surrounded by just-released butterflies
- The bridal party sitting in the sand
- The couple surrounded by a sea of tulips
- The couple standing at a distance by a dramatic cliffside overlooking the clear blue ocean and the setting sun
- The ushers perched up in a tree
- The couple looking at their reflection in a clear koi pond
- The couple dancing on the edge of an ornate fountain
- The couple dropping coins into a wishing well
- The bridal party standing ankle-deep in the ocean water
- The children of the bridal party searching for seashells on the beach
- The children of the bridal party playing among the garden flowers

the creative vision. It's his technical skill that finds the correct lighting and film-speed setting in a heartbeat to capture that special moment. It's his experience that allows him to take the best pictures of the day. And it's the quality of his lab that creates perfect prints for you to display on your walls and in your albums. That said, it's of the utmost importance to find a top-quality photographer.

FINDING A PHOTOGRAPHER

Sure, you'll see lots of ads listed in the Yellow Pages and in newspaper bridal-section advertisements, but the best photographers come by word-of-mouth. Ask your recently married friends whom they hired and whether or not he met their expectations *and* investment. Be sure to see your friend's album, judge the content and quality of the photos, and ask plenty of questions about how cooperative and professional the photographer was.

Next, contact Professional Photographers of America (800-786-6277; www.ppa-world.org) for referrals to qualified experts in your area. The benefit of finding a professional through an organization is that its members are well trained and adhere to a strict code of conduct. Members of such a prestigious organization must remain in good standing, and they receive up-to-the-minute training on new technology, procedures, and trends in their industry. So consider this a higher level of word-of-mouth, and collect more names for your list of potential hires.

QUESTIONS TO ASK THE PHOTOGRAPHER

Again, you'll have to ask very specific questions in order to find the professional who is the right "fit" for your photographic needs. Start off with a few basic questions about the photographer's availability during an initial phone conversation, and then make appointments to visit your top contenders in their studios. The in-studio visit allows you to see a wide variety of their photo samples, framed portraits, and albums, and that face-to-face meeting is the first assessment of what kind of rapport you have with the expert.

Make Sure Your Photographer "Gets the Picture"

Your photographer is different than many of the other professionals you're hiring for your big day. He will be very visible throughout the event, he will interact with you and with your guests, and he will give a certain amount of instruction as he plans the portraits and shots you've requested. During this meeting, see what his personal style is. Is he friendly and down-to-earth, or is he an intense creative type who might be overwhelming on the wedding day? Does he listen to what you say, or is he too busy "selling" his services? What kind of feeling do you get about him? How is your shared rapport? The partnership you'll create is just as important as the quality of his photographs, so consider the following less-tangible elements when interviewing the pros:

1. Are you available on our wedding date?
2. Have you done outdoor weddings before? How many?
3. How many weddings have you done in total?
4. Can we see samples of your outdoor-wedding pictures?
5. How many weddings will you be working that weekend?
6. Will you be shooting any other weddings on our wedding day?
7. What kinds of packages do you offer?
8. Can we see an itemized price list?
9. Are we free to customize your packages in order to get the shots we want?
10. Do you offer a budget package? What is included in it?
11. How many hours of work are included in the package we want? (The average package is four or five hours.)
12. How many photographs will you take in total? (On average, a good photographer will take between 250 and 300 pictures.)
13. Can we get some black-and-white photographs?

14. Will you be taking our photographs, or do you plan to send a staff photographer from your studio? If so, can we meet with that photographer, see his samples, and hear about his professional credits?

15. What will you be wearing to the wedding? (Important: Tell the photographer whether or not your wedding will be informal. He'll look silly in a tux if you're all in sundresses and khaki pants.)

16. Will you be working with an assistant? Several assistants? (Important: Find this out, as the assistant will also be included in the caterer's headcount.)

17. What will the assistants be wearing?

18. Do you have backup cameras and equipment?

19. How early will you arrive before the ceremony?

20. How long will it take to shoot the post-ceremony pictures?

21. How long will it take to get the photographs back?

22. How long will it take to receive our albums after we place our order?

23. What kind of photo touch-ups can we expect for our pictures?

24. Can we see the proofs on disk or online?

25. Can we keep the proofs?

26. Can we buy the negatives from you? (Some studios will not let you buy the negatives. They keep them, copyright them, and therefore make a lot of money when you need to have extra copies made. Still, some companies do have a policy of selling negatives to the couple. It's best to ask.)

27. How long do you keep the negatives?

28. Where do you store the negatives?

29. Do you digitize the negatives?

30. Do you have insurance?

31. What does overtime cost?

32. What is the payment schedule?

33. What kind of refund/cancellation policy do you have?

The True Outdoor Wedding, Open-Air Style

Once you've chosen your photographer, you'll work with him to create the perfect package. Now you'll decide how many pictures will be taken, how many pictures you'll have in your albums, how many albums you'll buy for yourself and for your parents, and all of the particulars.

At the outset, the photographer will need to collect a great deal of information from *you*. Beyond the wheres and whens, he will need to know the style and formality of your wedding and—most importantly—what *your* personal style is. He will assess you for how casual a person you are, whether or not you prefer more spontaneous pictures, how upscale you may be, and what your personal vision is. He will show you a selection of photographs and watch your reactions. Do you oooh and aaah over the romantic shot of the couple on the beach? Are you drawn to the fun group pictures? He can tell a lot about you by the way your hand lingers on a particular album page and even by the questions you ask. In this sense, *you* are also being interviewed. The photographer needs to get a sense for what you like. The pictures he sets up and takes will be a statement of who you are and what your day is like. He wants to find out your style, so that he can tailor his shots to meet your dream images.

Provide a description of the types of special shots you want taken. Tell him about your college girlfriends and ask for fun shots of your group. Tell him about your close relationship with your grandmother and that you want a special shot of the two of you. Let him know if you don't want table shots of your guests, but rather prefer more candid shots of them dancing or interacting with one another.

> *Simplify It*
>
> Ask the photographer whether or not he has reliable transportation. It's important that the expert arrive on time.
>
> —Rich Penrose, Dean Michaels Studios, Madison, New Jersey

And, be sure to tell him what shots you *don't* want. One couple confided that the groom's brother had just had a quickie marriage a few weeks before theirs. The brother had asked if their photographer could take some shots of the two of them, as they didn't hire a photographer of their own. Knowing that the groom's brother was a bit of a con artist and wasn't likely to pay them for these shots, the couple warned the photographer of the potential situation and asked that he not allow any special "photo sessions" without their permission. Other shots you might not want include large group photos of your side of the family and your groom's side, forced-smile pictures of your recently divorced parents standing side-by-side (if that would be a problem), any pictures that might make someone uncomfortable. It's important to explain any fierce tensions within your family so that the photographer doesn't unwittingly open a Pandora's box simply by asking your dad's new girlfriend to get in the family picture. Similarly, the photographer should know about your groom's surly teenage daughter and her probable unwillingness to pose for pictures. Weddings can be hotbeds of family dynamics, and the photographer should know about the most dangerous hot spots.

Next, choose the number of pictures you want for your album, and start thinking about the types of pictures you might like to include. Some couples create a more formal, official album with their posed pictures, and then a more casual separate album that contains fun pictures of their guests celebrating. For ideas, scan through the sample albums the photographer shows you. See what kinds of pictures strike your fancy, and make a mental note if you absolutely have to have a shot of your bridal party on the lifeguard stand at the beach.

Simplify It

Ask if you will be allowed to keep your proofs. That could mean 200 to 300 more pictures included in your wedding-package price, and although not all of them will be great (your eyes may be closed in some, for instance), they will meet your needs for sending pictures to faraway relatives without having to pay extra for additional prints.

If you'll be allowed to keep your proofs, then you won't need to order as many larger prints. Mix up your selection by ordering some 8 × 10 photos, some 5 × 7 photos and the like, and know that there will be a ton of candid photos being taken during the event. Think about the elements of the packages you're offered, and look at an itemized price sheet of separate, individual pictures you might want to order.

At this point, you should know how many albums you'll be ordering. Many couples save a few hundred dollars by ordering just one official album for themselves and creating special parents' albums using prints they have made and those fun, candid shots taken by the guests.

Create a package that includes a large number of pictures. You may wish to save money by ordering a limited amount of shots, but once you see those gorgeous proofs of your wedding day, it will be difficult to choose the best pictures. After the contract is signed, ordering more pictures can be a large extra expense. So err on the side of ordering too many. They will not go to waste.

Once your package is created, have the photographer draw up a complete order form for you—with every single detail written down—and forge a solid written contract for your investment. A good photographer's contract will include all of the main details of your day, where and when the photographer needs to show up, the price and payment plan for your package, the refund and cancellation policy spelled out, and any other important information you've agreed upon. Be smart and have the photographer add a line to the contract stating that *he* will be the professional working your wedding. Putting this in your contract ensures that your hiring decision

---

Wedding Day Reflections

Both of our sets of parents are divorced and remarried to other people, so we would have had to order four separate albums for all of them! To save the big bucks, we just ordered copies of some of our favorite photos, and assembled parents' albums using inexpensive but pretty store-bought photo albums."

—Nina and Tre

will be honored and that he will not send another photographer in his place on that day.

As with all hiring situations, get the photographer's card, including his cell-phone number, and obtain a signed copy of your contract. Congratulations! You've just hired the professional whose work will be a lasting part of your life forever. You may even show his photos to your kids someday.

Hiring a Videographer

Wedding videos have sure changed in the last few years. Where they started out as grainy, shaky, handheld footage, wedding videos now are shot and produced in high-quality style. Some look like expertly created television programs, with perfect clarity and Emmy-worthy special effects. Indeed, wedding videographers attest to the changing look of wedding videos by calling themselves photojournalists. Their creations come out like seamless documentaries of your day, suitable for a showing in your living room or at the Sundance Film Festival.

To begin, you'll need to find a reputable and well-trained videographer. Your photographer should be able to help you out with this one. Often, photography studios employ a stable of top-name video professionals, and they function as a partnership. The benefit of asking for a referral through your photographer is that he is *not* going to refer an untested expert. The pro you hire through him is going to be known to him, have excellent credentials, perhaps work in tandem with him on a regular basis, and make the photography studio look good.

Also ask your recently married friends whom they hired, whether or not they were happy with the finished product, and if you can view their video as a sample of his work. Firsthand impressions are often very valuable, as it's the true story from the bride and groom that counts the most. Only they can tell you if the videographer got the

Wedding Day Reflections

We considered skipping the wedding video just to save money. After all, we reasoned, we would be there and we'd have the memories in our minds forever. Why pay $5,000 for a video we'd watch a few times? But then we decided to go for it, and we hired a good videographer for the day. The footage became even more valuable a year after our wedding when my husband's mother died. Now this wedding video is a great memorial of how happy she was on that day, how healthy she looked, how much fun she had with all of her sisters and brothers and with us on the wedding day. So, while it's a special memento to us, it's also the most precious tribute to her. We'll show it to our kids someday, saying "Look at how beautiful your Grandma was! Look at how she danced with Grandpa!" And to think we almost lost this by trying to save money.

—Gail and Warren

right shots or if he was always out on a smoke break during the big moments of the reception. They can tell you if he was intrusive, if his lighting system was too blinding, and if he took six months to edit the video. All of these elements work together, so the interview process for a good video professional should be taken seriously.

QUESTIONS TO ASK THE VIDEOGRAPHER

Though it's always wise to view a sample videotape from any professional, you'll need to gather plenty of information from him as well. Again, it's not just the facts you're collecting, but a general feel for how this expert listens to you, works with you, and interacts with you.

1. Do you work outdoor weddings?
2. Have you shot our particular kind of wedding before (such as a beach wedding, boat wedding, etc.)?
3. Are you available on our wedding date?
4. How many other weddings will you be working that weekend?
5. Do you have another wedding planned on our wedding date?
6. Have you worked with our photographer before?
7. What kind of equipment do you use?
8. Will you bring a backup camera along?

9. How much footage will you shoot?
10. Will you be working our wedding, or will you send another videographer from your studio? If so, can we meet with that professional and view his samples?
11. Will you bring a lighting assistant along on that day?
12. What will you be wearing on the wedding day? (Let him know if your wedding will be casual so he can dress appropriately.)
13. What will your assistant be wearing?
14. What is your editing process?
15. How long will it take you to edit the footage and deliver the tape to us?
16. What are your basic package rates?
17. Can we customize your plan to suit our needs?
18. Can we have a list of itemized prices?
19. What is your overtime fee?
20. Are there extra charges for your lighting assistant?
21. Can we have a photo montage added to the beginning of our tape?
22. Can we select the additional music that you'll add to the tape?
23. Do we get to select any special effects for our tape?
24. What is your payment plan?
25. What do you charge for making duplicate copies of the tape?
26. Do you deliver the master tape to us, or do you keep it in storage?
27. What is your refund/cancellation policy?
28. Do you have insurance?

The most important part of the planning process here is making sure that your footage will be shot on high-quality tape with high-quality equipment. Right now, new technologies are booming, and videographers are shooting weddings using high-tech cameras. When you ask the expert what kind of camera he uses, you'll hear a lot of words like *SVHS*, *digital*, and *3-chip*. It's enough to make your head spin.

Simplify It

With a videographer, you are not just dealing with the capturing of images. You're dealing with his particular style of photojournalism. Every videographer is an artist, capturing images according to his style of shooting. He could be very creative, very romantic, or even very direct in a journalistic way. Ask him about his videotaping "philosophy." What does he look for in wedding images, and how does he express his style? These are all very good indicators of how your wedding video is going to turn out. Try to find a video pro who shares your same vision and style, as you may not want your tape to look like a segment on the 6 o'clock news.

All you need to know is that the most common camera used for wedding videos is the SVHS camera, which delivers quality images. A 3-chip is a more refined piece of equipment, often used in more professional capacities, such as shooting television and documentary segments. Though a 3-chip will deliver outstanding footage, it's an expensive piece of equipment, so your rates will be higher. Also higher in price range and the creator of fine imaging, digital equipment offers more in the realm of editing the scenes of your day. Now, even movies and documentaries are shot on digital camera, so the film-world experts do attest to the quality of its production values. However, for a wedding, an SVHS camera is still the industry standard, and the image captured will be quite suitable.

One camera or two? Some videographers will shoot your wedding using more than one camera. Perhaps he'll set up a camera at the back of your ceremony site to capture sweeping, wide-angle footage of your site and your guests facing you as you take your vows, and then he'll be up close with a handheld camera to capture the two of you. This option does provide additional views, but it's often an unnecessary expense. A good videographer can shoot a wedding with one camera, and then edit the final product to make it *look* like there was more than one camera taking your shots.

Lighting is an integral part of your videography plans. Especially in the outdoors, or in your tent, where the lighting can range from bright sunlight to shade to shadows, a good amount of light is crucial to capturing the best footage of your day. Videographers offer on-camera lights that are used when the camera is running, or they can set up an elaborate system of additional lights at your site. Ask the expert if you can see sample tapes of weddings shot with an on-camera light and those shot with additional exterior lights. Only in this way will you be able to tell how the foreground and background of the shots come across, if the lights are so bright that the guests are squinting and shading their eyes, or if the evening part of the festivities look like they took place in the dark. As you've put a lot of thought into arranging romantic, complimentary lighting for inside your tent, will you want the videographer's floodlights to ruin the ambience?

You've got lights . . . camera . . . now it's time for—no, not action (that comes later). Sound is a big part of the videography plans, especially because you will not be in an indoor space with good acoustics. An outdoor wedding means your spoken words may be drowned out by the sound of the ocean's surf, the breeze rustling tree leaves, a nearby waterfall, even a plane flying overhead. The videographer will surely want to attach microphones to you, in order to capture your vows and those quiet "You look beautiful" and "I love you" comments that you'll whisper to each other at the start of the ceremony. Ask the videographer about his microphone system to be sure that the mikes are small and that you can be wired for sound without the mike showing too obviously.

Finally, you'll have to get more technical. The editing of your video is the last important step. These days, the trend in the industry is toward nonlinear editing. This process means that the video footage taken is transferred onto a computer program, edited to perfection,

> ## Simplify It
>
> These days, you hear a lot about digital cameras. Although the digital models have moved into the mainstream, video experts say that the technology is not at 100% yet. The same goes for the option of having your wedding footage video-streamed onto DVDs. Because these options aren't quite standardized yet, and as such are more expensive, skip the ultra high-tech equipment and go with SVHS.

and then transferred out to a tape or CD-ROM. This system allows more editing options, a greater range of special effects, and the capturing of more details. See if the video pro works with a nonlinear editing system, and ask about his training and experience with that system. Some new programs are out on the market, and you won't want your pro to be "practicing" with your tape.

Once you select your wedding videographer, draw up a complete contract in writing, including all pertinent information about your wedding and your chosen package, and take a signed copy with you to seal the deal.

Choosing a Videography Package

Most videography packages come in three-hour, four-hour, or five-hour sets. The meter starts running from the first moment the video pro arrives on the scene. So you might want to think twice about having him show up at your house for your prewedding getting-ready time. It's enough to have him arrive at the ceremony site and begin his work from there.

The videographer will shoot your footage on a master tape or a series of tapes, and then the option of editing follows. I say "the option of editing" because you do have a less-expensive alternative: You can opt to purchase the "raw footage" of your wedding. This means that the videographer shoots as the day goes on, and then at the end of the reception hands you the tape he recorded. There is no editing, no special effects, no extra time and labor spent. Though your tape will not come out as perfect as an expertly edited version, with seamless cuts and only the best parts of

---

Wedding Day Reflections

We asked for special effects, and the videographer said he would use his "standards." When we got the tape back, we weren't too pleased to see an animated bunny hopping around the screen during the father/daughter dance and a tennis player running across the screen during the bouquet toss. Some of the effects were psychedelic in nature and made our wedding look like one of those "raves."

—Angela and Justin

the day included, you will get professionally captured images in an acceptable style.

If you'd rather have the editing included, talk to your expert about the editing process. Specify the special effects you'd like, or those you don't want. Some wedding videos come out positively cartoonish with too many effects.

Create a shot list with your videographer, spelling out the footage you want captured. This is a good way for the videographer to plan his timetable and the amount of attention he devotes to each element of the day. He'll need to know about any special dances you have planned for the reception, any special toasts, or if you really want some tape of you and your grandfather dancing to "Take the A Train." A quick written list gives the video pro a guideline of your wishes, and you'll receive a complete video account of all the most special parts of your day.

Because most edited wedding videos make use of additional music to enhance the footage, you should discuss with the expert the exact titles of the songs you want him to use. Ask about the number of songs he will add to the production, and submit your list in writing. Not taking this step could result in your unhappiness with the selected song or—worse—songs being used that remind you of a previous partner!

A great wedding-video touch is the compilation of pictures of the two of you. Set against a favorite song, the video montage will show snapshots or additional video footage of the two of you as children, growing up, during your dating days, and in the days leading up to the wedding. A great videographer can edit these images together into a wonderful look at the past that led up to your big day. Ask the expert about the price of such an added feature, whether the montage is a standard part of the package, and when he'll need the photos. Affix your address labels to the backs of each photo or home videotape, and make solid arrangements for their safe return to you.

Finally, arrange for a set number of copies included in your package price. Of course, your parents may want their own copies to cherish and you might want to buy an extra copy to store in a safe or a fireproof box. Don't plan on making copies from your master tape, as those copies can come out flawed *and* you could damage your master tape.

Save Money in a Flash

Because wedding photography and videography are such an important part of your day and such lasting, treasured mementos, it's no wonder the prices are so sky-high. With the cost of equipment, film, developing, editing, and manpower, prices can soar. Though it would be a mistake to cut your photography budget to the bare minimum, or to cut out the expense of videography as a whole, there are smart ways to stretch your budget and get great pictures and footage without spending a fortune:

> ### Simplify It
>
> *A*sk the videographer to "copy protect" your tape by pulling off the plastic tab on the tape's back. This simple step will prevent the catastrophe of someone accidentally recording a football game over your wedding footage.

• *Hire them for a shorter period of time.* It would be a waste to pay for the photographer and videographer to wander around your reception for four hours, snapping pictures and scanning while your guests are dancing. Instead, just have them stay for the first hour of the reception, and cut the cake early so those important shots can be captured. Then the pros leave, and the guests can take the fun candid shots with their own cameras.

• *Do your math.* Break down the prices of package deals compared with itemized prices of the prints you'll really want. With a calculator and some strategic thinking, you can get great pictures in the sizes you need without buying in bulk.

- *Skip the extra albums.* Yes, your parents will want their own albums, but there's no rule saying they have to be professional albums. Instead, fill inexpensive, store-bought albums with your extra proofs or copies of your favorite prints.

- *Skip the proofs.* If your photographer will not allow you to keep the proofs, then don't pay to have 200 pictures developed. Ask to view your photos on contact sheets for a good view at a lower cost. If the photographer is high-tech enough to have his proofs posted on a Web site for your viewing, you'll get better clarity.

- *Get a smaller album.* Limit the number of pages in the album. You won't need fifty 8 × 10s, so go with a lesser number.

- *Skip the special photo effects.* Whether it's cropping, line-erasing, or the addition of stars and other graphics to your pictures, extra work will cost extra money. So consider the quality of the photos you choose, and reconsider paying for expensive touch-ups and accents.

- *Go raw.* For your video, just have the videographer shoot the footage and hand you the tape when he's done. You can save thousands of dollars by not asking for time- and labor-intensive editing at great expense.

- *Keep your videotape short.* No one wants to sit through the entire five hours of your wedding again, and even you will tire of it eventually. So have the video pro compile a shortened version of your footage, highlighting the best moments. An hour to an hour and a half is sufficient.

- *Skip the special video effects.* So you won't have dancing bunnies and tennis players appearing on your screen . . . at a cost of $500!

14

Arriving in Style

ONE OF the best things about outdoor weddings is that, very of-ten, your transportation needs will not be monumental. After all, your ceremony and reception might both be held on the same grounds. You may not need a ride to a separate reception site. You may not need transportation *at all*! That's a few thousand dollars saved or redirected to your gown or reception fund. If you do plan to arrive at the site in a sleek limousine, a snazzy classic car, or even in a ro-mantic horse-drawn carriage, you will need to research these trans-portation companies well to create a suitable transportation package for your entire wedding weekend. Here, you'll create the picture of your arrival and departure, and you'll solidify one of the most impor-tant plans: Getting to your wedding on time.

What's Your Style?

When you picture your dream wedding, as it's being pieced together right now, do you see yourself climbing out of a sleek, black limousine?

Do you see an elegant Bentley pulling up in front of your ceremony site? Or do you picture a majestic white horse and flower-strewn carriage delivering you to your wedding? Are you the flashy type or the romantic type? Are you traditional or unique? Do you want a fairytale image? Do you want to make a statement and arrive in a manner your guests will never forget?

What Suits You?

Start your "car shopping" by considering the following rental options:

- Traditional limousine
- Rolls-Royce
- Bentley
- Excalibur
- Lexus GX 400 (ten-passenger)
- Mercedes Benz E420
- BMW 750IL (ten-passenger)
- Red Corvette (ten-passenger)
- Stretch Lincoln Navigator (fit the whole bridal party inside!)
- Stretch Humvee limousine (fit the whole bridal party inside, plus a few of the nephews!)
- Luxury limo coach
- Thirty-passenger limo bus
- Classic convertible
- Horse-drawn carriage
- Trolley
- Hot-air balloon
- Horseback
- And anything else you can think of!

Some couples want the tried-and-true limousine, and others dare to dream of departing from their wedding in a hot-air balloon or via speedboat from a nearby marina. Whatever your wish, it can be done. Today's transportation companies can accommodate any idea you can come up with. From horseback departures to trolleys to stretch Navigators, you can find whatever your heart desires. So sit down together and think about the style of your wedding, your personalities, and the site where your wedding will be held. What works best for you? What is the stuff of your wedding daydreams? Decide on limo or carriage, horse or trolley, or even your own mint convertible decorated with flowers and a "Just Married" sign.

Once you have the image in mind, you can start your search and map out the details of your transportation needs.

Choosing the Right Transportation Company

Always start by getting referrals from recently married family and friends. They'll be able to tell you if the service was worth the investment, if the cars were in good condition, if the company was eager to please, and if they were happy. You can't beat a firsthand recommendation. Also, ask friends who do a lot of corporate entertaining. Their company may hire limousines on a regular basis, and they will certainly be able to recommend a classy, professional company for your use as well. And don't forget the best hotels in your area. Call the concierge and ask him which limousine company his hotel regularly uses for its most esteemed guests.

Once you collect your list of contenders, it's time for the lengthy and involved process of interviewing, researching, and assessing them. You're shopping for reliability here, as it's of the utmost importance that their cars work, their drivers are well trained, and their company is organized. As when hiring any other wedding professional, you want to do as much in-person research as possible. Go to the company's headquarters and walk through its lot. Inspect the cars. Are they shiny and clean? New models? Are there a lot of cars? Is there a wide range of sizes and colors? During the interview process, a good transportation company will let you climb into some of its cars for a good firsthand look at what you're "buying."

When you're talking to the manager, is he friendly and willing to answer your questions? Or does he seem rushed and disorganized, with papers falling in mountains from his desk? Does he have a sizeable staff, or is he a one-man operation? The presence of a staff means that the company gets a lot of business and that a quality staff is working together to meet its customers' needs. You might not get the opportunity to meet your limo driver for your wedding day, but you should ask about the company's drivers as a whole. Here are the main questions you should cover for the top-two types of wedding-day transportation:

> ### Simplify It
>
> The National Limousine Association (800-NLA-7007) can also help you find a reputable company in your area. It's always a good idea to hire a company that is certified with a professional association, so be sure the company you're considering does have an active membership in a group such as this one.

INVESTIGATING LIMO COMPANIES

1. Do you have cars available on our wedding date?
2. What kinds of cars do you have?
3. Do you have the model of car we desire (e.g., Bentley, Rolls-Royce, etc.)?
4. What color cars do you have?
5. What size cars do you have? Eight-seaters? Ten? Twelve? Fourteen? Larger?
6. What are the features of the standard limousine? Bar? Champagne-glass rack? Sunroof? Television?

7. Do you offer the standard wedding-package extras, such as a champagne stand, red carpet, or balloons?

8. What will the drivers be wearing?

9. What are your package rates?

10. Do you offer a discount for multiple car orders?

11. What are your rates for a party van or bus for our guests?

12. Do you have insurance? (Request to see a copy of the certificate.)

13. Are you a member of a professional association, such as the NLA? (Request to see a copy of the certificate.)

14. What are your overtime rates?

15. Do you charge by the hour or a set fee for a length of time?

16. What is your refund/cancellation policy?

17. Do your drivers carry two-way radios? (IMPORTANT! Cell phones are fine, but they do not work in some areas. A two-way radio will connect the driver with his home base, so that contact is always assured in case of emergencies.)

18. Do you have a liquor license, so that we can have a champagne toast in the car? (Some companies don't, and the rules vary by state as to which types of cars are allowed to hold drinking passengers.)

As I mentioned earlier, inspect the cars. Climb inside and check the seats for tears, holes, or general dirtiness. How does the car smell? If you're sensitive to cigarette smoke, insist that you be given a nonsmoking car for your wedding day. Consider the needs of your family members if they too will be picked up in a rented luxury vehicle.

And don't "cheap out." There are, of course, ways to save money on transportation, but hiring the cheapest car you can find will only yield you major headaches. Trying to scrimp here might mean that you're not going to arrive at your wedding on time, or that you've gotten grease smears on the bottom of your dress from a filthy vehicle. Take your time, research well, inspect thoroughly, and get the most value for your money.

INVESTIGATING HORSE-AND-CARRIAGE COMPANIES

1. Do you have a horse and carriage available for our wedding day?

2. Can your horse and carriage ride along the path we've chosen? (Some companies do not allow their horses and carriages on busy highways or on rough dirt roads.)

3. Do you have distance restraints for your horses? (Some companies limit the trek to one or two miles, or even a couple of blocks.)

4. What color horse will we have? (The most popular is a white horse with a white carriage, but having a black horse with a black carriage is very elegant as well.)

5. Do you have enclosed carriages? (This regal look protects you from wind and rain.)

6. How is the carriage decorated—with fresh flowers and garlands? Is decorating the carriage to our specifications permitted?

7. Can we attach a "Just Married" sign to the back of the carriage, or do you provide that?

8. What will the driver be wearing? (Some companies go all out, providing Victorian outfits for their drivers. Specify if you want the formal tuxedo look, or if you have a different look in mind. But always ask. The driver should match the style of your day as well.)

9. Do you provide music in the carriage? (Some can be rigged for stereo sound.)

10. Are we allowed to have a champagne toast in the carriage?

11. How old are your horses? Are they healthy?

12. How experienced are your drivers?

13. What are your package rates?

14. For how long do we have use of the carriage?

15. What are your overtime rates?

16. Do you have insurance? (Request to see a copy of the certificate.)

17. Do you have a valid license that we can see?

18. Can we come see the carriages and horses?

19. What is your refund/cancellation policy?

Of course, the most important part of this shopping trip is seeing the carriages and horses up close and personal (well, maybe not *too* up close!). Inspect the carriage. Is it relatively new and in good condition? Clean? Are the seats comfortable? Is it easy to climb up into the carriage? Is a courtesy step provided for the bride and groom to use to climb into the carriage? Look at all details, and find the best carriage for your style.

Next, check out the horse. You can specify which horse you would like to use, so pick an experienced one with a clean, well-groomed coat and a friendly demeanor. An experienced carriage horse will be comfortable around you and any other strangers. As he will be out on the road, he'll have to be happy with his job and used to any number of distractions. You won't want a jittery horse who's afraid of loud noises and crowds, or your ride to the ceremony will be quite . . . memorable. Ask about the horse's experience level, as in how many weddings he has worked. A good horse-and-carriage company will treat its horses like valued members of its family. They will be housed in comfortable stalls, they will be groomed, and the handlers will speak kindly to them. Use your best judgment to choose the horse for your day.

Keep in mind that a horse-and-carriage ride does mean that it will be a slow trip to the wedding. And many couples warn that such a slow-moving vehicle means that traffic will get tied up behind you. If your route to the wedding will take you through busier streets, think ahead to the logistics of that slow procession. You might need to arrange for a township police escort, and don't be surprised if you hear some angry car horns behind you. Most couples could care less about impatient drivers in their wake, but it is something to keep in

Simplify It

Be sure that your carriage company is a registered member of a professional association, such as the Carriage Operators of North America (CONA) or the Carriage Association of America (CAA; www.caaonline.com). Several individual states have their own horse-and-carriage associations, so run an Internet search to find the one nearest you.

mind when checking if your route and the traffic patterns of the time of day match your ideal wedding plans.

PLANNING YOUR TRANSPORTATION PACKAGE

Together with the manager or booking agent of the transportation company you choose, you will create the package that will assure your delivery to and from the wedding. Know your wedding-day schedule, and be prepared to give times and places to the reservations agent. Because transportation arrangements come in hourly packages, you'll need to streamline your day and book your cars according to the times they'll be in use.

Once you know how much time you'll need for your transportation, then you'll need to configure your car arrangement. How many cars will you need? Just one for the two of you? A full lineup of limos for your bridal party, parents, and grandparents? Discuss with the limousine manager the number of bridal-party members and parents you need to transport, as he may be able to help you book the right number of cars. I spoke with a limousine-company manager recently, and he told me that he was able to save one engaged couple the price of an extra limousine. They had seventeen people to transport on their wedding day, and they were considering getting three limousines. He rented them two 10-person cars at a savings compared to the price of three regular cars.

When it comes to the color of the vehicle, you do have options. The all-white wedding limousines have been the standard so far, but the black cars are gaining momentum. Not only are they less expensive than the white limousines in many cases, but they create a strik-

---

Simplify It

Transportation fees can reach into the stratosphere, so it would be a waste of money to have the limos sitting idly in the parking lot during the reception hours. Instead, use the pricey, flashy limos for the approach to the wedding, and then let them go at the start of the reception. Afterwards, arrange for safe, non-drinking drivers to deliver you to your hotel room. The hotel where your rooms and honeymoon suite are reserved might even allow you free use of its guest shuttle to take you "home" at the end of the event.

ing contrast that makes those by-the-limo photographs come out great. Against the backdrop of a shiny black limousine, your white gown looks amazing. Many couples choose the black limousine for its movie-star quality and its look in the photographs.

Next come the instructions. The transportation company will need to know the exact timetable and details for whom they're picking up, when, and where. Take your time and compile a list of where the groom and ushers need to be picked up, where they should be taken, and so on for yourself and the rest of your family. The manager should be able to help you with this, as he's done this sort of thing many times before. For your use, here is a sample directions timetable:

LIMOUSINE DIRECTIONS

Jim Johnson and Shelly Kennedy

Wedding date: May 25, 2006

Wedding location: State Arboretum,
2100 Spring Blossom Road, Springfield, NY (219) 555-0000

Limo #1 picks up Jim Johnson and four ushers at 2 Locust Lane, Springfield, NY (219) 555-1111 on May 25 at 10 A.M. and delivers them to State Arboretum by 10:15 A.M.

Limo #2 and Limo #3 pick up Shelly Kennedy, four bridesmaids, mother, grandmother, and father at 17 Madison Circle, Springfield, NY (219) 555-7777 on May 25 at 10:15 A.M. and delivers them to State Arboretum by 10:45 A.M.

Limo #1, #2, and #3 deliver Kennedy bridal party to State Marina, 2 Marina Lane, Springfield, NY (219) 555-8888 at 12 noon.

Limo #1 returns to State Marina at 7 P.M. and delivers bride and groom to Biltmore Hotel, Grand Ave, Springfield, NY.

Simplify It

For still greater savings—and even greater fun—consider booking a party bus through an agency. These new buses are decked out with leather seats, mood lighting, surround-sound systems, even bars and restrooms for a great continue-the-party atmosphere. You'll save plenty per head if you have a large bridal party and a good number of family members, and it will be a ride they'll never forget! Some brides and grooms say they would rather have been in that bus with their loved ones than in their own private limo.

Do we need to provide driving directions to the limousine company?

Most limousine companies are knowledgeable about the streets and routes in your area. If they are not familiar with the location you have chosen, they will call the site and get the best directions, or they will run an Internet search for the details.

The pickup and drop-off locations should be included in your written order as a part of your contract. Have the manager sign the Directions Worksheet (on page 249)—or his own computer-printout version of the directions you supply—to make it an official part of your agreement. Be sure the contract you arrange with the company spells out all of the most pertinent information, including all of the specific details you've discussed and arranged with the manager. Once signed, the company is bound by your agreement, and the terms of your transportation package are set.

Getting Your Guests There

Depending upon the location of your wedding, the date and time, and the travel plans of your incoming guests, you might find that your transportation needs extend beyond the basic to-the-ceremony and to-the-reception arrangements on your big day. Your guests may need to get from the hotel to the ceremony site, and then to the reception site, and then back home again. Many hotels do offer free use of their shuttle buses for wedding guests, and they may rent their shuttle buses to you even if you're not holding your wedding at their banquet hall. Ask the hotel manager about this convenient service.

If the free hotel shuttle is not an option, then you may have to mobilize helpful friends and family to drive some of your guests from place to place. Choose only reliable friends who are not likely to get drunk at your reception, and assure your guests that they do have a safe ride.

Another issue that springs up is the guest parade that needs to get back and forth from the airport or train station. Again, see if the hotel where they're staying has free shuttle service to and from major airports and train depots. If not, ask those great friends and relatives to help out with rides.

Directions Worksheet

Date:

Before the Ceremony

Limo #1:

Time:

Place:

Phone number there:

Pick up whom?

Drop them off where?

Limo #2:

Time:

Place:

Phone number there:

Pick up whom?

Drop them off where?

Limo #3:

Time:

Place:

Phone number there:

(continues)

Pick up whom?

Drop them off where?

From Ceremony to Reception

Limo #1:

Time:

Place:

Phone number there:

Pick up whom?

Drop them off where?

Limo #2:

Time:

Place:

Phone number there:

Pick up whom?

Drop them off where?

Limo #3:

Time:

Place:

Phone number there:

Pick up whom?

Drop them off where?

After Reception

Limo #1:

Time:

Place:

Phone number there:

Pick up whom?

Drop them off where?

Limo #2:

Time:

Place:

Phone number there:

Pick up whom?

Drop them off where?

Limo #3:

Time:

Place:

Phone number there:

Pick up whom?

Drop them off where?

Invitations

YOUR INVITATIONS are more than just pretty cards with fancy writing on them. They impart a world of information beyond the what, when, and where of your wedding. Although they certainly serve that basic purpose, they also convey to your guests the important message of how formal your wedding will be. As you sort through the many hundreds of invitation styles, you will see a wide range of invitations that reflect every level of formality, from ultraformal to fun, whimsical, informal types. The design of your invitation, then, will tell your guests what to expect and—most importantly for some—what to wear.

The invitation serves the outdoor wedding particularly well. It is through the wording that your guests will learn that your wedding will be an outdoor affair and whether informal or casual dress is expected. Clearly providing the information that the wedding will be out in the elements will help your guests plan for their own comfort and suitable attire for the day.

In this section, you'll choose and design your own invitations, plus the various other printed items you'll supply, such as maps, programs, and place cards.

The First Steps

Before you shop for your invitations, you'll need to know all of the basic information that will be printed:

- The wedding date
- The exact street location of the ceremony site
- The exact street location of the reception site (if different from ceremony site)
- The time of day of the wedding
- The formality level of the wedding
- The style of the wedding (beach, backyard, arboretum, outdoor-indoor, etc.)
- The full, correct spellings of the names of all people who will be mentioned on the invitation (more on this later)
- Who will be listed on the invitation as hosts (your parents, both sets of parents, the bride and groom, the children of the bride and groom, etc.)
- Whether you need separate cards for reception invitations (some couples may need this decisive paper, as some of their guests may be invited only to the church)
- Your full guest headcount

You will use your full guest headcount to figure the number of invitations you will actually need. Not every guest gets his or her own invitation, as many of your guests may be listed as *Mr. and Mrs.*, thereby requiring only one invitation between them. Thus, two people get one invitation. Children over age 18 living at home get their own invitations as well. Children under age 18 may be listed on their parents' invitations, for one easier send. Take a few minutes to go through your guest list and add up how many invitations you'll actually need. Have you included the bridal party in the guest-list count? The officiant? Many brides forget these obvious guests, but they do have to be officially invited along with any of their dates for the day. As it's always a good idea to have extras—for additional invitation mailings and as keepsakes—order 20% more invitations than you'll need.

What's the Style?

The style of your wedding will determine the style of the invitations package you choose. A classic, formal outdoor wedding will prescribe a more elegant style of invitation, such as a simple cream-colored invitation stock with raised black lettering. A more informal outdoor wedding might allow for some design or bordering to your invitation, on cream or blush-colored paper. A beach wedding opens up a whole new realm of design, such as a style with starfish or seashells in gold embossing or a raised pattern. The style of invitation you choose will give your guests a good sense of the style of the wedding. And it also shows your own sense of personal style.

Flip through the many designs in invitations catalogs or on the Internet to see samples of what's out there. A good invitations sales assistant can help you narrow down your choices in order to choose the invitation that's best for you. Take your time on this job, as there are literally thousands of options out there.

Looking through all of those catalogs can be a bit overwhelming. There are so many designs, and so many factors that go into the decision. After all, you'll have to choose from different types of paper, different types of printing styles, different fonts, all with different prices. On top of that, you'll have to abide by the formal rules of invitation planning and wording. Although etiquette rules may be bent in other areas of your wedding, they still reign over your decisions for the invitations. Let's look a little more closely at all of the details involved in designing your invitations package.

WHAT TYPE OF PAPER?

Invitations don't just come in one style of paper. As you flip through those sample books, you'll see textured papers, woven linen blends, papers with dried flowers incorporated into them, and any number of different materials used just for the base of the invitation alone. You will see from looking at them, holding them, feeling them in your hand, which kinds of papers will complement a more formal wedding-invitation style. No doubt you've seen many invitations before, and you may have noticed that some papers are thicker or shinier than are others. The selection you make—whether you go with the classic, traditional cotton stock or a woven blend—must work well with the formality level, print type, and your budget. The following are the most popular kinds of papers you'll have to review:

100% cotton. The most common type of invitation paper, this is also one of the least expensive and most complementary to the different types of print and inks.

Corrugated. Suitable for informal or at-home weddings, this type of paper is thicker and may have that artsy, "homemade paper" look. Very often, it is presented with a center fold or two middle folds, with the print inside.

Jacquard. Uses a layered-paper look that suggests an overlay of fabric or lace on parts of the invitation.

Laid. A smoother blend similar to cotton papers, but with a noticeably textured grain. It comes across as a natural paper, which is a great choice for outdoor weddings where the natural look is in.

Linen. A popular choice for all wedding styles. This classic paper is used most often in boxed stationery, and its less-smooth finish holds print well and is lighter in weight as a whole.

Moiré. A smooth finish with watermarks pressed into the grain. Very often, the watermark gives a classic look to a plain-lettered invitation, offering a hint of something extra if you look carefully enough.

Parchment. It's not just used as an insert in the invitation anymore. It's becoming the main attraction, as parchments have gotten slightly thicker, have gentle shading, and are now able to hold print. An invitation that comes on a piece of parchment is a romantic image, one that even the most famous brides are going for right now.

WHAT TYPE OF PRINT DO YOU LIKE?

The print may all look the same to you, but invitations are printed using different types of processes. The kind of typeface you get could be very expensive, or it could be more affordable, depending on the choice you make from the following:

> ### Simplify It
>
> Heavier stock paper is going to mean a heavier invitation packet, which translates to more postage when you're ready to send it. Remember that your invitations package will include the weights of the invitation, the outer and inner envelopes, response card, map, and other items. So choose a lighter paper stock if you have a lot of invitations to send.

- *Engraved.* The most expensive and formal of options, engraved invitations have raised lettering and letter indentations on the back of the invitation. Because the printing process is more involved, delivery time may need to be extended.

- *Thermographed.* The most popular option and the norm of the industry right now, thermographed invitations are printed cleanly and have no indentations on the back of the invitation. It's a far less expensive option, with less turnaround time, and the quality comes out just as beautifully as engraved styles.

- *Calligraphy.* Beautifully scripted, handwritten invitations are a lovely touch when it suits the formality of your wedding. Unless you've studied calligraphy for years, or have a friend who has, you'll have to hire a calligrapher to pen the wording for you. This option is best if you have few invitations and envelopes done, so that the prices are not astronomical. If you're the do-it-yourself type, you might choose to create your own invitations using a calligraphy font on your home computer.

- *Color.* Several print types can be done in color. Although the basic and most widely accepted wedding invitation is always done in black ink on white or cream-colored paper, color is growing in popularity and reflecting the floral nature of an outdoor wedding. Some couples are now opting for a blush pink paper with a deeper rose-colored print. Another option for a great outdoor-wedding invitation is to use hunter green print on a cream-colored paper. The colored options are for more informal weddings, so if you're going with the formal wedding style, then stick to black print. Just note that colored print is generally more expensive than black print, so factor that into your invitation's budget.

ELEMENTS OF STYLE

- *Go with a simpler style.* A plain invitation with a simple border and easily readable wording will convey a sense of elegance and the formality level of your wedding. Busier invitations come off as gaudy, and they're also more expensive due to the additional detailing and colors.

- *Bigger isn't better.* A smaller invitation will not only be less expensive to buy as an item, it will also add up to a lighter and regular-sized

Simplify It

*W*hen *hiring a calligrapher, always ask to see samples of his or her work, find out how long the calligrapher has been such an artist, and choose a specific style of calligraphy from a sample book. There are many different styles of calligraphy, from Gothic to Roman to more personalized flowery scripts, so choose the style that best suits the formality of your wedding. Get a signed contract with a delivery date specified, and be sure you provide a clear printed copy of the wording of your invitation, with all spelling, grammar, and facts triple-checked for accuracy.*

invitation package. That means less postage and no oversized-item mailing rates. Plus, many wedding guests report that they prefer an envelope that fits easily into a purse on the big day.

• *Skip the glitter.* It may look special, but that glitter gets all over the guest's hands and clothes. It's an unnecessary addition, more expensive, and makes your invitation look a bit cheesy.

• *Reflect your theme.* If you've planned a less-formal themed wedding, your invitation should reflect that. For a beach wedding, consider an invitation imprinted with delicate starfish and some scalloped shells in the top corners. An outdoor wedding allows for so many great stylistic options in the beach, nautical, and floral themes that you are free to choose from literally hundreds of embellishments.

• *Reflect yourselves.* The invitation is really the first impression your guests receive of the wedding's style, but it's also a great way to incorporate your own personal style and tastes. If you're a traditional, classic person, you might choose to reflect your tastes in the style of invitation you choose. If you and your fiancé enjoy the night sky—and perhaps may have even shared a moonlight stroll under the stars on your first date—why not choose an invitation that features shooting stars?

• *Surround your words.* Choose from a variety of attractive borders to encircle your words. Today's myriad of styles offers everything from a classy, thin black scroll line to a border of tiny daisies (perfect if you'll have daisies as the main flowers at your garden wedding!) or even starfish or seahorses. A colored border should match the color of the print, as a unified color theme works better than coordinating colors. Use your wedding's color theme here, as well.

THE LITTLE INSERTS

Of course your invitation packet will include not just the invitation itself, but several extras. The invitations catalog will almost certainly offer matching styles of the following:

- Response cards:

The favour of a reply is requested by
Sunday, the twelfth of May
_____ *will attend*
_____ *will not attend*

- Reception cards:

Reception
following cocktail party
at
The Victoria House
Newport, Rhode Island
8 o'clock in the evening

Simplify It

The wedding-site manager can provide you with preprinted maps or clear, written step-by-step directions from all major approaches to your area. Very often, they have these directions on hand as a basic part of their wedding package, and your simple request can save you hours of researching and printing your own versions.

- Hotel information cards: On these, you'll list the name of the hotel where the block of rooms is reserved, the last name to provide for identification as a member of that block of rooms, prices, the reservations phone line, and the availability of nonsmoking rooms and handicap-access rooms.

Printed directions to your locations:

From Route 287: Take Exit 22 to
Bedminster,
Turn left at the second light
Continue on Route 202 through three
traffic lights . . .

- An at-home card: On this you will print your after-wedding residence and phone number:

Emily and Ryan Scott
4 Spruce Tree Lane
Jenkintown,. PA 00000
(600) 555-0000

• Invitation cards: These will list whatever other events will be going on that weekend, such as brunches, barbecues, family golf tournaments, and other outings:

You are invited
to a prewedding brunch
in the main dining room of the
Marriott Hotel
Saturday morning
7 A.M.—10 A.M.
Dress is casual.
Mr. and Mrs. Davis are hosting
this event.

ENVELOPES

Again, the invitations package you choose will come with its own matching envelopes. Speak with the invitations salesperson about the number of enclosures you'll have, and she should be able to arrange the size and number of envelopes you'll need.

Remember that most formal and informal invitations packages include an inner and outer envelope for your use, and a smaller envelope for the return of the response card. Right now, some brides and grooms are choosing to skip the inner envelope for more informal wedding-invitation packages, but you might consider that option for a savings of money and a slight decrease in the final weight of your filled envelopes. To be on the safe side, order thirty to fifty more

> ## Simplify It
>
> For any additional events, order only the number of invitations you'll need for each guest list. If you'll only host twenty close family members for the brunch, you'll only need ten to twenty invitations. It takes some preplanning, but you should know these details before you put in your invitations package order.

A Corner-Cutting No-No

Don't attempt to save time and effort by using your computer to print out a merged list of all of your wedding guests and then just stick the labels on the envelopes. It doesn't matter how pretty a font you have, or if it looks just like calligraphy. It doesn't matter if you have found wedding-themed address labels. Printed envelopes are a big no-no in wedding etiquette, and even though the rules of etiquette are bending in many areas of a wedding, this is still one area where a rule is a rule.

envelopes than you think you'll need, as mistakes are almost always made during the hand-addressing process.

Stay away from designed envelopes with raised décor on the outside, colored envelopes, and ones with glitter on them. Not only do these look tacky, but officials at the U.S. Post Office say that large envelopes with lots of details sometimes get jammed in the processing machines. It is also difficult for the postal machines to read addresses written on some darker or patterned shades of colored envelopes. So keep your choices simple.

POSTAGE STAMPS

You may be aware that the "love stamps" issued by the post office are the traditional postage used on wedding invitations. Several styles are offered, from styles bearing swans, Victorian bouquets, and heart shapes, so your choice can vary according to your wedding's formality level as well. Another option for less formal outdoor weddings is the theme stamp. For a beach wedding, you might find an issued summertime theme stamp. For a garden wedding, you'll have plenty of flower stamps to select. For a viewing of the different stamps issued at the time of your wedding, visit the U.S. Post Offices Web site at www.usps.gov. You can even order your stamps directly through the site, rather than waiting in line at a crowded post office.

You will, however, need to make an in-person visit to the post office to weigh your final, completely assembled invitation package. With all of those inserts, maps, and response cards, your invitation envelope may require extra postage. Only a professional weighing of your package will reveal the true amount of postage due on each.

Remember as you add up your stamp order that you'll need one for each of the response cards as well as the full postage for the outer envelope. This extra amount is most often forgotten, so keep it in mind before you buy your stamps.

FINDING THE RIGHT WORDS

Of all of the elements of weddings, finding the correct wording for the invitation is probably the most involved part of the entire event. Now that it's not the absolute norm for the bride's parents to be the only ones hosting the event, various etiquette rules exist regarding the correct wording as relates to who's hosting the wedding, what wording is used, what formality of spelling is used, and so on.

Even as etiquette rules are bending throughout the wedding-planning process, I'll restate that the invitation is still bound rigorously to the standards of etiquette. It's probably the one area left where you really are pressured to "do the right thing" according to what's proper. Family dynamics and situations run the gamut, from divorced parents hosting, to the groom's parents hosting, to the couple themselves hosting, to

---

Wedding Day Reflections

We didn't go to have our invitation packages weighed, and we were stunned when ALL of our invitations came back to us stamped "Insufficient Postage." Since all of the envelopes were ruined, we had to rush order more at great expense, buy new stamps, re-write all of the outer envelopes, and speed the new ones out in time to invite our guests by the RSVP deadline. It was a nightmare, one that could have been avoided if we'd taken the right precautionary step beforehand.

—Miranda and Wes

Compromise to Save Your Sanity

My fiancé's parents have paid for a few things, such as the traditionally prescribed "groom's family" expenses, but my parents have paid for everything else—and it was a lot. Now, his family wants to be listed on the invitation as hosts of the wedding along with my parents. They say their friends will expect their names to be on the invitation. I say that's not fair to my parents, since they're the real hosts. But my fiancé's parents are really putting up a fight, saying I'm ungrateful. What can I do about this?

That's a tough spot to be in, as family egos often get in the way when planning a wedding. Too many parents confuse "what other people will think" with what's best for the bride and groom. It's up to you to decide how much this fight is worth creating future tensions with them. Talk to your parents about the situation, and tell them that you're facing a situation where you might be forced to list the groom's parents under your parents' names as hosts. As long as your parents understand why you made this decision, they may not mind. If you feel strongly about keeping your parents listed as the primary hosts, then show your groom's family samples of traditional invitations where the groom's parents' names are listed under the groom's name. An example is as follows:

Mr. and Mrs. Anthony Smith
Request the honour of your presence
at the marriage of
their daughter
Alicia Ann
to
Scott Taylor
son of
Mr. and Mrs. Michael Taylor . . .

the children of the marriage being listed as the hosts. The correct listing—and order of listing—of their names on the invitation is a tribute that parents and couples take very, very seriously. So you must be sure you get it right. A slight here, even unintentional, has been known to ruin familial relationships. It sounds petty, but you'd be surprised how fiercely people feel about the wording of the invitations.

If you and your fiancé are paying for and planning the wedding, then obviously the two of you should be listed as the hosts of the wedding and the top names on the invitation. If your parents are hosting and paying for the wedding, their names are listed first. The groom's parents' names may be listed on the invitation either as joint hosts or as the parents of the groom. Confusing? I've listed a few examples here for you to follow as a model.

The best way to tackle this thorny issue from the outset is to have a discussion with both sets of parents about your decision as to the wording of the invitation. They may make requests or complain, but it is your decision. Of course, if you have gone the traditional route and had your parents pay for everything, you must honor them now. Just follow the traditional rules and exercise good family diplomacy for the sake of future happiness.

Now it's time to look at the standard wording for the various types of wedding situations that might suit your situation. Follow these models and create your own correct style of wording for your invitations.

SOME RULES ABOUT WORDING

1. For formal weddings, use the Old English spellings of words, such as *honour* and *favour*.
2. Spell out all abbreviated words, such as *Street* and *Avenue* rather than *St.* and *Ave.*
3. 4:00 P.M. should be spelled out as "four o'clock in the afternoon."
4. Provide an exact street location and town for all wedding-day sites.
5. Spell out all names in full, formal spelling.

6. Use appropriate titles where necessary, for example, if your fiancé is a captain in the navy, his name would be "Captain John Somers."

7. Don't use bold lettering. All print should be in the same typeface.

8. Make sure all of the information listed on the invitation is correct. Double- and triple-check spellings (especially of your parents' names!) and make sure you have the correct date and times written.

If the bride's parents are hosting the wedding:

Mr. and Mrs. Steven Andrews
request the honour of your presence
at the marriage of their daughter
Lindsay Elizabeth
and
Evan James Smith
son of
Mr. and Mrs. James Smith
Saturday, the twenty-seventh of May
at four o'clock in the afternoon
Saint Peter's Church
64 First Street
Chicago, Illinois

If both sets of parents are sharing hosting responsibilities equally:

Mr. and Mrs. Stephen Andrews
and
Mr. and Mrs. James Smith
request the honour of your company
at the marriage of their children

Lindsay Elizabeth

and

Evan James Smith . . .

When divorced parents are hosting:

Mr. Jeremy Davidson

and

Mrs. Kathleen Davidson

request the honour of your company

at the wedding of their daughter

Linda Marie

to

Benjamin Gregory Stone . . .

When multiple sets of parents are hosting, such as in the very common situation of the bride's divorced and remarried parents:

The loving parents of

Linda Marie Davidson

request the honour of your company

as their daughter unites in marriage with

Benjamin Gregory Stone . . .

When the couple is hosting their own wedding:

Ms. Linda Marie Davidson

and

Mr. Benjamin Gregory Stone

request the honour of your presence

as they unite in marriage . . .

More informal invitation styles have significantly more relaxed, even whimsical wording:

We're finally tying the knot!
You're invited to join us on our wedding day,
to share in our celebration,
drink a toast,
watch the sunset,
and dance all night with us
as we light up
the Harbor Club Marina
in Newport, Rhode Island,
on Friday the ninth of June
at 7:00 P.M.

Other, more personalized invitations fit for informal or at-home weddings can use any number of fun wording styles. Some invitations employ humor, and others let guests know that the style is casual and that the wedding will be held outdoors. One couple reminded their guests to bring sunscreen. Whatever your wording choice, as prescribed by both etiquette and personal preferences, remember that your invitation includes some very important cues for your guests, and it will become a forever keepsake for yourself.

Ordering Your Invitations

Now that you have the style and wording of your invitations all planned out, you're up to the task of placing your order correctly and efficiently. Most standard invitations companies whose books you

Take It from Someone Who Knows

"When planning an outdoor wedding, the weather is always a factor. On your invitation, you can help your guests prepare for any changes to your site location or wedding date by including an inclement-weather clause such as 'In case of rain, the wedding will be held at 123 Sycamore Road, Plainfield, New Jersey.' Some couples even alert guests to check their 'wedding day weather hotline,' which is a recording on their voice mail or a separate 800-number that gives a to-the-minute status report on whether the wedding is changed due to inclement weather."

—LINDA ZEC PRAJKA, OWNER, AN INVITATION TO BUY—
NATIONWIDE, WWW.INVITATIONS4SALE.COM

scanned in the stationery store do have an order turnaround of eight to ten weeks. Add that to the six to eight weeks' notice you should give your guests—ten to twelve weeks' notice if you're planning a destination wedding—and a full week for addressing, stamping, and sending all of those invitations, and you're looking at a large lead time. The following are some details about the ordering methods in practice right now so that you can plan your attack and schedule your order well:

• *Standard orders through stationery stores.* The best companies, such as Birchcraft, can deliver in that standard time of eight to ten weeks, but rush orders will cost you more money. Be sure to fill in the order form carefully, including all extra invitation items such as response cards, reception cards, and at-home cards. In most cases, the salesperson at the shop will help you fill it out, allow you to proofread and affix your final okay, and then start talking about payment.

• *Mail Order.* Though the selection may not be as great as what you'd see in a lineup of books in a stationery store, this is still a fine option. Very often, this is where you'll find a greater selection of unusual and themed invitations, natural papers, and inclusions. This type of order is likely to take less than the standard eight to ten weeks, and it may also be less expensive. Remember to factor in shipping charges, as well. If you do choose this option, be *sure* to fill out your order form very carefully and be sure the company has enough time to reprint in case of any errors. Also, be sure you have a refund and reprint guarantee in your contract.

> *Simplify It*
>
> **I**f you're placing your order over the phone, take some extra steps as precautionary measures. Ask the salesperson not only to read your order back to you, but to spell out every word, specify every capitalized letter, note when a new line is started and whether the first word is capitalized or lowercased, and verify again the type of print and catalog style order by number.

• *Online orders.* This isn't sending invitations online. Some sites are trying that trend on for size, and it is just not accepted in the wedding industry. Some people do not have e-mail. Some don't get all their e-mail messages. Some will save the e-mail and forget to print it out. Some will lose all their e-mail to a computer virus. Some do not open forwarded e-mails. Not only are the methods dangerous when dealing with technology, it's just tacky to send out all your invitations via carbon copy (cc:). By online ordering, I mean checking out online invitation-ordering catalogs and companies. Many online companies will send you a printed catalog for a more detailed viewing of invitation details, so don't be afraid to ask for print versions in addition to site pictures. Create a complete contract, specifying delivery time and reprint and refund clauses in the company's contract. When ordering online, be sure the site has security measures in place to ensure the privacy of your personal information.

THE DO-IT-YOURSELF ROUTE

If you're really short on time—and money—or if you just like having the opportunity to create your own invitations and inclusions, then plan to design them yourselves. Many couples have done this, following the lineup of steps here:

- Have all of the pertinent information ready.

- Get a supply of good invitation paper stock or suitably designed paper at a stationery store, or even at business-supply stores such as Staples and OfficeMax. These chains know that there is a proliferation of couples who are using their computers to print out wedding invitations and other paper items, and they now stock attractive, high-quality papers and wedding-themed papers at a steep discount.

- Use a good computer-design program. Even a standard word-processing software program such as Microsoft Word can give you a beautiful layout, hundreds of fonts and sizes to choose from, borders, even clip art and graphic-design elements. If you're a true computer guru, you can use other design programs, scanners, and your own clip art.

- Spend some time arranging the wording on the page, printing out onto regular paper to see how the design will lay out on the official paper.

- Create your invitation and print it out on your chosen card stock to see how it looks.

- Though I would suggest printing all of your invitations out using your own printer, you might not want to put your machine through that kind of a workload. Instead, take a solid, crisp printout of your invitation on regular white paper, along with your card stock, to a reputable printer in town and have him duplicate your invitations and smaller cards.

- Consider hiring a friend with great handwriting and some experience with calligraphy to hand write your invitations. Perhaps you could make this task her wedding gift to you, and remember to thank her at completion of the job with a nice note and perhaps a gift for her efforts.

Assembling the Invitations Packets

Once the invitations have come in and you've checked them for any spelling errors or other mistakes, then you're ready to assemble your invitations packets. As with everything else related to invitations, there is a correct way to do this. Most quality invitations companies will include with your order a printed brochure or letter that spells out the proper assembly of a formal or informal invitation. The instructions might include where to place the colored tissue paper on top of the print covers to prevent smudging of ink, the order in which to pile the inserts, and which direction the inner envelope should face when slid into the outer envelope. Follow these instructions thoroughly, as they will make your invitations packets more uniform.

Another step to take before you begin addressing your envelopes and assembling your invitations packages is making sure you have the full, correct addresses for everyone on your list. Your fiancé's side of the family should have provided its list already, and you should have all of your addresses. If there are any missing street numbers, apartment numbers, or zip codes, you can tackle the job quickly yourself with a phone call to that recipient.

Be sure that all of your inner envelopes and outer envelopes are written out correctly. Outer envelopes are addressed to the guests, with their full names and addresses written out, and all abbreviations spelled out. Inner envelopes list just the names of the people invited. If this envelope is for a family, the inner envelope will read *Mr. and Mrs.*

> ## Simplify It
>
> Create an assembly line of invitation inserts and folding and inserting spots. Set out all of the items in the correct order, and then ask your fiancé, family, and select bridal-party members to help you assemble the invitations. Put one person in charge of matching the inner envelopes with the outer envelopes, so that the names written on each do match. Streamline this process, and you could be done assembling hundreds of invitations in very little time.

Smith with the children's names *Sarah, Aimee, and Dennis* centered below their parent's names.

It is very important that the names of the actual guests you are inviting appear on this inner envelope; otherwise, your guests may assume their kids are invited or not invited. It leaves room for questions, and assumptions may be made.

After you write the names on each inner envelope, immediately do the outer envelope. A sample reads as follows:

Mr. and Mrs. Joseph Daniels
7 Indiana Terrace
Davenport, Iowa 87369

Again, all words are spelled out. And, never send an invitation without a zip code written down, as a zip code is fundamentally important. Without it, an invitation may get lost or delayed during its journey, and the guest may be offended that he or she wasn't invited to the wedding. If you're stumped on the zip code for a guest's town, check the U.S. postal site at www.usps.gov for an official listing of national zip codes.

One item that often trips up brides and grooms is guests who are bringing a "date." In every case, a guest may only bring a date if it has been stated on the invitation that he or she is welcome to do so. In no case should a guest call you and ask to bring a guest when you haven't offered. If someone does commit this grievous faux pas, simply state that there's just not enough room for extra people. You had to leave some of your second cousins off the list, so it's a matter of space. This seems to happen a lot with teenage guests. Parents feel that their teenage daughter would have a better time if her boyfriend could join her, but you are under no obligation unless it's your heartfelt choice to allow the boyfriend to come. Adults over eighteen should always be given an "and guest" on their invitation even if you're not aware that they are involved with anyone at the time.

When addressing the inner envelope to a guest who has indicated that he will be bringing a date, be sure to write the date's name, rather than "Paul Smith and Guest." That's far too impersonal.

When to Send Out Your Invitations

Traditionally, wedding invitations go out six to eight weeks before the wedding. This allows your guests plenty of time to clear their calendars in order to attend your event. They'll have to check their work schedules, their travel plans, their kids' vacation and activity plans, and even perhaps schedule medical tests for a different time. Giving your guests plenty of notice is just good form in showing consideration for their needs, and more of your guests will show up at your wedding.

If you're asking guests to travel across several states to attend your wedding, or if you've asked them to attend your destination wedding in St. Lucia, you'll need to respect their planning time by giving them even more notice than those eight weeks. Ten to twelve weeks should be fine. The more time in this situation, the better.

RSVPs

You will need a final guest headcount in advance in order to finalize your catering, floral, and favor orders. So be sure to list an RSVP date on your invitations with enough lead time for you to place your orders in advance. Do not heed any advice stating that response cards and RSVPs are passé. You will need these solid numbers for your own planning and budget purposes.

Most guests do respond in ample time, but there are always those stragglers who do not send the little response card back. That will require a simple call from you, whereby the guest ought to know if he is or isn't coming to the wedding. Many brides have had to take a hard stand here, due to the irresponsible nature of the guest. Some non-committal types respond with a very unhelpful "I don't know yet. . . ." or "I have to check my schedule still. . . ." As nice as you may want to be, this is not the time to say, "Okay, whenever you're ready just let me know." Simply explain that you're on a rushed deadline and you need to know right away.

Your Wedding Program

The wedding program is handed out to all of your guests on the wedding day so that they can learn the names of the people in your bridal party and so that they will know the progression of your ceremony. They'll certainly want to know the name of that lovely song that's playing as you walk down the aisle, and if it's a hot day they'll want to know how long the ceremony is going to be.

Designing your wedding program is something that you can do on your own. Although you're certainly free to order a printed program from an invitations catalog, most couples design and lay out their programs on their home computers and print the final versions out on plain white paper, hued paper, or bridal-designed paper complete with pictures of bubbling champagne glasses, wedding rings, or doves. These printed papers may serve as the program itself, or they may be folded and tucked into beautifully designed program covers that you can order online or at gift shops.

Your program's design is up to you, but here are the main elements that most couples include:

Rather than pay for response cards and extra stamps, can't I just ask the guests to e-mail their responses to me?

That is becoming a trend, but in my opinion it's not a very good one. Some people, again, do not have e-mail. Some messages get lost in cyberspace. It's better to have those tangible little response cards for a sure headcount.

- *The front cover.* Place a pretty graphic here, perhaps a picture of the two of you, a pair of doves, or a picture of a wedding cake. The front cover is also inscribed with *The Wedding of,* your names, and your wedding date.

- *The inside cover.* List your own names as bride and groom, plus the complete names of your parents, bridal-party members, anyone participating in your ceremony, musicians, and the officiant.

- *The first page.* Provide a complete rundown of all of the ceremony elements, from the processional (and that lovely song that's playing while you're walking down the aisle), any readings, any musical performances, the vows, the exchange of rings, the pronouncement of husband and wife, and the recessional.

- *The back cover.* Most couples use this space to print a personal message of thanks to their guests for sharing the day with them, to their parents for helping to plan the perfect wedding, and to their families for their unconditional love and support. Also listed on this page might be a special tribute that lets guests know the floral arrangements are in memory of a departed parent, grandparent, sibling, or friend. At the very bottom, you might choose to include your new address, phone number, and e-mail address where you will be living as husband and wife after the wedding.

The Additional Mailer

This is a trend whose time has come. As weddings are now becoming more expansive events, with activities planned throughout the weekend, brides and grooms are sending out packets of material for their guests' use. The following are some of the best inclusion ideas I've seen:

- A personal computer-printed message from the bride and groom, sharing how the planning is coming along and how excited you both are for the big day

- A brochure of the hotel where they'll be staying (just ask the manager for as many as you need; it's free publicity, after all)
- A list of nearby hotels if the guests will be making their own plans
- A list of nearby restaurants
- A travel guide or tour book of the surrounding area, landmarks, spots to see, etc.
- A list of what movies are playing at the local theater
- A list of kid-friendly places in the area, such as playgrounds, zoos, museums, and parks
- A card stating the availability of baby-sitting services during the wedding and other weekend events
- Invitations to family events during the long weekend—barbecues, brunches, mini-golf tournaments, spa days, etc., listed with complete directions, prices, and coupons
- Maps to all wedding-specific sites
- Official invitations to all wedding-related events, along with dress-code advice
- A phone-number list for guests who wish to contact you or your family during the weekend
- A list of emergency phone numbers for that area
- A photocopy of the cable company's list of which television stations are carried on which channels (ingenious!)
- A travel care package for kids, including books, games, crossword-puzzle books, joke books, crayons and pads, and healthy snacks

Other Printed Items

At this time, you should also think about the other printed items that you may need for your big day. Think about your print needs, and consider the following:

• *Personalized stationery.* Choose a simple style, an elegant letterhead, and personal stationery. One of the advantages of placing this order now is that you will have professional and official stationery that declares your name and whether or not you'll take your husband's name.

• *Thank-you notes.* These are a must for the bridal couple's print order. Choose a simple style with a basic message on the cover and a cutout for a wedding photo, and one that is blank inside, rather than one with a preprinted message. As you do have to write a handwritten message anyway—it's a must by etiquette standards!—this will save you time, room, and money.

Simplify It

Y*ou don't have to buy stationery and letterhead that matches the style and print of your other wedding papers. You're actually likely to find a better deal through another company: An Invitation to Buy—Nationwide at www.invitations4sale .com offers a wide range of cards, papers, and letterheads in a variety of prints and colors.*

• *Place cards.* Most couples do hand write their own place cards or print them out with the use of a home computer. If you'd prefer a more formal, elegant style, and if you have the budget for such an extravagance, then consider getting your place cards professionally printed.

• *Maps.* You can create personalized maps through several Web sites such as www.Go.com and www.MapQuest.com. Just choose your site and destinations, the type of route you want, and then click a button to generate a great, printable map for your use.

• *Menu cards.* Some couples are placing elegantly printed menu cards at the center of each guest table. This way, the guest can see what's on the menu for dinner and dessert and pace his eating at the cocktail hour accordingly.

• *What's this dish?* These are cards for the buffet table that identify seafood quiches, entrees, and soups. Many couples do like to let their guests know what is in each of the menu presentations not only as a courtesy, but also to alert family members who may have an allergy to peanuts, garlic, dairy products, or sugar.

- *Invitations to the rehearsal dinner.* The honored guests do have to be invited officially, with directions to the restaurant and the correct date and time included on the invitation.

- *Invitations to post-wedding events and the bridal brunch.* Again, invited guests will need a printed reminder of where they're to be and when.

- *Printed cards to accompany favors.* If you're giving out seed packets or chocolates to your guests, you might want to print out a little thank-you note to attach to each gift. This isn't the official thank-you note, mind you, but rather a nice way to express your gratitude for their presence on the wedding day.

Favors and Gifts

I**T'S** TIME for a shopping spree! Throughout your wedding-planning process, your loved ones have been there for you, supported you, helped plan the big day, and traveled far and wide to be a part of your wedding. Now, it's time to give a little something back to express your gratitude and love. In this section, you'll decide on the many gifts you'll give to your bridal party, parents, and each other, plus the favors you'll present to all of your guests after the reception.

No matter what your budget, no matter what your style, you'll find plenty of fun, creative, and touching options available to you. The favor and gift part of the wedding industry has exploded with new selections in response to brides and grooms wanting to give their guests something a little more special than the bag of pastel-colored candies and the wine glass with their names and wedding date on it. Couples nowadays have more elegant tastes, and their choices of favors and gifts get far more personal than that. This section will help you decide which favors and gifts are right for your guests, and which fit in with the style and expense of your wedding. Get your credit card ready: This is the fun part!

Choosing Great Favors

Of course you'll want to present lovely gifts to all of your guests, but when you have a large amount of people attending your wedding, you might be looking at a hundred or so individual presents. With the nicer gifts—such as Lalique crystal vases, silver picture frames, and even fine bottles of wine or champagne—in the upper stratosphere of expense, you're looking at quite a high budget amount. Even for more moderately priced items, your need for one hundred of them could run you in the thousands of dollars for favors alone. But don't worry. There are wonderful, inexpensive options that look more expensive than they are, and with a bit of creative presentation and added meaning, your guests will have no idea that you acquired these selections on the cheap. (It's the meaning that counts, of course, but the appearance of extravagance is still impressive.)

The following are some popular favor ideas to consider:

• *Candles and candleholders.* Who doesn't love a great, scented pillar candle or a delicately hued candleholder to place next to their bed? The popularity of candles is expanding now, with catalogs and gift shops offering a wide range of aromas and shapes. The Illuminations catalog (800-621-2998, www.illuminations.com) even offers floating butterfly candles and theme candles such as those to attract love, prosperity, good health, and serenity. For greater savings, check out the selection of candles and holders at a craft store where you can buy in bulk.

• *Godiva chocolates.* They're the hallmark of wedding favors. Those small gold boxes, called ballotins containing mouthwatering truffles and selections of milk-chocolate goodies are the gold standard in the bridal industry, and you might be surprised by the very affordable price tag on the two- and four-piece boxes. Godiva also prints personalized ribbons for adorning your favor boxes. An added bonus for beach-theme weddings is the selection of Godiva starfish-shaped chocolates, usually filled with a sweet raspberry filling. Place a special order for a mountain of these, and package them yourselves in great little gift boxes or see-through plastic gift containers.

- *Candies.* If the weather is likely to be sweltering, chocolate favors may not be your best bet. Instead, fill tulle pouches or plastic gift boxes with candies that match the theme of your wedding. If your first date was on Valentine's Day, why not honor that memory by filling favor boxes with heart-shaped candies? You'll find candies in every shape, size, and flavor, even matching the theme of your wedding. You can match your color scheme as well.

- *Potpourri bowls.* Again, head to the craft store to find a wide range of pretty, little glass potpourri bowls in every shape and size. Some have delicate silver lids, which at any price add the impression of extravagance. Fill the bowls with fragrant potpourri in your wedding colors for a pleasing and lasting favor.

- *Silver frames.* The old standard has polished its image, so to speak. In years past, brides and grooms offered their guests small silver frames that may have held a place card or a picture of the happy couple. Now, frame choices offer an even more expansive variety of shapes, styles, and budgets, and you'll also find functional frames that play music or have a voice chip inside that plays a recorded message. For a less formal wedding, why not supply more whimsical picture frames, such as those with sea-themed or floral decorations lining the outer borders of the frame? Frames are among the most practical favors offered these days, and you'll find choices for all budgets, from the high-end Tiffany styles to the craft-store bulk buys.

- *A nice bottle of bubbly.* Wines and champagnes make great favors, and you can find high-quality vintages at lower prices, depending upon where you choose to shop. Some discount liquor stores will negotiate great per-case deals. Your coupled guests might take their bottles back to the hotel room for their own private toasts and celebrations after your wedding is over. For underage guests, don't bother with the sparkling cider or the nonalcoholic wine. Have a separate basket of goodies just for them.

• *CD mixes.* The hot trend right now is for compilations of your favorite romantic songs burned onto CDs and packaged with a personalized cover. You can create these song mixes through established companies, or you can create them yourselves using your own home-computer technology. This is a fun project that can be shared by brides and grooms, who report that they loved filling a CD with "their songs" and sharing it with their loved ones.

• *Plants and flowers.* In keeping with the outdoor, natural theme of your wedding, consider giving your guests potted flowers, plants, or seedlings for their own home gardens. One bride chose to give out small gardenia plants to all of her guests, in tribute to her departed grandmother who had a passion for gardenias. It makes the bride smile knowing that all of those gardenia plants went out to her 175 guests and are now growing in their gardens. "It makes me feel like I just spread my grandmother's love even wider, even after she's gone," the bride said emotionally. Another, less expensive option for an informal outdoor wedding is a packet of flower seeds. One bride with a sunflower-themed garden wedding gave each of her guests a gift basket with packets of sunflower seeds, a sunflower magnet, a matching notepad, and a small bottle of perfume called Sunflowers. The theme grouping was great, and the guests loved the multipack of gifts.

• *Pampering products.* The basket of minigifts also works when you create men's and women's collections of theme-scent pampering products such as perfumes, lotions, massage oils, and soaps. One couple planning

Simplify It

Rather than wander all through a gourmet wine shop or liquor store searching for a nice bottle of wine, check out the ratings, descriptions, and price ranges of each vintage on Wine Spectator's Web site at www.winespectator.com. Here, you can review a primer on wines and even plan a prewedding wine tasting so your bridal party can assist in choosing the wine favors.

a beach wedding put together "summer kits" filled with sunblock creams, sunblock lip balms, aloe lotion, fun sunglasses, and men's and women's paperback novels for their guests' vacation use. Children received kid-friendly sunblock, beach toys, and kid-themed sunglasses.

• *The big-ticket items.* If you have a sky's-the-limit budget, you might choose to go the ultra-extravagant route and give each of your guests tickets to a nearby theater production, ballet, concert, or sporting event.

Simplify It

Pretty groupings of favors can serve as your centerpieces, thereby eliminating the cost of expensive floral center-décor.

Whatever your choice of favors, be sure to label the adults' and children's versions, attach a note of thanks to each, and plan your method of disbursement. You might choose to arrange the favors on a special table near the exit for your guests' own selection. Or, arrange the favors in the centers of the guest tables.

Avoid one bride's hassle by speaking with the site manager ahead of time if you're expecting her staff to arrange the favors for you. Ellen shares her story of her own lack of foresight: "We just dropped off the case of favor wine bottles and kids' bottles of soda pop. We had forgotten to affix the name and table-number tags to the tops of each one, so the reception site staff had to do it when they found the labels at the bottom of the box. Not knowing who was an adult and who was a child, they just randomly attached labels. Needless to say, we were surprised at the wedding when my father got a bottle of soda as his favor and my four-year-old nephew got a bottle of Merlot. It was an avoidable mix-up if we'd only been more careful."

Choosing Great Gifts

Throughout your engagement, everyone has been giving you gifts—at your engagement party, showers, and bridal brunches—but now it's time for you to plan your gift list for all of your most special loved ones. Including each other. The gift from the bride and groom is your way of thanking your family and friends not just for the assistance they've given during the planning process and on the wedding day, but for the years of love and support they have given throughout your lives. Couples devote a great deal of thought to coming up with the perfect gifts for their parents, bridal parties, and each other, as this presentation is filled with meaning and will be treasured and remembered for a long time to come. Here, start your brainstorming process with my suggestions for great gifts.

For Your Parents

Regardless of whether or not they helped plan and pay for your wedding, parents always deserve a special gift from the two of you. Very often, it's a highly personalized gift, something that fits with their interests and loves. Consider the following options to get your own thoughts rolling:

- Tickets to a concert by their favorite performer
- A weekend away at a bed-and-breakfast or resort location
- A dinner cruise
- A day of beauty or massage at a spa or salon
- A round of golf at a pro-tour golf course
- A collection of free movie-theater passes
- A "wine of the month" club membership
- A gift certificate for a course at an adult school (cooking classes, tai chi, gardening, ballroom dancing, a travel or educational lecture and slide show, etc.)
- His and hers engraved watches
- Tickets to a sporting event for a team they both love—for extra "favorite child" points, make it a play-off game!
- A professionally edited videotape of your family's old home movies, with a soundtrack of their favorite songs

- A professionally edited videotape of your parents "growing older together." Start with old reels of their childhood days or stills of their childhood snapshots and continue through their lives together to the present day.

For Your Bridesmaids and Maid of Honor

They're your favorite women, and they went through a lot to be in your bridal party. So thank them now for their years of laughter and love with a special gift:

- Jewelry to wear on the wedding day
- Engraved silver bracelets
- Tickets to a play, concert, ballet, opera, or favorite sporting event
- A day of pampering at a spa or salon
- A silver picture frame with your favorite picture of the two of you (some brides get a double picture frame to hold a picture of both of you when you were little girls and a present-day shot of you as successful, beautiful women)
- A fine perfume and matching-scent lotion kit
- Personalized jewelry box
- Something to support her future goals: a membership in a yoga class (if she's expressed interest), payment of the entry fee for a professional conference she's been dying to attend, a new leather portfolio for an up-and-coming ad executive, a class at an adult school for one of her new artistic passions
- A professionally edited videotape of your growing-up years together
- A gift certificate to a bookstore she loves
- A professional makeover and an appointment with a personal shopper at a department store (if she's expressed interest)

For the Groomsmen and Best Man

It's up to the groom to choose his gifts for his brothers and buddies, so consider the following popular options here:

- Engraved beer mugs
- Engraved money clips
- Engraved cuff links
- Engraved watch
- A day of golf at a ritzy pro-tour golf course
- Tickets to a concert or sporting event (preferably the play-offs or a championship game)
- A framed picture of "'the guys" in your prime
- A professionally edited videotape of your growing-up years together
- A bottle of fine port, brandy, or cognac to be shared on a special occasion

FOR PARTICIPANTS IN YOUR WEDDING CEREMONY OR RECEPTION

Your loved ones may have graciously offered their assistance with the desserts, the setup and cleanup, or reading a passage during the ceremony. Thank them on the big day with a special gift of gratitude, even if you've arranged for their service to be their wedding gift to you. They're giving of themselves to make your day more special, so present them with a little something special to show your thanks:

- Tickets to a movie or show
- A bottle of wine or liqueur
- A gift certificate to a favorite store, such as a bookstore or music store
- A silver locket
- A silver picture frame
- Chocolates or candies

FOR CHILDREN

If one or both of you have children, and you're blending your families together, it's a wonderful idea for each of you to give the children a special gift. Though the "family medallion" necklace is often used as part of the wedding ceremony, symbolizing the shared vow between the entire new family, a little something extra is in order for kids:

- A diamond necklace or child-appropriate diamond ring
- An engraved watch
- An engraved charm bracelet
- A much-wanted big-ticket toy, such as a PlayStation or the complete Barbie Dream House with pool and cabana, Corvette convertible, and riding stables
- A gift certificate to a favorite store
- The promise of a much-wanted item, such as a ski trip with friends or the keys to the old family car
- Tickets to the hottest teen concert coming through town
- A wardrobe shopping spree
- A day of beauty at a spa or salon
- Their own bedroom in the new house

For Each Other

Of course, you've already exchanged the best gifts possible: agreeing to spend the rest of your lives together. But the emotion and meaning of the wedding day certainly calls for a special present that once again says "thank you" for all you've shared so far.

Today's brides and grooms do exchange the traditional gifts, such as a string of pearls or diamond earrings for the bride to wear on the wedding day and gold cuff links for the groom to wear with his tuxedo. But now, weddings gifts between bride and groom are far more functional and fun, reflecting shared interests and goals, plus a splash of romance:

- His and hers engraved watches
- Something to support each other's career and personal goals, such as membership in a certification course or entry fee to an important networking conference

- His and hers membership to a ritzy health spa or country club (the couple who plays together stays together!)
- Mountain bikes
- Kayak and oars
- A new car
- Something priceless: changing the name of your boat to the bride's name
- Hyphenating both of your names together, officially
- A much-wanted collector's item, such as an authentic signed baseball by a childhood sports hero

- A favorite book in bound leather version, signed by the author
- A new dog or cat, either pedigreed or a lovable mutt from the animal shelter
- Professional framing of each other's most esteemed accomplishments, such as a certificate for a writing-contest award, a diploma, a letter of praise from the CEO of the company, acceptance to a prestigious program or club
- A year of maid service or lawn-care service (you'll be too busy as newlyweds to dust or mow the lawn on a regular basis!)
- A mailbox with your new names on it
- Presentation of all of your saved love letters, tied with a red ribbon

Wedding Day Reflections

I actually photocopied several pages and entries from my journal and arranged them in a photo album with pictures of us throughout our early dating and engagement years. I then presented the album to my fiancé the night before the wedding, and he loved reading what I was thinking back then. Especially the fact that I wrote in my journal "I think he's The One" after our third date. He was smiling from ear to ear when he read my descriptive and complimentary account after our first romantic weekend together.

—Sandy

Guest Hotel-Room Gift Baskets

It's always nice to provide a little welcome basket for your guests who have traveled into town and are staying at a nearby hotel for your wedding weekend. Such a gift gives them a message of your gratitude for their traveling hassles and expenses, and it invites them to relax and enjoy themselves—without having to hit the pricey minibar. Here are some great filler ideas for their baskets:

- Little bottles of spring water
- Sodas and juices
- Packets of crackers and snacks
- Gum and breath mints
- Chocolates
- Guidebooks to nearby sites of interest
- Tickets to the local movie theater
- Aromatherapy kits, such as The Healing Garden's ZZZTherapy line of relaxing body mists, lotions, and bath salts
- A reminder card of where to be and when for the rehearsal dinner and other family activities
- Games and toys for the kids
- A silk eye pillow
- Fuzzy slippers

> ## Wedding Day Reflections
>
> We did the Night of Passion baskets for all of our coupled guests—providing one for ourselves on the wedding night as well. And at the all-inclusive brunch the morning after the wedding, everyone was walking around with big smiles on their faces and holding hands! We loved that!
>
> —Jaimie and Peter

For your coupled guests—those without kids staying in their room—you might want to share the romance with a "Night of Passion" basket:

- A bottle of champagne
- Scented massage oil
- Scented bath soaps and lotions
- Scented candles with safe glass candleholders and a lighter
- Chocolate-covered strawberries
- Chocolate body paints
- A book on revving up sexual techniques, such as the *Kama Sutra*
- A plumed feather

Toss-Its

For the wedding day, your guests will want to throw something at you right after you're pronounced as husband and wife. Because many outdoor sites forbid the use of rice (it kills the birds), rose petals, and even bird seed, you'll have to get more creative with the post-wedding toss-its.

For most couples, a sea of bubbles works just fine. Your guests can blow bubbles from mini-bubble holders sold at most wedding Web sites. You can also find cases of them in decorative plastic containers at craft stores, near the wedding–ribbons-and-favors section.

Ask the site manager about her location's rules for toss-its. Some have strict policies about rose petals, confetti, and other commonly tossed items. Another item to inquire into is whether the site has a policy about the release of butterflies after your wedding. Though the release of these lovely winged creatures is a popular wedding activity these days, some arboretums and botanical gardens have rules prohibiting this practice. Their gardens are highly controlled environments, and the introduction of a new breed of butterfly could upset the delicate balance of growth and nature in the area.

If your wedding will be held in your own backyard, then you're free to supply your guests with any toss-it you'd like, arranging for cleanup afterward. Please do keep in mind the safety of any animals or wildlife in the area, as rice does kill birds that eat it and small animals could be harmed by metallic confetti. Environmentalists do ask that you refrain from releasing helium balloons into the air, as they too cause harm to animals when they float back down to Earth.

> ## *Wedding Day Reflections*
>
> The bridal party actually planned the *"What a Wonderful World"* serenade as a surprise to us, knowing that's our favorite song. They handed the guests a separate pink piece of paper with all of the words to the song, and they encouraged the guests to sing it in Louis Armstrong's raspy voice! It was touching and hysterical at the same time.
>
> —Lynne and Jamal

If you're not looking forward to getting bird seed down the front of your dress or sticky bubble solution on your face, then you might choose to skip the toss-its altogether. Your guests can break into song as you dash by as husband and wife. Several brides report this fun addition to even a formal wedding ceremony, as guests were prompted on their wedding programs to start singing "What a Wonderful World" by Louis Armstrong when the bride and groom began the recessional.

Throwaway Cameras

Place one single-use camera in the center of each guest table with a note instructing the guests to take their own fun, candid shots throughout the reception. These throwaway cameras are inexpensive, and they guarantee you'll capture the kinds of shots that take place behind the scenes while the official photographer is focused on you.

Place a large basket by the reception exit with a note "Please place throwaway cameras here" so that guests remember them leave it for you.

The Emergency Bag

It's the smart bride who brings her own emergency tote along to the wedding. In it, store such essentials as breath mints or spray, aspirin, a nail file, several extra pairs of stockings, clear nail polish for minor snags, pressed powder to get rid of shine, a lipstick, a cell phone, a list of all necessary phone numbers, hairspray, contact-lens solution and holder, extra earrings (in case you lose one during the night), a small bottle of baby powder for chafing thighs under your dress on a hot day, tissues, safety pins, tweezers (for removing splinters and stingers), sunscreen, a small water bottle, a pair of comfortable flat shoes for dancing, perfume, and any allergy medications or insulin kits needed that day.

Some special items to consider for an outdoor wedding:

- A small container of meat tenderizer (not for the caterer to use, but to treat any bee stings suffered at your outdoor wedding)
- Mosquito-repellant cans
- Pretty paper fans for a break from the heat
- Sunblock lip balm
- Shine-free face-blotting papers
- Sunglasses
- Fabric-stain wipe cloths, for spills and grass marks
- Band-Aids

Destination Weddings

Your dream may be to have an outdoor wedding—in Hawaii. Perhaps you've seen pictures of brides and grooms exchanging their vows in a tropical forest, next to a beautiful waterfall with hibiscus plants flowering all around. You may have heard of the "island luck" that is supposedly conveyed by marrying at the Seven Sacred Pools of Hana, an ancient spot favored by old Hawaiian royalty. Or you have your sights set on an outdoor wedding in Paris. Whatever your dream destination, planning a wedding at a distance does take a little extra legwork. How do you plan a wedding over the phone? How can you truly assess the beauty of a beachside spot in Bermuda only from the pictures in the brochures? What are the legalities of marrying in a faraway land? Here, you'll learn the basics of destination outdoor-wedding planning, so that you can work with an on-site coordinator to create your perfect day.

As the term *destination wedding* refers to any wedding you're planning far away from home, we're also talking about planning your wedding in your old hometown clear across the country. So don't flip past this chapter thinking "Well, I'm not having my wedding in Bali, so this doesn't apply to me." It certainly does if you're marrying at any distance. Here are the classic breakdowns of destination weddings, so that you can see which category you fit into:

- *The vacation wedding.* The bride and groom forego the traditional celebration at the banquet hall in their hometown and instead plan their nuptials for an island or foreign getaway spot.

- *The my hometown/your hometown wedding.* The bride and groom come from two different areas of the country (or the world), and instead of shipping half the guests for miles, they host one celebration in the bride's town and another in the groom's hometown.

- *The last-minute getaway wedding.* The bride and groom don't want all of the fuss, all of the family involvement, and all of the details that go into planning a traditional wedding. They just want to be married. So whether it's a one-week planning process or a one-minute decision to hop a plane to Las Vegas, spontaneity is the essence of the last-minute wedding.

Planning a destination wedding does take some extra effort, and that translates into extra time needed to make all of your arrangements. This is especially true if you're planning your wedding for an outside spot in a foreign country. Brides and grooms tell me that it often took weeks to receive information packets from far-flung sites, and in some cases the legal red tape did cause some stress and headaches when unexpected and lengthy delays threatened to hold up the works. So schedule "waiting times" into your planning calendar to prevent any problems.

Where Should You Go?

Do you want that tropical beach with its crystal-clear blue waters? Or do you want an outdoor wedding at Walt Disney World? A private ceremony for the two of you by a pyramid in Egypt? A yacht wedding in the Mediterranean? When choosing the perfect location, you are determining the amount of effort that will go into planning your destination wedding. Obviously, if you're choosing a spot in a foreign country, you'll have to learn and follow the rules for that country's many stringent permissions and tests. If you want the Hawaiian wedding, there is far less diplomatic hassle.

Luckily for you, destination weddings are so very popular now that the bridal and tourism industries offer well-oiled procedures. Most resorts and international tourism boards are well versed in arranging destination weddings, so most of the information you need will already be assembled and available to you. Many resorts boast their own highly trained wedding-coordinating staffs and a wide range of wedding packages. If you do choose a site that's known for its destination weddings, you might be surprised at just how easy the process is.

Many couples say that they were nervous to hire a wedding coordinator at a faraway resort, sight unseen. How could they be sure the wedding coordinator would fulfill their requests exactly as specified? Was ordering everything over the phone or through a fax or e-mail a smart idea? In the end, these same couples said that they couldn't have been happier. Everything worked out exactly as they had planned—in some cases, even better—but only because they did a stellar job of handling the planning. They completed thorough research, asked friends and family for referrals to favorite resorts and locations, located reputable resorts with a large amount of experience in

> ## *Wedding Day Reflections*
>
> The Four Seasons in Las Vegas had their act so together that it took little more than a few phone calls to arrange everything. We chose the coordinator with the most experience; communicated by phone, fax, and e-mail; and always asked for pictures of what we had to choose from. We made our choices very clear, and just a few days later we arrived in Vegas to find the wedding we had requested waiting for us! It was amazing!
>
> —Jennifer

planning destination weddings, and kept in constant contact with their coordinators.

As you begin your research, you will find a great many resorts of all types opening their doors to you. Save yourselves time by talking over your wishes at the outset. Do you definitely want the outdoor wedding on the beach? Or are you open to a lush garden setting? Do you have a particular attraction to a certain island? What other elements of a resort attract you? Perhaps you want the beach wedding, but you also want to honeymoon at the same resort. Does that resort offer the amenities you desire? A professional-grade golf course? A spa? A five-star restaurant? Sports activities? Nightlife? For this purpose, you are combining your ceremony plans with your plans for your honeymoon. So even as you're picking out flowers, cakes, and officiants, you're also looking at room rates and hotel offerings. Keep your plans organized and coordinate your questions so that you can find the best spot for you.

Simplify It

If you are a member of AAA, visit your local AAA office to request free brochures and guidebooks for the destinations you have in mind. Most of these books include detailed accounts of the average weather patterns and temperatures for every month of the year.

Another thing to keep in mind is travel time. How far away do you want to travel? Do you want to spend eight hours on a plane getting to a foreign country? Will you and your guests mind that it takes a larger plane, then a little puddle-jumper plane, and then a small motorboat to get to your secluded resort of choice? Some locations are a bit more involved to reach, and some couples would rather avoid tricky travel itineraries, both for their own relaxation and for their guests' comfort.

The weather is also a factor. Will it be hurricane season at the island you're considering for your August wedding? Is it the rainy season in Borneo? What about heat and humidity? Some brides say they skipped their plans for a Florida wedding in the summer, knowing

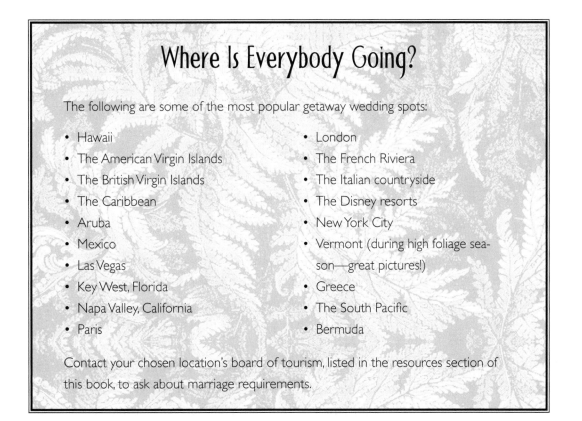

Where Is Everybody Going?

The following are some of the most popular getaway wedding spots:

- Hawaii
- The American Virgin Islands
- The British Virgin Islands
- The Caribbean
- Aruba
- Mexico
- Las Vegas
- Key West, Florida
- Napa Valley, California
- Paris

- London
- The French Riviera
- The Italian countryside
- The Disney resorts
- New York City
- Vermont (during high foliage season—great pictures!)
- Greece
- The South Pacific
- Bermuda

Contact your chosen location's board of tourism, listed in the resources section of this book, to ask about marriage requirements.

that the humidity would make everyone way too uncomfortable. Check the average temperatures, rainfall amounts, and storm-season details through your chosen location's tourism bureau. Most offer organized charts of the average weather on their brochures and Web sites, and you can ask a tourism associate for a breakdown of the expected weather at the time you're considering.

The last, and perhaps most important, issue when deciding where to go is the safety of the area. Some locations experience civil unrest, and you don't want your getaway marred by a riot or unsafe conditions. If you're looking at any foreign destination or island, check the U.S. State Department's Travel Advisory page at www.travel.state.gov. There you will find listings of active warnings against traveling to or through any spot that's experiencing war or danger to American tourists.

Who's Coming Along?

Most couples who plan getaway weddings do invite their closest family members and friends to make the trip and attend their nuptials. Depending upon how far you're traveling and the details of your location, you might choose to limit your guest list to only your most immediate relatives and friends. It's quite an imposition to ask all two hundred of your guests to book a trip to Fiji for your wedding, and the planning of such a big wedding on-site is a huge effort. So decide on your guest list and bear in mind that many couples marry in the company of their family and friends at a faraway resort, and then return home to hold an official reception with the entirety of their guest list.

Choose your travel mates well, taking into account their own budgets, work schedules, education schedules, and accrued vacation days. Talk personally with each person on your list, and decide if there's room in your budget for you to pick up your loved ones' travel expenses.

If either of you have children, and you're combining your families, think about choosing a destination that offers programs for kids. This is your wedding/honeymoon, after all, and you will certainly want some quiet, romantic time to yourselves. Ask the travel agent or resort wedding coordinator about day camp or activities for kids at the resort so that you will be assured that your kids are safely entertained while you're taking a bubble bath together back in the room. For instance, the Maui Loves Kids program offers the services of a wedding-planning coordinator, and when the ceremony is over, the kids are kept busy with a long list of fun activities and day trips.

If you have decided to ask a larger group of friends and family along for the trip, keep the following issues in mind:

1. Have you given your guests enough time to make their travel plans?

2. Are your guests going to be in school, studying for their bar or medical exams, or planning their own weddings at the same time?

3. Can your guests afford the travel expenses?

4. Can you get a block of rooms at the same location where the wedding will be held? Especially in high tourist seasons, you don't want your guests to stay at a one-star hotel while you're staying at a five-star. You also don't want the headaches of having your guests scattered among four different resorts on the island.

5. Will your guests have to go get passports?

6. Are any of your guests afraid to fly?

7. Is there handicapped access at the resort you're choosing, or on the modes of transportation needed to get to the island?

The Legalities

For any wedding, you will have to acquire your state's required licenses and blood tests or physical exams. For a destination wedding, you will actually have to do twice the work. You'll need to research the current requirements of your destination—and I say current, because you cannot depend on Internet information or book information but will have to call the state or country's board of marriage licensing for the most recent and applicable laws. You'll have to make all of the arrangements from where you are. Many brides say this took a lot of time and effort, requiring hours of correspondence, research, and confirmations. Pictures and sample wedding videos needed to be mailed and received, reviewed and considered. Menus needed to be planned. Flowers needed to be chosen. On top of that might be the issue of a great time difference between your home and the country or island in question. In such a case, you might have to make all of your business calls to the coordinator in the middle of the night! For any destination you will have to ask the following questions:

1. What documents are needed for the filing of our marriage license?

2. Can you supply us with a copy of the officiant's license to perform weddings?

3. Is there a residency requirement? (Some locations require that you be present in the country for a specified number of days, which establishes residency. Be aware of this number of days, so that you can make your travel plans accordingly.)

4. Are blood tests from our home state applicable there?

5. If not, what is the time limit and time requirements for blood tests at your location?

6. Where do we get blood tests at your location?

7. How many witnesses are needed?

8. What are the requirements for witnesses? (Some locations require that the witnesses have known both of you for a certain period of time. You can't just grab the taxi driver and have him be the witness.)

9. Do you need to see proof of divorce?

10. Do you need to see proof of annulment?

11. What kind of religious licensing do you require?

12. Do we need a translator? This is important, as many brides and grooms find that their ceremony is performed in a language they don't understand, and their marriage certificate is also in a different language.

Finding a Destination-Wedding Planner

Your destination wedding is only going to be as good as the person who's planning it. Therefore, it's vitally important that you thoroughly research and interview the men and women you're considering for that valuable role. Many of the best-known resorts all over the world hire excellent, well-trained wedding planners with credentials that would make your head spin, and it is your job to research them as you would any other wedding expert—more so, in this case, because the coordinator is charged with so many responsibilities on-site. As always, ask to see a copy of the planner's professional license, membership in a professional planners' association (such as the Association of Bridal Consultants or the International Special Event Society), and a rundown of the planner's experience. Do not be afraid to ask too many questions, as a qualified planner is going to expect the informed bride and groom to be knowledgeable and request a lot of information.

If a planner sighs a lot and acts like you're wasting time, move on to the next candidate. You want a professional planner who will work well with you, and a friendly, understanding personality is going to make for a better partnership. You will be in contact with this person a lot, at all hours of the day and night, and at times when the planner is extremely busy. Her willingness to treat you like an important client is vital, and you should have a good, intuitive level of confidence and comfort with her.

> ## Simplify It
>
> Ask for a copy of the resort's press packet in addition to its wedding-planning packet. The best resorts will provide not only brochures and photos of their wedding offerings, but more information about the resort's amenities and reviews in high-level publications.

Always work with only one planner. Some of the larger resorts offer teams of coordinators who work on each wedding, and that can make for miscommunications and mix-ups. The one hand does not always know what the other hand is doing or has done already. So ask to work specifically with the one planner you've chosen, get her name, and make her your wedding-planning partner.

WORKING WITH THE PLANNER

Your partnership with the wedding coordinator requires a great deal of communication in order for your wedding to come out as you'd like. She can't read your mind, and you can't see the cake she has in front of her. So follow these rules for better cooperation and a better outcome:

1. Send pictures—for instance, many brides send pictures of the kinds of floral arrangements they want.

2. Ask for a sample menu and request that you be allowed to choose the elements of your reception meal.

3. Ask for weekly e-mailed updates and confirmations of orders placed and plans made.

4. Be clear at the outset about all of your must-haves and must-not-haves. The planner will appreciate having these guidelines in hand so that she doesn't waste your time or hers.

5. Don't be talked into anything you don't want.

6. Ask to be informed of any last-minute changes.

7. Give her your cell phone or beeper number in case of emergency notifications or questions.

8. Get a good contract with absolutely all plans spelled out, including the names of the professionals the planner has hired, the exact location of the ceremony, the types of flowers used in your bouquet, and all other details.

9. If a planner speaks of "verbal agreements" between herself and local professionals, ask for written contracts instead. Verbal agreements are grounds for disaster. All agreements should be in writing, for your own protection. If the planner balks and says "That's the way we do it here," then find another planner who will respect your wishes.

10. Ask for a videotape of the location, the grounds, and a wedding in progress at that site, keeping in mind that videos are professionally edited to show the resort in its best light. You are only using this sample as a way to see the grounds and the offerings more clearly.

11. Ask for the location's Web site address and check out what it features, whether it has testimonials from other brides and grooms or if it has been reviewed in popular travel magazines. Also examine the quality of the Web site design.

12. Get a complete, itemized listing of all fees, including tips, local taxes, and hidden charges.

13. Get the planner's personal and cell phone numbers and assurance that you can call when you need to. (Just be sure to keep time zones in mind, as one bride reports having woken her French planner up at 2 A.M.)

14. Remember that the planner is there to serve you, but she is not your personal slave. Treat her with respect, honor her knowledge, and do not blame her for delays and problems that are not her fault.

15. Pay with your credit card, never cash. It's the only way to reserve and protect your reservations and plans in case of a problem or cancellation.

Special Concerns for Destination Outdoor Weddings

In most cases, the first time you see your wedding location will be the moment you arrive at the resort. Some couples do take a short trip a year or so ahead of time to tour the grounds and inspect the merchandise, but most couples do step-in sight unseen.

As you will be at the mercy of the weather, be sure to arrange for an indoor alternate spot for your wedding. Jeffrey and Shana Landi of New York City were married near an old sugar mill on the island of Nevis. They report that another wedding taking place the same week as theirs had to be moved indoors into a lavish lounge. Those tropical storms can be unpredictable, and even the tropical heat can cause sweltering and melting. So discuss a plan B location with your planner in case of unexpected situations.

Anyone who has ever visited an island, particularly in the warmer months, can attest to the presence of any number of insects. Flying gnats make themselves at home near the resort's gardenia bushes, but they're unwelcome guests at your wedding. Talk to the coordinator about the resort's practice of spraying for insects. Some hotels do have an outstanding bug-repellant program, and others expect visitors to make do. If you're concerned about flying critters, arrange for your outdoor reception tent to sport pretty white-mesh mosquito-net sides to keep out the majority of pests.

One of the best steps you can take is putting off the planning of your ceremony and reception until a few days *after* you arrive. This gives you time to do some firsthand planning and reviewing of the coordinator's choices, make some switches, and relax into your environment during the days before the wedding.

Allow for your guests to deal with the heat. Plan your ceremony for a shaded location, or supply your guests with pretty, tropical-print fans and even color-coordinated umbrellas to block the sun. Some couples hire waiters to hand out crystal glasses of ice water with slices of lemon and tropical fruit to guests waiting out in the sun before the ceremony.

Speaking of drinks, know that being out in the hot sun can cause additional effects from alcoholic drinks. So although those daiquiris and piña coladas may make for great reception fare, hot and thirsty guests may gulp down too many before the effects kick in. So offer plenty of cold, nonalcoholic drinks as well, and be sure you offer some cold-food choices.

As for your wedding wardrobe, a destination outdoor wedding may make a full-length gown and train a bit . . . uncomfortable. If you're having a beach wedding, try a little white slipdress. If you're in the island mood and want to show some more skin at your informal seaside vows exchange, then wear a white bikini top and a pretty white sarong. (Don't forget the leis!) Your groom can dress the tropical part as well with khaki shorts and a lightweight white cotton shirt,

> ## Wedding Day Reflections
>
> We arrived at the resort in Nevis a week before our wedding, so we had time to switch our wedding-cake flavor to a great cheesecake we had at the resort's restaurant, and we even switched our location to the sugar mill once we saw how nice that site was. After the wedding, our guests left for home, and we stayed on for a week's honeymoon.
>
> —Jeffrey and Shana

or he can do the surf thing as well with a pair of black swim trunks. Dress for comfort, regardless of your destination. But do keep in mind foreign dress codes, so your sleeveless white dress doesn't get you thrown in jail.

Incorporate local flavor into your outdoor wedding. Use tropical flowers and fruits, local seafood, and island tropical drinks or authentic French or Italian wines while you're standing in a true European vineyard. Ask your coordinator about the safety and preparation of local foods and water, and create a menu that suits who you are and where you are.

Finally, if many of your guests can't be at your wedding, be sure to send a postcard or pick up some inexpensive souvenirs, and take plenty of great pictures to share with the folks at home. Some couples are going the high-tech route, setting up their laptop computers with cameras to capture the big event and broadcast it live online to their loved ones. Some resorts even offer this Webcam option as a part of their wedding package, so ask about such offers during your planning process.

The most important part of a destination wedding is safety. You may be at a lovely resort, but if the hotel staff warns against venturing off the grounds into nearby towns, adhere to local rules. If your resort is surrounded by a barbed-wire fence, it's probably for a good reason. So listen to government warnings and travel advisories and don't take your life in your own hands by going where it's not safe to be. Follow all safety precautions when participating in tours and sporting activities, so that your getaway wedding doesn't turn into a nightmare for all of you.

The 24-Hour Countdown

It all comes down to this! After a year or so of planning, choosing pictures from books, making phone calls, and sweating decisions, you're about to see your dream wedding come together. The last twenty-four hours before the wedding are likely to be a whirl of activity, with all of the last-minute arrangements that need to be made and family responsibilities that need to be carried through. Start here to map out your plans for the rehearsal and rehearsal dinner, and think your way through to an organized wedding-day morning, so that you'll be efficient, prepared, and able to walk into your wedding as relaxed as possible. The big tasks are complete. Now it's time to breathe deeply and watch it all materialize before you.

The Rehearsal

If you've ever been to a rehearsal, you know that the level of excitement and energy is palpable. Everyone's smiling, everyone's gathered together, and everyone's all abuzz. The party atmosphere must level out for just long enough to take care of the business at hand—walking through the steps of the ceremony. You'll invite the members of your bridal party and their guests, your family and their guests, any musicians or readers who will perform in the ceremony, and the officiant for a night-before-the-wedding walk-through. Once you arrange a time with the officiant, send your invited guests official invitations along with directions to get to the site. Have everyone confirm with you that they will be able to attend, as it's vitally important that all of your bridal-party members and ceremony participants know what they are to do and when.

Begin by showing the ushers where and how they are to seat the guests, and alert them to which relatives are to be seated in the first few rows. Some couples choose to ribbon off the first few reserved rows, and they give their grandparents, godparents, and other special guests with "VIP seating" pew cards with row numbers on them, so that the ushers will seat everyone correctly. You'd be surprised at how bent out of shape some guests get when the ushers do not know that the stepmother should be in the second row, not the first, so be clear about seating. Also, remind the ushers to walk slowly as they escort the guests, make small talk with the guests, and not rush even if a line is forming.

Be sure the groom and best man know where they will await your arrival before they take their places at the end of the aisle, and review your own walking path to approach the ceremony. Line your bridal party up in order and walk through the processional accompanied by the music you'll use the next day. Get your walking speed right, and be sure the person "giving you away" is comfortable with how you will link arms and how you will walk. The officiant will then take over to guide you through the steps of the ceremony, and you will then practice the recessional as a group.

Don't be afraid to ask questions, even those on behalf of your bridal party. You're the bride and groom; everyone expects you to be a little nervous, and they'll forgive a stream of questions and clarifications.

Be sure to have the musicians actually perform the entire song they will play during the ceremony, so that you can hear how it will sound on location. You might ask the trumpeters to tone it down a bit, or the harpist to play a bit more loudly. You might decide that the sounds of the waves nearby are drowning out the music, so some last-minute additions of microphones are in order. These are the kinds of details that must be handled now, so that everything is fine on the wedding day. The same rule applies for those who will read passages, poems, or psalms during the ceremony. Have them read through their parts so that they are comfortable with the wording, with the speed at which they should talk, and with when they are to do their part.

Don't break for the rehearsal dinner until you've run through the ceremony rehearsal at least twice. Some couples ask their bridal-party members and families to step outside for a bit while they practice their vows in place with the officiant. Be sure all details have been reviewed.

Another area to consider during the rehearsal is the site itself. Is the site set up as you've instructed? If not, when will it be? Can you drop in early the next morning to inspect the premises? Have all permits and licenses been filed with the site manager? Ask to see where the caterer's tent will be set up, if it's not already in place. Find out where the valets will be working. Make changes, if necessary.

Inspect the grounds thoroughly to see if you'd like to switch your approach line to the ceremony. Is there a great cobblestone path that

Simplify It

If your flower girl or ring bearer is young, you might have some trouble with the child's ability to walk down the aisle in an orderly fashion. Many brides I've spoken to said that a potential child tantrum isn't something you can prevent, so just encourage the child to do his or her part. If the child is resistant, then have a bridal-party member walk him or her down the aisle. Here's one trick shared by a rather ingenious couple I spoke to: "Let the child know that there is a lollipop waiting for them at the end of the aisle. The child may race down the aisle to get it, but at least he gets down the aisle!"

leads to the center aisle? Perhaps that would be better than descending the site's marble staircase a few dozen yards from the ceremony area. If you're already planning on the cobblestone or gravel walkway, how are your maids faring with their footing? If it's a difficult walk, especially in heels, then switch the path to the grassy walkway from a side approach. If the walkway seems a bit muddy after a rain, see if another path can be planned.

Be sure the site manager is aware of when the caterer, florist, and other professionals will arrive for their setup procedures. Hand her a list of whom to expect and when, and let her know about any large-scale deliveries or special access that will be needed the next day.

At the very end, ask again if anyone has any additional questions. Remind all of your ceremony participants that there's no such thing as a stupid question, as you all want the wedding to go smoothly. You might ask the officiant to give verbal cues during the ceremony if your guests of a different faith are having trouble following the progression, and you might even have to remind the officiant of the correct pronunciations of your names! Attend to every little detail so that you will be confident the next day that everything will go exactly as planned.

The Rehearsal Dinner

Traditionally hosted by the groom's family, the rehearsal dinner is a chance for everyone to get together, relax, have a great meal, and share some special toasts before the big day tomorrow. You might choose to give your parents and bridal party their gifts at this function, knowing that the wedding morning itself will be too chaotic for the personal presentation of special tokens. The rehearsal dinner was made for just this kind of interaction, as everyone is now taking a breather and enjoying each other's company before the real activity begins.

Who Comes to the Rehearsal Dinner?

My fiancé's family wants to have a big rehearsal dinner. I thought it was supposed to be just the bridal party and performers, but they want to invite all of their out-of-town guests. What's proper?

Some families do see the rehearsal dinner as their opportunity to put on a big, splashy affair. If they have the resources, they plan to invite all of their out-of-town guests as well as the members of the wedding party. As bride and groom, it's your call as to what works best for you. It may be that you want an intimate dinner where you can spend relaxed time with your friends and family, and not have to mingle with guests you barely know. In this case, thank the groom's parents, express your wishes that you'd like the rehearsal dinner to include just those involved in the wedding and their guests, and that there's plenty of time during the wedding weekend for the groom's family to host their guests at brunches and at other times. I know it's always tough to express your wishes when so much ego and so much money is involved—particularly if you've struggled with your future in-laws throughout the planning—but you must stand your ground if you feel very strongly about your rehearsal dinner being a relaxing one.

The style and formality of the rehearsal dinner is according to the bride and groom's personal preferences and the groom's family's resources, if they are acting as hosts. Some couples desire a more informal rehearsal dinner, not wanting a miniwedding the day before the real one. I have seen great rehearsal dinners at family-style restaurants, at the groom's family's home, in backyards, and in parks. You might search out a nice restaurant with an outdoor terrace, or a deck overlooking a lake or marina. You can choose to keep the outdoor

Wedding Day Reflections

After the rehearsal dinner, I went home with my parents and slept at their place for the night. We sat up for a while, had some coffee, talked about family memories and how we wished my grandmother could have been with us. It was a really nice, quiet time that I enjoyed sharing with my parents and my sisters. We got a little emotional, but it made it all the better. I'm glad I decided to spend my last single night with my family.

—Rose

theme, or give yourself one less thing to worry about by planning an indoor event.

Work with the groom's family, or whomever is hosting the dinner, to create a nice menu and dessert offerings, avoiding very heavy or spicy foods. Limit alcohol to just wine, beer, and perhaps a champagne toast. Such boundaries keep costs lower, and they also discourage guests from getting inebriated the night before the wedding.

Choose a post-dinner time to make your toast as a couple or individually, thanking your family and friends, and remember to propose toasts to one another at this time. Some couples present the bridal party's gifts officially, in front of everyone and with personalized speeches, and others just quietly hand out the presents throughout the night.

Don't stay out too late. Wrap up the party at a reasonable hour, go over last-minute instructions with your bridal party (such as when and where to show up the next day), and head home to get some sleep.

The Night Before the Wedding

Although a good dose of relaxation and cozy family time will be in order, you'll also have to make sure the last-minute details are in place. Be sure your dress is pressed and hung up for easy access tomorrow, and that all of your accessories, from your lingerie to your jewelry, are set out and ready to go.

Be sure the groom has the license and the rings in a safe place where he will remember to bring them along the next day. Set out your emergency bag by the front door, as well as any other items that you'll need to bring with you.

Make any last-minute confirmations with your wedding professionals, check your e-mail for guests' last-minute messages, and go through your to-do list for any forgotten tasks or items to be located.

And just before bed, call your intended for a last-minute "I love you" and a wish for pleasant dreams. Then get some sleep. You'll need your rest for the wonderful day to come.

You Look Gorgeous!

Every bride wants to look her best on her wedding day, so the primping and preening process is always an important one—especially for an outdoor wedding. In bright, natural sunlight your makeup will have to look flawless in the unforgiving glare, and in heat and humidity, your hair will need to hold its style and avoid the frizzies. The groom too will need to perfect his look with a clean shave, good skin care, and the right hair products for the weather.

Even though you may have your hair and makeup done by a professional in a salon or at home—the wedding-morning trip to the salon is an event in itself!—you ought to know the best makeup-application methods and shades for the conditions of your day. I spoke to several makeup artists with celebrity clientele, and they all have the same advice: Go for a natural look, with a little bit of extra pizzazz to set you apart from the crowd.

Makeup

Wedding-day makeup is always a few notches greater than your everyday makeup style, even if your wedding will be held in daylight hours. Visit a professional to find the right shade of foundation for your skin's tone. The experts warn against switching to a new brand of makeup right before your wedding day, as your skin may be sensitive to a new formula and become prone to irritation or breakouts. So stick with your usual brand of makeup, and search for the right color.

For blush, ask a professional to help you choose the right shade of blush for your skin tone. Too many brides use their everyday blush and find that it's either nearly invisible and not dramatic enough, or it's too intense for an outdoor-wedding look. Go for a pink blush if you have light skin, or a rose color if you're olive- or dark-skinned. Though it might seem appropriate to try the new, fun blush with glitter in it, you'll look more suitable for a nightclub than an outdoor wedding. So keep to standard blush styles. A good tip is to wear a white shirt to the beauty counter (if you're wearing white for your wedding), have the professional try several shades on you, and then step outdoors into natural sunlight with a mirror to check your look. Yes, it's a hassle, and the makeup artist might raise a perfectly plucked eyebrow at your methods, but it's the best way to find the perfect shade for the natural lighting of an outdoor wedding.

Use lighter shades of eye shadow, sparing the more dramatic darks and eye-crease shadings. Natural, lighter colors make for a brighter complexion and a more open-eyed look. Consider the trends of the day, as makeup styles change all the time. If lighter eye shadows are in, then think about a brush of light shade by your eyebrow line, or by your upper lash line. Again, a professional can show you the new looks and can advise as to the best styles for your outdoor wedding's formality level.

Avoid too-dark eyeliner. The raccoon look is hardly flattering to most people, and many brides are favoring the darker brown liners to complement their eyes. The idea is to bring out your eyes, not make you look like a painted model. And it goes without saying that waterproof mascara is a must.

One of the top tips for wedding-day beauty is perfectly shaped eyebrows. Done well by a professional, whether waxed or tweezed, a great arch in the eyebrow will bring out your eyes and even make you look younger, the experts say. Professional makeup artists advise the use of brow fill-in pencil, and they strongly suggest that you visit a professional for selection of the right shade and application. The idea is not to have the shading be noticeable, but just to add a little bit of extra color where your brows might be a little sparse.

As for your lips, avoid pale or brown lipsticks, as they do not photograph well. Many brides are nervous about wearing too bright a shade of lipstick, particularly if neutrals or pale colors are their norms. The experts say to apply the usual shade of neutral lipstick, and then apply a more vibrant shade of pink or coral on top of it. If, however, you normally wear darker lipsticks, then apply your favorite shade and tone it down with a swipe of paler color or lip gloss. Practice with many shades, aided by a professional, until you find the right color for your wedding-day look. Be sure the tone you choose looks natural, not too dramatic for your formality level, and that it works with your skin tone and the color of your teeth. Some lipsticks can make slightly yellowed teeth look even more stained, and others make teeth look whiter. Whatever shade of lipstick you choose for the professional's application on the wedding day, be sure to purchase a tube or sample for frequent touch-up applications during the day.

A big look for outdoor brides is the bronzed look. You've been warned against tanning out in the sun, and you may even fear tanning booths. Perhaps artificial tanning creams don't give you the results you desire, and you're not willing to risk looking like a striped, orange tiger on your wedding day. If you're considering self-tanners, look into having one professionally applied at a beauty salon, or practice for months beforehand to get the exfoliation and application process just right. Or, skip the tanning process and rely on a good bronzing powder to give you that great, natural glow that everyone's after. Because a professional can best match a bronzing powder to your skin tone and apply it more naturally to your neck and jawline than you might be able to, add that to your list of beauty regimens on the big day.

Again, don't be tempted by sparkly or frosted makeup, as it can give a washed-out appearance in pictures, and it often holds up badly in the heat. It would be an odd beauty statement for you to have a caked-up line of frosted powder over your eyelids and glitter all over your face. The sparkly lines of cosmetics are reflective during photographs, preventing you from having a seamless, flawless face in all pictures and at all times during the wedding day and night.

Outdoor weather means warm air, and that can translate to a shiny nose and forehead. So arm yourself with a good pressed-powder compact and puff pad, and ask your maids to gently notify you of your need to powder your nose. Get rid of shine with oil-blotting papers, if they work well for you, and be sure to even out your make-up after each shine-removal session.

Though many brides choose to do their own makeup, I strongly advise your hiring a professional for this day. Ask the makeup artists at beauty counters if they moonlight for wedding days, or check with a local modeling school for names of suitable candidates for hire. Interview several before you give your face to this pro, and schedule a practice session a few weeks before the wedding. Remember, it's your face, and it's your look. An expert can suggest a great new trend, but if you're uncomfortable with a look, wipe it off and ask to try something a little more natural. The most important thing is for you to feel comfortable with your look, as a great sense of comfort in your personal style makes you even more beautiful. And that's the goal for your wedding day.

Perfume

You have to be careful about perfume at your outdoor wedding. Though it's important to smell great, heavy perfume can attract insects, get even stronger out in the sun, and cause allergic reactions or sunburns when skin is exposed to the bright outdoor light. So keep your scent natural, and layer it for extra-lasting effect. To layer, apply a skin lotion in a certain scent after your shower, then the same scent of perfume on your wrists, ankles, behind the ears, and behind the knees.

Experiment with different scents to see which ones say "wedding-day perfect" to you. You could take a personality fragrance-finder test on the Internet to discover a list of applicable scents for your style, but it's far better to visit a perfume counter and test the merchandise on your own body. Your natural chemistry and natural scents will mingle with the aromas of a perfume to create your own signature scent. Do you want a floral essence around you? Or a fruity one? One bride found a fragrance called Ocean Dream that she loved. She wore it to her beach wedding and presented small vials of the same scent to her maids and mothers. Whatever your choice, just go easy on the application, knowing that you can spritz a bit more on during the day if necessary.

HAIR

Again, a professional hairstylist can help you find the best wedding-day hairstyle for you. Whether you wear your hair up in a tight braid; gathered into a chignon; or loose, flowing, and curly will depend upon the formality of your wedding, the cut of your gown, and your own sense of personal style. For an outdoor wedding, though, you'll have the additional factor of the weather.

When the air is humid, does your hair turn into a frizzy mess? Does humidity flatten out your locks? Think ahead to the possible weather conditions of heat, humidity, and wind to determine your hair's personality. Talk with your hairstylist about what the conditions of your day will be—windblown on a beach or boat, for instance—and how you feel most comfortable. Some brides say in retrospect that they hated having to practically shellac their hair so that it held its shape on the wedding day. Sure, it looked great in the pictures, but the hair was stiff and sticky all day long. Ask your stylist about hair-control products that do not turn hair into a helmet, and decide together on a style that works best with your look.

Beauty Tip from a Professional

I spoke to Alain Pinon of Salon AKS in New York City, and he recommended fighting frizzies on the wedding day by washing your hair the day before the wedding. A same-day wash can strip hair of its natural oils, taking away softness and styling capabilities. Washing your hair the night before the wedding will give your tresses some time to develop their own natural styling condition for better manageability. Ask your stylist if this procedure is right for your hair type.

Experiment with different styles a few weeks before the wedding, bringing your veil in to show the stylist. Remember that hair designers can create veritable sculptures with the curls of your hair, turning a plain upsweep into a gorgeous focal point. Some brides choose to get extensions for their wedding day, giving them dramatic curls and length, and others agree to the incorporation of hairpieces or natural-hair braided buns to add some size to their own hairstyles.

The experts say to have a professional dye your hair weeks before the wedding, if that is your choice, and have a pro do any highlighting or root touch-ups ahead of time as well. Even if you've always dyed your hair yourself at home, don't tempt fate—and definitely don't tempt fate the day before the wedding.

Play up your 'do with great hair accents, such as sparkling tiaras, headbands, or hair clips. I found wonderful beach-themed styles, such as the Oceana tiara by Winters and Rain (www.WintersandRain.com), which features tiny seashells and muted sea colors of aqua and pink. Some beach brides choose to wear delicate starfish hair clips or seashell-studded bobby pins throughout a French braid. It's these fun accents that give you a once-in-a-lifetime wedding-day look, so explore your options well. You're not just limited to the standard pearl pins and a veil headpiece, especially for an outdoor wedding where hair might be adorned with fresh flowers or a simple daisy tucked behind your ear.

Your hair is your crowning glory on your wedding day, so invest as much time choosing your style as you did choosing your dress. Pick a style that will look natural, elegant, and complementary to the neckline of your gown and the formality of your day.

Nails

The gold standard of wedding-day nails is the French manicure for both fingers and toes. Whatever the style or formality of your wedding, you can't go wrong with this natural, classic look. Some brides choose to go with a pale pink nail color, and some go with a daring red, depending upon color schemes and personal style preference.

For an extra bit of fun, barefoot beach brides have added a little pizzazz to their exposed toenails. You can now have a sparkly gem glued to a toenail to make a statement, or go dazzling with a line of miniature crystals attached to your nail.

Stress Relief

The best way to look beautiful is to be relaxed. Throughout the planning process, no doubt you'll have at least several moments when your nerves are shot, your shoulders are up by your ears, and you're ready to explode. Stress takes a huge toll on the body and on your sense of well-being, so ward off the accumulated effects of wedding stress with a good massage. Either trade backrubs with your sweetheart, or find a professional who will knead out those kinks and deliver you to bliss.

You've probably been dealing with stress your entire life, and you know the practices that calm you. Whether it's aromatherapy, yoga,

Simplify It

Find a qualified massage therapist through the American Massage Therapy Association's Web site (www.amtamassage.org), where you can find a massage expert by zip code and even have him come to your home for a session.

meditation, or just a warm bath surrounded by scented candles, lean on your relaxation methods now more than ever. Planning a wedding is a stressful time, and as the day comes closer you may find that the pressures are even greater. Not only are you dealing with the many details of your day and your own sensitivities, you're also dealing with the nervous energy of everyone around you. Find a healthy way to deal with your stress, keep it in check, and stay in control of your own well-being even as the pressure mounts. Remember, this is supposed to be fun. Stress relief will return you to a place where you can enjoy the process and keep the bigger picture in mind.

The Bridal Brunch

Start your day off well with a nourishing brunch for yourself and your entire bridal party. If you'll bring your maids to a salon for hours of beauty and relaxing massages, then arrange to have your brunch catered there. Or, serve a nice breakfast spread back at your house before it's time to dress. Remember that the men need to eat too, so have a supply of goodies sent to their hotel room or home.

Keep the fixings light, choosing bagels, quiches, and juices over heavier, greasy fares and alcohol. Though a champagne or mimosa toast is always in order, it's a good idea to limit the dehydrating effects of alcohol and get your group off to a healthy start. Use this brunch time to be sure everyone has something in their stomachs, and even if you have "butterflies" do try to eat a little something for your own strength and well-being.

For obvious reasons, skip the onion or garlic bagels, and limit your caffeine intake to prevent even greater jitters.

Once you're done with the brunch, it's time to get dressed and pose for pictures before heading off to start the celebration!

Last-Minute Wedding Morning To-Do's

Your outdoor wedding may require some wedding-morning errands and last-minute checks. Recruit assistants to help you with the following, so that you can relax, get pampered, and dress in peace, knowing that everything is in order:

❑ Be sure the marriage license is in an envelope and that someone is taking it to the ceremony.

❑ Be sure the best man has the rings and is taking them to the ceremony.

❑ Call to confirm the limousines or cars for the day. Don't worry about being a pest. The most important thing is that you get to your wedding on time.

❑ Transfer your engagement ring to your right hand before you head off to the ceremony, so that your wedding ring will slip on as necessary.

❑ Be sure that all payment envelopes are filled with the appropriate amounts, marked with the recipients' names, and that a responsible family member or the best man will take them to the wedding for payment of professionals.

❑ Be sure that someone, such as the best man or the father of the bride, has enough cash on hand to complete any unforeseen tips and payments.

❑ Be sure your garter is on your leg before you leave the house.

❑ Be sure that someone is bringing your emergency bag along for you.

❑ Be sure that someone is bringing your separate throwaway bouquet along and perhaps keeping it in a cooler to keep it fresh.

❑ Be sure that your honeymoon bags are packed completely, that your airline tickets, passports, and wallets are in your carry-on bags, and that they are set in your hotel room or trunk of your car for easy pickup after the wedding.

❏ Be sure you have a cell phone and a card on hand, with all of the important phone numbers for your wedding professionals and bridal-party members.

❏ Be sure the ceremony and reception sites are set up to completion. Send a responsible family member out to the site to inspect everything and ask him to call you if any permissions need to be made for changes.

❏ Record on your home and cell phones a voice-mail message that lets guests know the status of any location changes due to rain or muddy grounds, or that the wedding is on as scheduled.

❏ Pose for pictures with your bridal party, allowing for plenty of time to get to the wedding in a relaxed manner.

❏ Ask your bridal-party members if they have any last-minute questions.

❏ Arrange for rides to the wedding for any guests or family members who say they don't have one.

❏ Call to confirm your honeymoon flight and honeymoon reservations.

❏ Call your sweetheart for one last "I love you" before you take your vows.

❏ Take a deep breath, stay calm, and remember that you've done a great job planning your wedding. Now, it's time to enjoy it!

Appendix I: Your Phone List

Bride: _____

Groom: _____

Bride's Parents: _____

Groom's Parents: _____

Maid of Honor: _____

Bridesmaid: _____

Bridesmaid _____

Bridesmaid: _____

Bridesmaid: _____

Bridesmaid: _____

Flower Girl: _____

Flower Girl: _____

Guest Hostess: _____

Guest-Book Attendant: _____

Best Man: _____

Usher: _____

Usher: _____

Usher: _____

Usher: _____

Usher: _____

Ring Bearer: _____

Ceremony-Site Manager: _____

Ceremony Officiant: _____

Organist: _____

Ceremony Musician: _____

Ceremony Musician: _____

Ceremony Reader: _____

Other Ceremony Participants: _____

Wedding Coordinator: _____

Reception-Hall Manager: _____

Caterer: _____

Baker: _____

Bar Manager: _____

Bridal-Shop Manager: _____

Seamstress: _____

Bridesmaids' Bridal-Shop Manager: _____

Bridesmaids' Seamstress _____

Shoe-Shop Manager: _____

Accessories-Shop Manager: _____

Tuxedo Manager: _____

Florist: _____

Photographer: _____

Videographer: _____

Reception Entertainers: _____

Limousine Company: _____

Hotel Manager: _____

Travel Agent: _____

Baby-Sitters: _____

Drivers: _____

Housesitters: _____

Beauty Shop: _____

Spa: _____

Other Numbers: _____

Appendix II: Bridesmaids' Dress Order Form

Name: _____

Title: _____

Address: _____

Phone: _____

E-mail: _____

Cell phone: _____

Measurements:

❏ Card sent in

❏ Measurements called in

❏ Order placed

❏ Size ordered:_____

❏ Deposit left

❑ Fittings scheduled

❑ Shoes bought

❑ Accessories bought

❑ Final payment

Notes:

Appendix III: Tuxedo Rental Order Form

Name: _____

Title: _____

Address: _____

Phone: _____

E-mail: _____

Cell phone: _____

Measurements:

❏ Card sent in

❏ Measurements called in

❏ Order placed

❏ Size ordered:

❑ Deposit left

❑ Fitting scheduled

❑ Shoes bought

❑ Accessories bought

❑ Final payment

Notes:

Resources

Please note that the following information is for your research use only. The author and the publisher do not personally endorse any vendor, service, company, or professional.

Gowns and Menswear

Bridal Gowns

Alfred Angelo: (800) 531-1125; www.alfredangelo.com

America's Bridal Discounters: (800) 326-0833; www.bridaldiscounters.com

Amsale: (212) 971-0170; www.amsale.com

Birnbaum and Bullock: (212) 242-2914; www.birnbaumandbulluck.com

Brideway.net: (800) 598-0685; www.brideway.net

Christos, Inc.: (212) 921-0025; www.christosbridal.com

David's Bridal: (888) 399-2743; www.davidsbridal.com

E-Brides.net: (800) 598-0685; www.brideway.net

Emme Bridal: (281) 634-9225

Forever Yours: 800-USA-BRIDE

Galina: (212) 564-1020; www.galinabridals.com

Helen Morley: www.helenmorley.com

Janell Berte: (717) 291-9894; www.berte.com

Jessica McClintock: (800) 333-5301; www.jessicamcclintock.com

Jim Hjelm: (800) 686-7880; www.jimhjelmvisions.com

L'Amour: (800) 664-5683; www.lamourbridals.com

Lila Broude: (212) 921-8081

Lili: (626) 336-5048

Manale: (212) 944-6939; www.manale.com

Melissa Sweet Bridal Collections: (404) 633-4395; www.melissasweet.com

Michelle Roth: (212) 245-3390; www.michelleroth.com

Mon Cheri: (609) 530-1900; www.MonCheriBridals.com

Mori Lee: (818) 385-0930; www.morileeinc.com

Pallas Athena: (818) 285-5796

Priscilla of Boston: (617) 242-2677; www.priscillaofboston.com

Private Label by G: (800) 858-3338; www.privatelabelbyg.com

Roaman's Romance (Plus-Sizes): (800) 436-0800

Signature Designs: (800) 654-7375

Silvia Designs: (760) 323-8808; www.silviadesigns.com

Sweetheart: (212) 947-7171

Tomasina: (412) 563-7788; www.tomasina.com

USA Bridal: www.usabridal.com

Vera Wang: (212) 628-3400

Yumi Katsura: (212) 772-3760; www.yumikatsura.com

Bridesmaids' and Mother of the Brides' Gowns

After Six: www.colorfinder.com

Alfred Angelo: (800) 531-1125; www.aflredangelo.com

Bianchi: (800) 669-2346

Bill Levkoff: (800) LEVKOFF

Chadwick's of Boston Special Occasions: (800) 525-6650

Champagne Formals: (212) 302-9162

David's Bridal: (888) 399-2743; www.davidsbridal.com

Dessy Creations: (800) 633-7791; www.dessy.com

Galina: (212) 564-1020; www.galina.com

Group USA: www.groupusa.com

JC Penney: (800) 527-8347; www.jcpenney.com

Jessica McClintock: (800) 333-5301; www.jessicamcclintock.com

Jim Hjelm Occasions: (800) 686-7880; www.jimhjelmoccasions.com

Lazaro: (212) 764-5781; www.lazarobridal.com

Macy's: (877) 622-9274; www.macys.weddingchannel.com

Melissa Sweet Bridal Collection: (404) 633-4395; www.melissasweet.com

Roaman's Romance (Plus-Sizes): (800) 436-0800

Silhouettes: www.silhouettesmaids.com

Spiegel: (800) 527-1577; www.spiegel.com

Watters and Watters: (972) 960-9884; www.watters.com

Men's Wedding Wear

Gingiss: www.gingiss.com

Marrying Man: www.marryingman.com

Children's Wedding Wear

David's Bridal: (888) 399-2743; www.davidsbridal.com

Finetica Child: www.Fineticachild.com

Katie and Co.: www.katieco.com

Posie's: www.posies.com

Willow: www.caprichoza.com

Shoes and Accessories

Shoes and Handbags

David's Bridal: (888) 399-2743; www.davidsbridal.com

Dyeables: (800) 431-2000

Fenaroli for Regalia: (617) 723-3682

Kenneth Cole: (800) KENCOLE

Nina Footwear: (800) 23-NINA

Salon Shoes: (650) 588-8677; www.salonshoes.com

Shoe Buy: www.shoebuy.com

Watters and Watters: (972) 960-9884; www.watters.com

Veils and Headpieces

Bel Aire Bridals: (310) 325-8160; www.belaireveils.com

David's Bridal: (888) 399-2743; www.davidsbridal.com

Dream Veils and Accessories: (312) 943-9554; www.renee-romano.com

Fenaroli for Regalia: (617) 723-3682

Homa: (973) 467-5500; homabridal@aol.com

Renee Romano: (312) 943-0912; www.Renee-Romano.com

Winters & Rain: (401) 848-0868; www.wintersandrain.com

INVITATIONS

An Invitation to Buy—Nationwide: (708) 226-9495; www.invitations4sale.com

Anna Griffin Invitation Design: (404) 817-8170; www.annagriffin.com

Botanical PaperWorks: (888) 727-3755

Camelot Wedding Stationery: (800) 280-2860

Crane and Co.: (800) 572-0024; www.crane.com

Embossed Graphics: (800) 325-1016; www.embossedgraphics.com

Julie Holcomb Printers: (510) 654-6416; www.julieholcomb printers.com

Now and Forever: (800) 451-8616; www.now-and-forever.com

PaperStyle.com: For ordering invitations online; (770) 667-6100; www.paperstyle.com

Papyrus: (800) 886-6700; www.papyrusonline.com

Renaissance Writings: (800) 246-8483; www.RenaissanceWriting.com

Rexcraft: (800) 635-3898; www.rexcraft.com

The Precious Collection: (800) 537-5222

Willow Tree Lane: (800) 219-9230; www.willowtreelane.com

RINGS

American Gem Society: www.ags.org

Benchmark: (800) 633-5950; www.benchmarkrings.com

Bianca: (213) 622-7234; www.BiancaPlatinum.com

Blue Nile: www.bluenile.com

Cartier: (800) CARTIER

Christian Bauer: (800) 228-3724; www.christianbauer.com

DeBeers: www.adiamondisforever.com

EGL Gemological Society: (877) EGL-USA-1; EGLUSA@worldnet.att.net

Honora: (888) 2HONORA

Jeff Cooper Platinum: (888) 522-6222; www.jcplatinum.com

Keepsake Diamond Jewelry: (888) 4-KEEPSAKE

Lazare Diamond: www.lazarediamonds.com

Novell: (888) 916-6835; www.novelldesignstudio.com

OGI Wedding Bands Unlimited: (800) 578-3846; www.ogi-ltd.com

Paul Klecka: (888) P-KLECKA; www.klecka.com

Rudolf Erdel Platinum: (865) 220-8090; www.rudolferdel.com

Scott Kay Platinum: (800) 487-4898; www.scottkay.com

Tiffany: (800) 526-0649; www.tiffany.com

Wedding Ring Hotline: (800) 985-RING; www.weddingringhotline.com

Zales: (800) 311-JEWEL; www.zales.com

For information on how to design your own rings, check out www.adia-mondisforever.com.

HONEYMOON

AIRLINES

Air Canada: (800) 776-3000; www.aircanada.ca

Air France: www.airfrance.fr

Alaska Airlines: (800) 426-0333; www.alaskaair.com

Alitalia: www.zenonet.com

Aloha Airlines: (800) 367-5250; www.alohaair.com

America West: (800) 247-5692; www.americawest.com

American Airlines: (800) 433-7300; www.amrcorp.com

British Airways: (800) 247-9297; www.british-airways.com

Continental Airlines: (800) 525-0280; www.flycontinental.com

Delta Airlines: (800) 221-1212; www.delta-air.com

Hawaiian Airlines: (800) 367-5320

KLM Royal Dutch Airlines: (800) 374-7747

Northwest Airlines: (800) 225-2525; www.nwa.com

Southwest Airlines: (800) 435-9792; www.southwest.com

TWA: (800) 221-2000; www.twa.com

USAir: (800) 428-4322; www.usair.com

United Airlines: (800) 241-6522; www.ualservices.com

Virgin Atlantic Airways: (800) 862-8621; www.fly.virgin.com

DISCOUNT AIRFARES

Air Fare: www.airfare.com

Cheap Fares: www.cheapfares.com

Cheap Tickets: (800) 377-1000

Discount Airfare: www.discount-airfare.com

Mr. Cheap: (800) MR-CHEAP

Priceline: www.priceline.com

You Price It: www.youpriceit.com

CRUISES

Cruise Lines International Association: www.cruising.org

American Cruise Line (East Coast from Florida to Maine): www.americancruiselines.com

Carnival Cruise Lines: www.carnival.com

Celebrity Cruises: www.celebrity-cruises.com

Cunard: www.cunardline.com

Delta Queen: www.deltaqueen.com

Discount Cruises: www.cruise.com

Disney Cruises: (407) 828-3400; www.disneycruise.com

Holland America: www.hollandamerica.com

Norwegian Cruise Lines: (800) 262-4NCL; www.ncl.com

Princess Cruises: www.princess.com

Radisson Seven Seas Cruises: www.rssc.com

Royal Caribbean: www.royalcaribbean.com

A Wedding for You: (800) 929-4198 (weddings aboard a cruise ship); www.aweddingforyou.com

RESORTS

Beaches: (800) BEACHES

Club Med: www.clubmed.com

Disney: www.disneyweddings.com

Hilton Hotels: www.hilton.com

Hyatt Hotels: www.hyatt.com

Marriott Hotels: www.marriott.com

Radisson: www.radisson.com

Sandals: (800) SANDALS; www.sandals.com

Super Clubs: (800) GO-SUPER; www.superclubs.com

Swept Away: (800) 545-7937; www.sweptaway.com/weddings.htm

Westin Hotels: www.westin.com

HOTELS

To find a suitable hotel in your destination, search by your criteria at www.all-hotels.com.

Bed and breakfasts, country inns, and small hotels: www.virtualcities.com

Bed and breakfasts (international guide): www.ibbp.com

Fodors: www.fodors.com

Hilton: www.hilton.com

Hyatt: www.hyatt.com

Leading Hotels of the World: www.lhw.com

Marriott: www.marriott.com

Radisson: www.radison.com

STATE AND LOCATION TOURISM DEPARTMENTS

Tourism Office Worldwide Directory: www.towd.com

Alabama: (800) 252-2262

Alaska: (907) 465-2010

Arizona: (602) 542-8687

Aruba Tourism Department: (201) 330-0800

Australian Tourist Commission: (800) 445-4400

Bahamas: (800) 228-5173

Barbados: (212) 986-6516

Bermuda: (800) 223-6106

British Virgin Islands: (800) 888-5563, ext. 559

California: (916) 322-1396

Caribbean: (212) 682-0435

Colorado: (800) 433-2656

Connecticut: (800) 282-6863

Delaware: (800) 441-8846

Disney Honeymoons: (877) 566-0969; www.disneyhoneymoons.com

France: (212) 757-1125

Fiji: (310) 568-1616

Georgia: (800) 847-4842

Germany: (212) 661-7200

Hawaii: (800) GO-HAWAII

Idaho: (800) 635-7820

Illinois: (217) 782-7139

Indiana: (800) 289-ONIN

Iowa: (800) 345-IOWA

Ireland: (212) 418-0800

Italy: (212) 245-4961

Jamaica: (800) 233-4582

Jersey/Cape May County: (800) 227-2297

Kansas: (800) 2- KANSAS

Kentucky: (800) 225-8747

Key West: (800) 648-6269

Lake Tahoe: (800) 824-6348; www.go-tahoe.com

Lousiana: (800) 227-4386

Maryland: (800) 543-1036

Massachusetts: (617) 727-3201

Mexico: (800) 44-MEXICO

Michigan: (800) 543-2937

Minnesota: (800) 345-2537

Mississippi: (800) 647-2290

Monaco: (212) 759-5227

Montana: (800) 541-1447

Nebraska: (800) 228-4307

Nevada: (800) 638-2328

New Jersey: (800) JERSEY-7

New Mexico: (800) 545-2040

North Carolina: (800) 847-4862

Oahu, Hawaii: (877) 525-OAHU; www.visit-oahu.com

Ohio: (800) BUCKEYE

Oklahoma: (800) 654-8240

Pennsylvania: (800) VISIT-PA

Puerto Rico: (800) 223-6530

Quebec: (800) 363-7777

Rhode Island: (800) 556-2484

St. Lucia: www.stlucia.org

South Carolina: (800) 872-3505

Tahiti: (800) 828-6877; www.islandsinthesun.com

Tennessee: (615) 741-2158

Texas: (512) 483-3705

Utah: (800) 222-8824

Vermont: (802) 828-3236

Virginia: (800) 248-4833

West Virginia: (800) CALL-WVA

Wisconsin: (800) 432-TRIP

Wyoming: (800) 225-5996

Train Travel

Amtrak: (800) 872-7245; www.amtrak.com

Eurailpass: www.eurail.com

Orient Express hotels, trains, and cruises: www.orient-express.com

Cottages and Villas

Country Cottages: (800) 674-8883 (cottages and villas in the U.S. and Europe)

Bridal Associations

Bridal Shows and Conferences

Great Bridal Expo: (800) 422-3976; www.bridalexpos.com

Twice Is Nice Encore Bridal Creations (for the encore bride):
  www.twiceisnicebride.com

Limousines

National Limousine Association: (800) NLA-7007

Organizations

American Federation of Musicians: (212) 869-1330

American Rental Association: (800) 334-2177

American Society of Travel Agents: (703) 739-2782

Association of Bridal Consultants: (860) 355-0464

Association of Certified Professional Wedding Consultants:
  (408) 528-9000; www.acpwc.com

Better Business Bureau: www.bbb.org/bureaus (to find the
  Better Business Bureau of your state or locale)

Professional Photographers of America: (800) 786-6277;
  www.ppa-world.org

Wedding Web Sites

The Best Man: www.thebestman.com

Bride's Magazine: www.brides.com

Della Weddings: www.weddingchannel.com

Elegant Bride: www.elegantbride.com

The Knot: www.theknot.com

Martha Stewart Living: www.marthastewart.com

Modern Bride: www.ModernBride.com

Premiere Bride: www.premierbride.com

Sharon Naylor's Wedding Page: www.sharonnaylor.net

The Wedding Channel: www.theweddingchannel.com

The Wedding Helpers: www.weddinghelpers.com

Today's Bride: www.todaysbride.com

Town and Country Weddings (upscale): www.tncweddings.com

Ultimate Internet Wedding Guide: www.ultimatewedding.com

Wedding Bells: www.weddingbells.com

Wedding Central: www.weddingcentral.com

Wedding Details: www.weddingdetails.com

Wedding Spot: www.weddingspot.com

Wedding World: www.weddingworld.com

Wedding Registries

Bed Bath and Beyond: (800) GO-BEYOND; www.bedbathandbeyond.com

Bloomingdales: (800) 888-2WED; www.bloomingdales.com

Bon Ton: (800) 9BONTON

Crate and Barrel: (800) 967-6696; www.crateandbarrel.com

Dillards: (800) 626-6001; www.dillards.com

Filene's: www.FilenesWeddings.com

Fortunoff: (800) 777-2807; www.fortunoff.com

The Gift: www.thegift.com

Gump's: www.gumps.com

Hecht's: www.hechts.com

Home Depot: www.homedepot.com

HoneyLuna (honeymoon registry): (800) 809-5862

JC Penney: (800) JCP-GIFT; www.jcpgift.com

Kitchen Etc.: (800) 232-4070; www.kitchenetc.com

Kohl's: (800) 837-1500

Linens 'n Things: (800) LNT-WEDDING

Macy's Wedding Channel: (888) 92-BRIDES;
   www.macys.weddingchannel.com

Neiman Marcus: www.neimanmarcus.com

Pier 1 Imports: (800) 245-4595; www.pier1.com

Sears: www.sears.com

Service Merchandise: www.servicemerchandise.com

Sur La Table: (800) 243-0852; www.surlatable.com

Target's Club Wedd Gift Registry: (800) 888-9333; www.target.com

Tiffany: (800) 526-0649; www.tiffany.com

Ultimate Online Wedding Mall: www.ultimateweddingmall.com

Wedding Channel.com: www.weddingchannel.com

Wedding List: (877) 933-5478

The Wedding List: (800) 345-7795; www.theweddinglist.com

Wedding Network: Internet wedding registry;
   www.weddingnetwork.com

Williams Sonoma: (800) 541-2376; www.williams-sonoma.com

Wedding Supplies and Services

Books and Planners

Amazon.com: www.amazon.com

Barnes and Noble: www.bn.com

Borders: www.borders.com

Calligraphy

Petals and Ink: (818) 509-6783

Cameras

411Bride: (800) 693-2468; www.411bride.com

Best Camera: (888) 237-8226

Candid Event Cameras: (800) 4-WEDCAM; www.wedcam.com

EPP Wedding Products: (412) 823-6748

FAVORS AND GIFTS

Beverly Clark Collection: (877) 862-3933; www.beverlyclark.com

Chandler's Candle Company: (800) 463-7143; www.chandlerscandle.com

Double T Limited: (800) 756-6184; www.uniquefavors.com

Exclusively Weddings: (800) 759-7666; www.exclusivelyweddings.com

Favors by Serendipity: (800) 320-2663; www.favorsby-serendipity.com

Forever and Always Company: (800) 404-4025; www.foreverandalways.com

Godiva: (800) 9-GODIVA; www.godiva.com

Gratitude: (800) 914-4342; www.giftsofgratitude.com

Personal Creations: (800) 326-6626

Pier 1: www.pier1.com

Seasons: (800) 776-9677

Service Merchandise: (800) 251-1212

Things Remembered: (800) 274-7367; www.thingsremembered.com

Tree and Floral Beginnings: Seedlings, bulbs, and candles; (800) 499-9580; www.plantamemory.com; in Canada, www.plantamemory.on.ca

Wireless: (800) 669-9999

PAPER PRODUCTS

OfficeMax: Check your local listings

Paper Access: (800) 727-3701; www.paperaccess.com

Paper Direct: (800) A-PAPERS

Staples: (800) 333-3330; www.staples.com

Ultimate Wedding Store: www.ultimatewedding.com/store

Wedmart.com: (888) 802-2229; www.wedmart.com

The Wedding Store: www.wedguide.com/store

WEATHER SERVICE

Check the weather at your ceremony, reception, or honey-moon sites, even get five-day forecast and weather bulletins, at the following:

AccuWeather: www.accuweather.com

Rain or Shine: Five-day forecasts for anywhere in the world, plus ski and boating conditions: www.rainorshine.com

Sunset Time: Precise sunset time for any day of the year:
www.usno.navy.mil

Weather Channel: www.weather.com

Wedding Items (Toasting Flutes, Ring Pillows, etc.)

Affectionately Yours: www.affectionately-yours.com

Beverly Clark Collection: (877) 862-3933; www.beverlyclark.com

Bridalink Store: www.bridalink.com/store2

Celebration Bells: (217) 463-2222; www.celebrationbells.com

Chandler's Candle Company: (800) 463-7143; www.chandlerscandle.com

Ketubah Ketubah: (888) KETUBAH; www.KETUBAH.com

Magical Beginnings Butterfly Farms: Live butterflies for release;
(888) 639-9995; www.butterflyevents.com

The Sarina Collection: (888) 6SARINA; www.sarinacollection.com

The Wedding Shopper: www.theweddingshopper.com/catalog.htm

Treasured Moments (unity candles): (800) 754-5151;
www.treasured-moments.com

If you will be making your own wedding cake, baked favors, or desserts,
check out the Wilton site for the best in supplies: (800) 794-5866;
www.wilton.com

Wine and Champagne

Wine.com: www.wine.com

Wine Searcher: www.winesearcher.com

Wine Spectator: www.winespectator.com

Beauty and Health

Beauty Products and Services

Check these sites for makeup and skin-care products, assessments, and
services:

Avon: www.avon.com

Beauty.com: www.beauty.com

Beauty Jungle: www.beautyjungle.com

Bobbi Brown Essentials: www.bobbibrown.com

Clinique: www.clinique.com

Elizabeth Arden: Choose the shades and treatment products that are right for you, and find the perfect perfume for your big day; www.elizabetharden.com

Estée Lauder: www.esteelauder.com

iBeauty: www.ibeauty.com

Lancome: www.lancome.com

L'Oreal: www.loreal.com

M.A.C.: www.maccosmetics.com

Makeover Studio: Choose your face shape and experiment with makeup shades and looks; www.makeoverstudio.com

Max Factor: www.maxfactor.com

Maybelline: www.maybelline.com

Michelle Roth: (212) 245-3390; www.michellerothbeauty.com

Neutrogena: www.neutrogena.com

Pantene: www.pantene.com

Reflect.com (customized beauty products): www.reflect.com

Rembrandt (tooth-whitening products): www.rembrandt.com

Revlon: www.revlon.com

Sephora: www.sephora.com

SELF-CARE AND HEALTH

Body Mass Index (BMI): To figure out your healthy weight range for your wedding day; www.phys.com/go/bmi

Cyberdiet: www.cyberdiet.com

Dance Classes Online (free!): www.bustamove.com

Drugstore.com: www.drugstore.com

E-Fit: www.efit.com

Fitness Online: www.fitnessonline.com

Mother Nature: www.mothernature.com

Tufts University Nutrition Navigator: To learn healthy eating habits; www.navigator.tufts.edu

Vitamins.com: www.vitamins.com

WebMD: To compile your family's health history; www.webmd

A Note from the Author

Y OUR OUTDOOR wedding is going to be beautiful! I wish you all the luck and success in the world, both with your wedding and with your future lives together. A marriage is a partnership, and it is the journey together that is most important. So as you journey through the planning of your wedding, I hope you'll keep in mind that it is the marriage that is most momentous, not the wedding day itself. When you consider that you're beginning a new life with your best friend, a few raindrops or wilted roses don't mean a thing.
Best of luck to you!

Sharon Naylor

Index